POLLUTION IN THE U.K.

AUSTRALIA

The Law Book Company
Brisbane · Sydney · Melbourne · Perth

CANADA

Carswell
Ottawa · Toronto · Calgary · Montreal · Vancouver

AGENTS

Steimatzky's Agency Ltd., Tel Aviv
N.M. Tripathi (Private) Ltd., Bombay
Eastern Law House (Private) Ltd., Calcutta
M.P.P. House, Bangalore
Universal Book Traders, Delhi
Aditya Books, Delhi
MacMillan Shuppan KK, Tokyo
Pakistan Law House, Karachi, Lahore

POLLUTION IN THE U.K.

by

DENISE FRANKLIN
J. D. (University of Michigan)
Attorney at law
Environmental legal advisor at Field Fisher Waterhouse

NEIL HAWKE
LL.B. (Hons.)(Hull), Ph.D.(Nottingham), FRSA,
Professor of Environmental Law
Environmental Law Institute
De Montfort University, Leicester

MARK LOWE
Solicitor
Partner at Field Fisher Waterhouse

European Specialist
Kevin Dehaan
Barrister

LONDON
SWEET & MAXWELL
1995

Published in 1995 by
Sweet & Maxwell Limited of
South Quay Plaza, 183 Marsh Wall, London E14 9FT.
Computerset by Wyvern Typesetting, Bristol
Printed and bound in Great Britain by Hartnolls Ltd, Bodmin

No natural forests were destroyed to make this product;
only farmed timber was used and replanted

A CIP catalogue record for this book is available from the British Library

ISBN 0 421 45690 6

ACKNOWLEDGMENTS

The authors would like to acknowledge the contribution of the following: Richard Caines, Consultant, Environmental Resources Management; Kevin de Haan, Barrister-at-law, 3 Raymond Buildings, Grays Inn, London; Andrew Lafferty, Solicitor, Environmental Law Unit, Field Fisher Waterhouse; Jill Shankleman, Director, Environmental Resources Management; Nigel Taylor, Solicitor, Environmental Law Unit, Field Fisher Waterhouse.

PREFACE

It is an obvious truism that the environment, and pollution of it, is all encompassing. By land, air and water, it affects every activity.

The U.K. was one of the first economies to industrialise and has one of the longest histories of environmental problems. Pollution levels and ecological disasters have escalated and, with them, has come increasing concern and increasing regulation.

This book is intended to offer a practical analysis of pollution control for those in industry, commerce, government, and private practice. It covers the wide range of applicable U.K. legislation and E.C. Directives. In an area of constant change, we have sought to set out central principles and trends as well as the current law.

Part One contains an overview of problems and trends. It traces the upsurge of reaction, within government and industry, to pollution and reviews important areas of debate such as allocation of responsibility. Part Two deals in detail with the concept of Integrated Pollution Control, contamination of land, waste, pollution of air and water, and related topics. In so doing, we have endeavoured to include practical guidance on the implications and requirements of the control regime. We have for instance examined environmental management systems and procedures for obtaining authorisations and licences.

The book, in essence, is a framework for understanding, advising on, and managing the control and regulation of pollution. As part of our research, we have consulted a range of policymakers and regulators on current, and future, practice and their views are reflected in the text.

Substantial contributions have been received from a number of sources – Jill Shankleman and Richard Caines of Environmental Resources Management in respect of Chapters 1 and 8; Kevin de Haan, barrister, in respect of Chapter 7; and Andrew Lafferty (Chapters 4 and 6) and Nigel Taylor (Chapter 6) of Field Fisher Waterhouse. We are most grateful to them, and to all others who have supported us in the production of the book both at our publishers and at Field Fisher Waterhouse. Passing reference only is made to the Environmental Bill which is currently before Parliament.

The law stated is at September 1, 1994. Passing reference only is made to the Environmental Bill which is currently before Parliament.

Mark Lowe
February 1995

CONTENTS

TABLE OF CASES

(References are to paragraph numbers)

E.C. CASES

TABLE OF STATUTES

(References are to paragraph numbers)

TABLE OF STATUTORY INSTRUMENTS

(References are to paragraph numbers)

TABLE OF E.C. DIRECTIVES

(References are to paragraph numbers)

PART ONE

Chapter One

AN OVERVIEW: THE PROBLEMS AND THE LAWS

After two centuries of industrial progress with little regard for the environment, concerns for the world we live in have slowly made their way to the forefront of the political agenda. When workers left farms for factory opportunities in towns and cities during the industrial revolution of the mid-eighteenth century, a new pattern of living and thinking was dictated. With the growth of heavy industries and mechanical transportation, nature transformed from an unknown quantity to a resource that could be harnessed for the benefit of humanity. **1–001**

The nineteenth century saw the first tangible signs of concern over this development. Political economist Thomas Robert Malthus (1766–1834) predicted food shortages caused by massive population growth. Utopian and idealist writers published environment-related commentaries, and by the late 1890s, protection agencies such as the National Trust and Royal Society for the Protection of Birds had been founded.

Fuelled by the consequences of two world wars and the development of nuclear weapons, modern environmentalism was born in the late 1950s. The romantic view of earlier conservationists was replaced by a stark realisation that humanity now had the power to destroy itself. Together with the peace movement and the women's movement, the "green" movement found a niche in the emerging "alternative" society.

The 1963 publication of *Silent Spring* by Rachel Carson, documented the impact of pesticides and similar compounds within natural ecosystems. Asserting that small concentrations of pollutants could accumulate up foodchains producing heavy doses in top predators such as humans, it gained widespread attention. With its contention that atmospheric transport of pesticides such as DDT produced detectable levels of the compound in Antarctic penguins, it invalidated the concept that the wilderness is immune to human repercussions. The news motivated many to protest against DDT's use.

More environmental activism emerged in 1970, when a popular recording of the sound of humpback whales prompted environmentalists to use the tactics of the civil rights movement in its appeal to save the earth and its creatures. Attracting an audience through its bizarre nature rather than any environmental message, "Song of the Humpback Whale," sold over 100,000 copies. The attention also instigated action against commercial whaling by the environmental advocacy group, Greenpeace[1] who stopped whale hunting by positioning small boats between whaling ships and their prey.

1–002 The principle of direct action encompasses a large spectrum of environmental activism—from consumer boycotts and letter writing campaigns to the more confrontational actions. A recent example of direct action occurred when Friends of the Earth (F.o.E.), a United Kingdom environmental advocacy group, published a list of companies that discharge the largest amounts of metals into sewers. By involving the public, the group's objective was to persuade the government to introduce legislation establishing public registers of firms' actual discharges, and tighter control of trade effluents.[2]

International initiatives such as the 1972 Club of Rome Report and Stockholm Conference introduced environmental issues to mainstream government, providing a platform for the increasing academic and governmental analysis of environment and development issues. The 1980 World Conservation Strategy (WCS), constructed ambitious national plans and targets. The United Kingdom's response to the WCS, called "The Conservation Strategy for the United Kingdom", issued in 1983, supported the concept of "sustainable development". This term was defined later in the 1987 report of the World Commission on Environment and Development[3], as:

> "Development that meets the needs of the present without compromising the ability of future generations to meet their own needs."

1–003 Despite such measures, some industrialists, politicians and members of the public still perceived environmental issues to be marginal. Ironically, it was during the personal wealth-focused United Kingdom "boom years" of the mid-1980s, that environmental issues began to gain the status they command today. With assured financial security, large sectors of the public started to support wider social causes. For instance, public sympathy over the bombing of the Greenpeace ship, *Rainbow Warrior*, in July 1985 doubled their membership in less than a year. The reduction of the threat of nuclear war brought on by the thawing of the Cold War shifted the attention of peace activists to environmental causes (see table 1.2a).

[1]Formed in Canada in 1970 in protest at nuclear testing.
[2]*The Ends Report*, (July 1992, Issue No. 210) pp. 4–5.
[3]*Our Common Future*, or the *Brundtland Report*

This, as well as the discovery of the ozone hole above Antarctica by British scientists which prompted Friends of the Earth to boycott ozone destroying chlorofluorocarbons from aerosol cans, contributed to the onset of the green consumer movement.

A result was the 1988 publication of *The Green Consumer Guide*, an environmentally pro-active purchasing guide that assisted the public to "think globally, act locally", and forced "green" competition among producers. The public's enthusiasm reached a peak in June 1989 when the British Green Party won 15 percent of the vote in the European elections—a higher percentage than was polled by Die Grünen, the established (and nationally represented) West German Green Party.

Table 1.2a **1–004**

Approximate membership totals for five leading environment groups, 1985 to 1994

	1985	1990	1992	1994
Friends of the Earth	28,000	180,000	210,000	200,000
Greenpeace	30,000	342,000	409,000	411,000
W.W.F.[4]	91,000	250,000	227,000	200,000
R.S.P.B.[5]	390,000	656,000	742,500	860,000
National Trust[6]	1,323,000	1,865,000	2,152,000	2,200,000

Today, the British public may not be so environmentally vocal, but the pressure they have exerted on government and industry have produced several earth-friendly changes. Environmental issues are being integrated into the British government, with a minister in each department given specific responsibility for environmental affairs. The British government's 1990 White Paper, "This Common Inheritance," outlines an national environmental strategy for which regular progress reports will be issued. Legislation arising from the European Community (E.C.) has encouraged Member States to act on many environmental concerns. Pressure groups have maintained lobbying pressure on a diverse range of environmental issues, such as biodiversity, marine pollution, tropical deforestation, transportation and global warming. **1–005**

At an international conference in 1992 over 150 heads of state or governments signed the Convention on Biological Diversity at Rio de Janeiro. Two years later the British government published its

[4]W.W.F.= World Wide Fund for Nature, formerly known as the World Wildlife Fund.
[5]R.S.P.B. = Royal Society for the Protection of Birds.
[6]National Trust membership entitles the holder to free admission to National Trust sites; motivation for joining may not always reflect environmental concern.

Action Plan for Biodiversity.[7] Important initiatives on the ozone layer – the so called Montreal Protocol in particular – have led in turn to new E.C. laws and their translation into U.K. law.

Large multinational companies have spearheaded industry efforts to integrate environmental management into their operations. Co-operative programmes between industry and conservation groups—such as the Shell Britain Campaign and the Heinz Guardians of the Countryside Programme—have added funds and publicity to conservation schemes. Other charitable bodies, such as the Keep Britain Tidy Group and the Groundwork Trust, have received significant government subsidies to develop their work. A broad spectrum of environmental programmes has been developed over the past two decades, representing many sectors of society.

[7] Cm. 2428 (1994).

Chapter Two

CURRENT TRENDS IN THE UK

The United Kingdom's environmental protection programme has focused primarily on enacting and enforcing legislation to prevent further damage to the environment through pollution. Existing legislation sets standards for environmental quality, requires the use of pollution control technology, and facilitates public participation in environmental decision-making through improved access to information driven more recently by E.C. policies in favour of pollution prevention and assuming (where possible) that the polluter pays. **2–001**

These measures are a first and essential step in pollution control. However, a focus on prevention clearly does not address the legacy of environmental damage in the past. As the country with the longest history of industrialisation, the United Kingdom has a record of pollution which cannot be ignored. Preventative legislation may also fail to deal with damage that occurs between enactment and implementation, and damage from accidents.

The key to remedying past pollution lies in clean-up and restoration. The clean-up activity, often called "remediation", is the removal or destruction of contaminants in order to restore a site to where it can be used for specific purposes, *e.g.* residential, industrial or public. Some types of damage to the environment can be repaired by natural processes, but others require human-made restorative action. Recent concerns relate to the question whether (as in the Netherlands) remediation should be to the highest standards (a "polished earth" policy) or whether remediation should (as in the U.K.) render land fit for its redeveloped purpose.

Restoration is necessary to prevent past pollution from leaving time-bombs for the future. It must compensate for the impact of past and present practices of industry, agriculture and the population at large. For example, local authorities and chemical companies in Grangemouth are considering investing in a jointly owned wet air oxidation plant. The process uses high temperatures and pressures that break down intractable organic compounds to form simple organic compounds which can be treated biologically. The site accepts about 110,000 tonnes of waste per year with about

30,000 tonnes originating from local companies. The cost is expected to be about £20–25 million for a site which might last for the next 20 years.[1]

LIABILITY FOR THE COST OF POLLUTION

2–002 Policymakers in the United Kingdom and the E.C. face the fundamental question of who should bear the financial burden both of ensuring that pollution does not continue into the future and of cleaning up existing "historical" pollution.

The need to address future problems with pollution control legislation is addressed by the Environmental Protection Act 1990 (EPA) as well as others. One such Regulation, the Control of Industrial Major Accident Hazards Regulations 1984 (CIMAH), shows how legislation can be a direct reaction to recent environmental disasters. It was created to ensure that the accidents like that at Italy's Seveso plant in 1976, where an out of control chemical reactor released poisonous gas which killed animals, plants and caused illness amongst the local population, will not occur again[2]. Subsequently in 1982, the "Seveso" Directive, as it is commonly known,[3] created tight controls for prevention of major accidents.

In respect of future pollution, the Environmental Protection Act 1990 places the financial burden on those who pollute and those running polluting processes. Polluters are liable to pay damages and restoration costs, and operators of polluting processes must pay to update their techniques to the "Best Available Techniques Not Entailing Excessive Cost" (BATNEEC) for controlling pollution. The difficulty in attributing costs lies with assessing past pollution combined with recent polluting activities, environmental accidents, and the cumulative effect of human use and abuse of the environment over the centuries.

The concept of attributing the cost of historical pollution to past polluting activities is controversial. The problem lies in identifying when and how the damage occurred and then accurately attributing the damage to a particular party. Even if records relating to the site are available, previous occupants or users may no longer exist. Evidence linking one particular party to the damage may be tenuous or hard to establish. There is the further difficulty that past polluting behaviour may have been legal at the time. This problem is seen in the facts of the recent House of Lords decision in *Cambridge*

[1] *The Ends Report*, July 1992, No. 210, pp. 10–11.
[2] Discussed below in Chapter six, p. 97 *et seq.*
[3] 82/501/EEC.

Water Co. v. *Eastern Counties Leathers plc*[4] where a toxic solvent (PCE) percolated into ground waters from the respondent's factory and polluted the appellant's water source. The PCE rendered the water unwholesome only according to recently introduced E.C. standards whereas the solvent had leaked from the site for many years. It was concluded that strict liability must be based on foreseeability of the harm or damage at the time when the offending substance was still under control.

Some Approaches to Liability

The United Kingdom and the E.C. have openly adopted the "polluter pays" principle.[5] The polluter pays principle states that the cost of damage resulting from pollution should be paid by those responsible wherever possible. This creates an incentive for potential polluters to prevent damage before taking over a site. Its modus operandi is to generate changes of behaviour in the community including better risk management and voluntary clean-ups. **2–003**

In the UK, the pollution liability sections of the Environmental Protection Act 1990 and the Water Resources Act 1991 (WRA) both place liability for damage caused by pollution on any person who "caused or knowingly permitted" the pollution to occur.

When identifying the "polluter" under the polluter pays doctrine, problems may arise. Fault-based liability seeks to establish whether a duty to behave according to a certain standard has been breached. Proof of fault can be difficult although scientific proof of causation is improving rapidly. It involves investigation and court time, which delay the actual clean- up of the environment, and create legal expenses which could be better spent on cleaning up.

The Environmental Protection Act 1990, section 61, introduces a further provision which holds the owner of land, not necessarily the polluter liable in any event for clean-up costs in certain circumstances. This provision has not been implemented yet but could have a phenomenal impact on owners, lessors and purchasers, who could inherit liability. It does not always follow the polluter pays principle; for example, a lessee rather than the owner may be running the polluting operations on the land at issue. Under section 61, it would be the owner not the operator who is liable for clean-up costs. It is the United Kingdom's first move toward strict liability for damage caused by pollution.[6]

At the E.C. level a recent Green Paper ("Remedying Environmental Damage") debates a number of options. It is observed that the latest E.C. Commission proposal for a Directive on civil liability **2–004**

[4][1994] 2 W.L.R. 53 (H.L.).

[5]HMSO, *This Common Inheritance: Britain's Environmental Strategy* (1990) Cm. 1200, para. 10.3 p. 136.

[6]Discussed below in Chapter 3.

for damage caused by waste refers to "impairment of the environment" as meaning "any significant physical, chemical or biological deterioration of the environment". Such a definition is an essential starting point in this important debate, as is the need to ensure that any regime of strict liability (as opposed to fault-based liability) is sufficiently widely defined to allow a "proper" allocation of the costs of restoring damage. The proposed Directive would impose liability on a waste "producer" or (if he could not be identified) the person in control of the waste at the material time. In the context of a strict liability regime such an emphasis should encourage better waste management and is consistent with a preventative regime. Where individual responsibility cannot be established, the Green Paper refers to a spreading of responsibility through joint compensation schemes of the sort already found in the oil shipping industry. The Council of Europe's Convention on Civil Liability provides a widely-defined strict liability regime where liability would rest on an "operator": any person supervising a dangerous activity at the time of an occurrence. The extent of the environment given protection is very widely defined to include the owned and unowned environment. Legal challenges to establish liability would be available to a wide variety of voluntary organisations and associations interested in the environment.[7]

A strict liability regime that is too broad in scope may come to be regarded as unjust or too expensive for society. It is argued, for example, that strict liability can stifle investment in industry. Additionally, strict liability for damage caused in the past could set unacceptable legal precedents. Traditionally, English Common law and European Civil law has considered retrospective liability to be against public policy.

Enforcement

2–005 New liabilities under the current regime are accompanied by radical changes in the enforcement of pollution control legislation and stronger enforcement measures, including substantial fines, prison sentences and the revocation of licences. Enforcement agencies are still being strengthened, with an Environmental Agency to be established on April 1, 1996.

Previously, local authorities and other public bodies charged with the task of enforcing anti-pollution laws tended to follow a "softly-softly" approach. Companies which broke the law were informally warned or threatened with prosecution without any such actual consequence. This leniency has been replaced by a tougher

[7] Remedying Environmental Damage, Commission of the European Communities, COM (93) 47 final, Brussels, May 14, 1993; Draft Convention on Civil Liability for Damage resulting from activities dangerous to the environment, Council of Europe, Strasbourg, January 15, 1993.

approach. Recent figures show a change towards more aggressive enforcement; by September 1991, prosecutions by the National Rivers Authority (NRA) had almost tripled from the previous year. This trend continued in 1992 and through into the early part of 1993. By the end of March 1993, 297 prosecutions for pollution incidents that had occurred in 1992 had been heard in court and 290 (98 per cent) of these had resulted in convictions.

Two powerful deterrents make it unwise for companies to ignore environmental law. Firstly, under the Environmental Protection Act 1990 and the Water Protection Act 1991, the courts have the power to impose higher fines than under the previous legislation.[8] Hence the sheer amount of a potential fine can be of concern to a polluter. Secondly, a polluter may have to pay for the clean-up costs incurred by the enforcing authorities in the future.

Since developments in the United Kingdom are not dissimilar to those in the United States a few years ago, examples in the United States should alert companies to take these sanctions seriously.

The United States government estimates that the average cost for cleaning up landfill sites which were singled out by the government as being polluted is $47 million per site. An example of a December 1990 clean-up cost award from damage to the soil and ground water in Massena, New York, by the General Motors Corporation was $84.8 million.

The Environmental Protection Act 1990 empowers the courts to impose prison sentences on company directors.[9] Although imprisonment was possible under previous legislation, it is only recently that this sanction has been enforced. In October of 1992 the first prison sentence in an environmental case in the UK was imposed on the director of a waste disposal company. Thomas McBride, a director of the GPD Group, a waste disposal company in Rutherglen, Scotland, pleaded guilty to the charge of "the unlicensed deposit of waste of a poisonous, noxious or polluting nature which is likely to give rise to an environmental hazard," and the charge of "storing dangerous chemicals in a warehouse and failing to ensure the health and safety of employees."[10]

DISCLOSURE OF ENVIRONMENTAL INFORMATION

One of the first pledges made by the British Prime Minister, John Major, after the 1992 general election was to "open up" government **2–006**

[8] The courts have the power to enforce up to £20,000 in the magistrates court and unlimited fines in the Crown Court.

[9] Discussed below in Chapter 4, para. 4–127.

[10] *The Ends Report*, November 1992, No. 214 p. 42.

by improving public access to information. This initiative, still in its embryonic stages, has seen the disclosure of Cabinet Committees minutes (including the Environment Committee) and indications that over 150 pieces of legislation are being reviewed in order to allow greater freedom of information. This is tempered by the fact that the Official Secrets Act (dating from 1911) remains in force within the United Kingdom, although the Act has been eroded over the last 20 years by the development of information disclosure through public registers. Europe has added momentum to this process as European Community Directives on disclosure have been implemented by English law.

While tracking information through a public register may involve considerable determination, E.C. Directive 90/313 on the freedom of access to information on the environment will significantly ease the passage of environmental information to the public. The United Kingdom interpretation of the Directive contains provisions which will allow some companies to claim non-disclosure rights.[11]

Legislation aside, the early 1990s have seen the wider environmental debate mature, allowing company initiatives to extend further than simply countering the allegations of outside parties. The development of several voluntary environmental management systems testifies to this, with information disclosure being a feature of many such schemes; the proposed E.C. Eco-Audit scheme and the new British Standard for Environmental Management Systems (BS 7750) are the most prominent. For the public, these two schemes may provide the most accessible source of information on participating companies. The E.C. scheme here probably has particular value in requiring participating companies to publish periodic statements (externally verified) of environmental objectives and performance, a requirement that does not feature in BS7750. BS5750, on the other hand, is concerned with "quality systems": organisational structures, responsibilities, procedures, processes and resources for the implementation of quality management. This standard extends generally and is not specifically concerned with environmental performance or impact.

Public access to information in Great Britain has improved, but legislation remains significantly behind the United States, where there is a presumption of access to information under the Freedom of Information Act. In addition, the Toxic Release Inventory allows the public, by law, to obtain a detailed breakdown of emissions and discharges of some 300 listed chemicals to the environment.

[11] See the Environmental Information Regulations 1992 (S.I. 1992 No. 3240). Registers are discussed below in Chapter six, para. 6–043 *et seq*.

PUBLIC OPINIONS AND THE FREE MARKET

Given the potential liabilities in dealing with polluted land, the cost of cleaning up land, directors' personal liability, heavy fines and the prospect of prison sentences, might be expected to generate an emphasis on environmental issues in the private sector. **2–007**

Nevertheless, four independent surveys carried out in 1991 suggest the opposite. Less than one in three British businesses in Great Britain considered the environment an opportunity, nearly half were unaware of any future environmental legislation likely to affect them, and two thirds had no training programmes to improve their environmental performance.[12] While this attitude was acceptable 15 years ago when industrialists could afford to take a fairly dismissive attitude on environmental issues. However Public opinion has, of late, been proven to have a direct association with company survival.

From the contention that it is necessary for companies to have a clean environmental record in order to succeed, it follows that those who are not conscious of the environmental effects of their business will suffer in the marketplace. Bringing these ideas to the attention of the consumer is one of the ways the government is attempting to "clean-up Britain".

Up to the end of the 1980s, the ability of public opinion to affect environmental behaviour was more or less limited to the United States and Germany. Whether out of genuine concern for the planet, or fear of being ostracised for not keeping up with the times, the American and German public, to a large extent, have not tolerated companies with bad environmental records.

In the late 1980s, statistics showed a growing awareness of environmental issues among the British public, and the beginnings of a similar development emerged in the United Kingdom. In 1988, the number of people actively supporting the environmental organisation Greenpeace in Britain was approximately 120,000. By 1994 the number was 411,000. Because the support is most conspicuous among the younger generations, the impact is likely to increase even more in the oncoming decades.

Environmental Consumerism

Thus environmental performance will be a key factor for businesses in the 1990s, not just for future commercial success, but for mere survival. The core message to industry was underscored in a course **2–008**

[12] *Industry and the Environment: a Strategic Overview*, Report from the Centre for the Explotation of Science and Technology (CEST).

given by the Industrial Relations Services Training conference, "Managing Environmental Risk":

> "The so-called green consumers, green shareholders and green workers are putting pressure on companies to take a more active role in environmental protection."

Public pressure was a factor in the voluntary removal of ozone-depleting chlorofluorocarbons from aerosol cans. Similarly, one of the reasons for the introduction by the E.C. of the "Eco-label"—a label to be put only on products passing environmental tests—was its appeal to an environmentally aware public.

In 1991, the then Environment Secretary, Michael Heseltine, gave a warning at the Shell Lecture held at the Royal Society of Arts. One national newspaper reported:

> "(He) injects a brutal note of *realpolitik* into the familiar admonitions to British industry to clean-up its environmental act for the sake of the planet and for the sake of its public reputation. Mr Heseltine is telling companies that in a world where toughening environmental regulation is changing the sort of goods that can be sold, they will have to do it for the sake of the balance sheet or go under".[13]

David Slater, Chief Inspector of Her Majesty's Inspectorate on Pollution (HMIP), cited that environmental consciousness is financially advantageous to competitive companies:

> "There is a big emphasis on management improving the safety of their processes. It is in the company's interests to be viewed as environmentally friendly. It is a big commercial advantage."[14]

The business world is hearing the message from a variety of sources, the consumer being one of them. The consumer market for eco-friendly products has remained fairly constant since 1991. Investors who finance businesses are increasingly questioning the environmental soundness of their investments—they are, after all, in the business of spotting trends. From the inside, there is employee pressure; as one industry executive put it, "people who are environmentally concerned citizens at the weekend do not change their views when they arrive at work on a Monday morning."[15] Nevertheless E.C. led Eco-labelling initiatives are being pursued by industry with great caution against a background of concern about misleading environmental claims for a variety of products.

[13] *The Times*, May 7, 1991, p. 8.

[14] *Financial Times*, April 24, 1991, p. 16.

[15] Julie Hill, Director of Policy for the Green Alliance and co-author of *Ethics, Environment and the Company—A Guide to Effective Action*

Economic Incentives

Acknowledging the power of the consumer, the government is considering how to use market forces to obtain desired environmental results. Economic instruments for reducing pollution include "green taxes" such as carbon taxes on fossil fuels, environmental charges on polluting materials, fiscal incentives to reduce pollution, and deposits on bottles and containers to minimise waste. Environmental taxes are a way of employing market forces to influence the behaviour of consumers and producers, and thus encourage environmentally cleaner methods of production. **2–009**

"The main point of charges is to influence behaviour without command and control regulation", explained Robin Bidwell, Director of Environmental Resources management. In December 1991 at the CBI Conference on "The Changing Water Business". "If people are required to pay a fee every time they do something, they will do it better. And if unleaded petrol is offered at a discount to leaded petrol, then people will buy it."

Various forms of charges, some in force and some proposed, have been created to obtain environmental results:

(a) *User charges*—Dischargers are required to pay for collection and treatment of polluted waste, for example, sewage;
(b) *Pollution or emission charges*—These are levied on the specific pollutant regardless of the direct cost of the clean-up and are mostly linked with permits or standards;
(c) *Deposit and refund systems*—These are specifically designed to encourage recycling. A number of countries have schemes for recycling beverage containers, bottles and even cars.

THE FUTURE

With increased environmental awareness and new laws in the United Kingdom and Europe, a trend of heightened involvement can be seen emerging from the public and the E.C. Commission. **2–010**

Increase in E.C. Legislation

The E.C. has played a major role in environmental policy in recent years and this role is increasing. Pollution from one Member State often affects another, so joint action is required if it is to be tackled effectively. The competition within industry and agriculture will **2–011** be balanced if the environmental rules governing the production of goods in Member States are aligned at Community level.

The environment is on the agenda of the E.C. today for several reasons:

(a) Public demand for systems of accountability and compensation which increases whenever environmental accidents occur, such as the industrial accident at Seveso, in Italy;
(b) the pledge of the European Council to take action in the area of civil liability when it adopted the Fourth Environmental Action Programme and other legislation;
(c) The efforts of international organisations, including the Council of Europe, to put in place international conventions establishing liability for environmental damage;
(d) Variances in the use of civil liability for environmental damage among the Member States, which could lead to distortions of competition.[16]

Increasing Public Involvement

2–012 The British Government is hoping that responsibility for environmental problems will ultimately become the responsibility of the governed. "Parliaments can pass laws and governments can produce White Papers. But the environment will only improve if we ourselves [the public] have the will to do what lies in our own hands."[17] Thus the government is encouraging a wider participation by the many voluntary bodies which tackle environmental issues at national and local levels.[18]

[16]Draft Communication from the Commission to the Council and Parliament on Environmental Liability, pp. 2–3.

[17]HMSO, *This Common Inheritance: Britain's Environmental Strategy,* (1990) Cm. 1200, para 2.13, p. 34

[18]HMSO, *This Common Inheritance: Britain's Environmental Strategy,* (1990) Cm. 1200, para. 2.13, p. 34

PART TWO

Chapter Three

FUNDAMENTALS OF POLLUTION CONTROL

HISTORY OF POLLUTION CONTROL IN THE UK

Before April 1991, pollution in the UK was regulated by reference to the environmental media into which it was released—air, land or water—and subjected to three distinct control regimes. This afforded no overall view of where the problems were most severe, and the solutions adopted took no account of the environment as a whole. **3–001**

Existing legislation tended to fall into two categories. The first category concentrated single-mindedly on specific problems and typically resulted from single issue campaigns or private member's bills. The Clean Air Acts of 1956 and 1968, the Litter Act 1983, the Wildlife and Countryside Act 1981, and the Water Act 1989 are examples of the genre. The second category, originating in the Control of Pollution Act 1974, (COPA 1974) recognised the environment as an entity requiring separate control while improving environmental awareness. This category lacked the ability to harmonise pollution control.

Over time, it became apparent that pollution in one medium can have implications in another:

> "Burning fossil fuels . . . emits gases which can return to earth in acid rain, harming fresh-water life and reducing soil fertility. Heavy metals such as cadmium or lead, which are emitted into the air through combustion processes, can similarly return to the sea or land and find their way into our food chain.[1]"

In addition to the lack of a coherent approach, existing pollution control laws were thought ineffectively enforced:

> "The piecemeal and still incomplete implementation of the

[1]HMSO, *This Common Inheritance: Britain's Environmental Strategy* (1990) Cm. 1200, p. 137.

Control Pollution Act 1974 is only one example of "optional" legislation, where ministers' unfettered discretion over commencement dates can effectively frustrate Parliament's intentions. It is, of course, for Parliament to ensure that future legislation does not fall into the same mould.[2]"

Not only was implementation slow, but also national and local enforcing authorities were lenient in ensuring that industry complied with the standards.

New Controls

3–002 With the Environmental Protection Act 1990 (EPA), a new type of statute was created. The Act, concerned exclusively with pollution, attempts to monitor all environmental media through Integrated Pollution Control (IPC). IPC looks at the effect of a polluting process on the environment as a whole, and attempts to organise pollution control from that standpoint.[3]

Together with the Water Resources Act 1991 (WRA 1991), the Environmental Protection Act 1990 contains measures to strengthen the powers and resources of the various inspectorates. The objectives of the legislation are to:

- make the air cleaner and safer;
- achieve further improvements in the quality of water, and in the state of the North Sea and United Kingdom coastal waters;
- establish the levels of emissions that air and waters can safely tolerate, and set up control mechanisms based on them;
- regulate and rationalise the management of waste;
- maintain, and strengthen where necessary, controls over pollution from industry and agriculture and dangerous chemicals and other substances; and,
- provide the necessary incentives to industry to improve its environmental standards and develop clean technologies.[4]

[2]*Tackling Pollution—Experience and Prospects*, Royal Commission on Environmental Pollution, Tenth Report, para 3.5 p. 61

[3]Integrated Pollution Control is discussed in Chapter 4 below.

[4]HMSO, *This Common Inheritance: Britain's Environmental Strategy* (1990), Cm. 1200, para. 2.11, p. 34

OTHER SOURCES OF CONTROL

The EPA was not created to consolidate all the existing legislation in this area nor to supersede the long developed role of the common law. Both of these are still relevant to pollution control today. 3–003

Existing Statutes

In the past, statutes were often enacted to deal with specific problems as they arose. While many of these have been superseded by the Environmental Protection Act 1990, there are a number that remain. Several important areas, such as noise, are dealt with (in part) in the Control of Pollution Act 1974.[5] 3–004

Other legislation that controls pollution can be found in the Control of Industrial Major Accident Hazards Regulations 1984[6] which deals with the handling of hazardous substances, Control of Substances Hazardous to Health Regulations 1988[7] which deals with employee health with regard to hazardous substances, the Planning (Hazardous Substances) Act 1990,[8] the Radioactive Substances Act 1993,[9] the Nuclear Installations Act 1965,[10] and the Health and Safety at Work, etc., Act 1974.[11]

COMMON LAW

The Common Law has extended its protection of property rights through a process of gradual evolution.[12] Because it has evolved over the years, the common law suffers from a number of drawbacks. Most often, there must be a financially quantifiable loss or a loss of enjoyment of property before legal action can be taken. Therefore, protection is only afforded to property which can be identified as belonging to a particular person, or for property where the owner is willing to initiate action in respect of an environmental problem. Nuisance, negligence, trespass to land, and the rule in *Rylands* v. *Fletcher*[12a] which imposes strict, no-fault liability for the con- 3–005

[5]Discussed below in Chapter 6, para. 6–013.
[6]Discussed below in Chapter 6, para. 6–024.
[7]Discussed below in Chapter 6, para. 6–026.
[8]Discussed below in Chapter 6, para. 6–027.
[9]Discussed below in Chapter 6, para. 6–031.
[10]Discussed below in Chapter 6, para. 6–032.
[11]Discussed below in Chapter 6, para. 6–037 *et seq.*
[12]Common law discussed below in Chapter 6, para. 6–002 *et seq.*
[12a](1868) L.R. 3 H.L. 330.

sequences of an escape of something from someone's land, have all evolved from common law. When an individual has suffered damage as a result of pollution, the common law remains an attractive course of action. Despite the growth of increasingly sophisticated environmental legislation, pollution control agencies still find the common law an attractive facility for the recovery of expenses, particularly where remediation of environmental degradation is concerned.[13]

The potential of the common law is seen in the House of Lords decision in Cambridge Water, referred to previously.[14] The essence of the conclusion in the case is that the type of harm or damage should be foreseeable as long as the polluting substance remains in the control of the defendant. Another element of strict liability here is the requirement for a "non-natural" user of the land in question which, now, is likely to include industrial uses. Increasingly, the growth of scientific and engineering techniques will tend to negate claims that the impact of industrial chemicals escaping into the environment is not foreseeable. The advance of these techniques will no doubt aid also the process of establishing causation. Allied to the ability of engineering techniques for the recovery of pollutants that have escaped into the environment so allowing maintenance of "control", the era of strict liability in environmental claims could be very significant and a further consolidation, at common law, of the "polluter pays" principle.

POLLUTION CONTROL AGENCIES

3–006 With the profusion of environmental legislation enacted in the United Kingdom, it is not surprising that the agencies created to control pollution have developed in a piecemeal fashion. Currently, the Department of the Environment (DoE) has general responsibility within Government for environmental protection policy. Under the umbrella of the DoE, there are two Inspectorates with distinct powers and responsibilities. Her Majesty's Inspectorate of Pollution (HMIP) is responsible for regulating industrial processes and implementing the new system of Integrated Pollution Control. There is also the National Rivers Authority (NRA) which has wide-ranging responsibilities for protecting and improving the water environment.

The Government is now committed to forming a new independent environmental agency which will take over many of the

[13]Note the inherent limitations confronting NRA statutory enforcement in Water Resources Act 1991, s. 161.

[14]Chap. 2 and n. 4.

responsibilities of HMIP, NRA and the waste regulation authorities. Draft legislation is now in place and the new body will commence its duties in 1996. The announcement followed an agreement on the future role of the National Rivers Authority (NRA) in the structure of the new body. Rather than being broken up, the NRA will be placed together with HMIP and the waste regulation bodies of local authorities in the Agency.

Independent Environmental Agency

In the October 1991 DoE Consultation Paper, "The Government's Proposals for a New, Independent Environmental Agency," the Government set out proposals for the establishment of a unified body which would bring together the key regulatory pollution control functions affecting the different media of air, land and water. The Consultation Paper laid out four main considerations: 3–007

(a) The Agency would assume responsibility for day to day decisions on the regulatory functions that it inherits. All rights of appeal to Ministers against individual authorisations, licences, or consents would be continued under the new arrangement;
(b) The Agency would be responsible for giving advice and making proposals to the Government on environmental quality standards, and enforcing them. The Government would retain overall policy responsibility for environmental issues, for negotiations in the E.C. and with other international bodies, and for setting domestic environmental quality standards;
(c) The Agency would have responsibilities for environmental monitoring both in relation to its own functions and in the context of environmental legislation generally;
(d) The Government would look to the Agency to employ its expertise knowledge and experience to promulgate advice on best environmental practices and to support other Government initiatives.

Department of the Environment (DoE)

The DoE has general responsibility for environmental protection policy. It is able to meet this responsibility in a variety of ways: 3–008

(a) Drafting legislation to govern environmental protection and to impose penalties for failure to comply;
(b) Setting up inspectorates to enforce standards, such as HMIP and NRA;
(c) Monitoring the research and assessment of environmental impacts to enable clear standards to be set;

(d) Developing economic instruments as a means of environmental control;
(e) Participating in E.C. and other international debate on environmental protection.[15]

In many areas of environmental activity, the Secretary of State has extensive legislative, quasi-legislative and discretionary powers. The Secretary of State also has wide powers in relation to appeals against decisions of the regulatory bodies, which reflect the policy-based nature of this area of law.

Her Majesty's Inspectorate of Pollution (HMIP)

3–009 Her Majesty's Inspectorate of Pollution is part of the DoE and was established in 1987 through the merger of these previous Inspectorates (the Industrial Air Pollution Inspectorate, the Hazardous Waste Inspectorate and the Radio-Chemical Inspectorate) and the newly created Water Pollution Inspectorate. It is divided into three regions which deal with all aspects of regulation in their areas. Three regions are supported by a central division which is responsible for co-ordinating technical standards, research and guidance material and developing regulatory procedures.

HMIP is responsible for controlling all major emissions to air, land and water from polluting industrial processes (prescribed processes) in the Environmental Protection Act's Integrated Pollution Control scheme.[16]

In addition, HMIP carries out several other functions including:

(a) The provision of authoritative and independent advice to Government on pollution control practices;
(b) The approval, inspection and oversight of potentially polluting processes under the Alkali Act, the Water Resources Act, and the Health and Safety at Work Act;
(c) The regulatory control for waste management authorities, and storage and disposal of radioactive substances.

In order to fulfil these responsibilities, HMIP performs the following roles:

(a) *Integrated Pollution Control*: HMIP is responsible for regulation of 200 of the most complex and polluting industrial processes. Existing plants that now fall within IPC will be re-authorised in a programme that started in April 1991. HMIP also ensures compliance with the standards set by authorisations through inspections and monitoring data;

[15] "The Government's Proposal for a New Independent Environmental Agency", DoE Consultation Paper, October 1991.
[16] Discussed below in Chapter 4, para. 4–004 *et seq.*

(b) *Waste management*: HMIP has a supervisory and research role in respect of waste management. Its functions include monitoring the management of hazardous wastes, publishing waste management papers and advising waste management authorities on waste issues;

(c) *Water*: HMIP is responsible for the discharge of prescribed substances into the aquatic environment by virtue of being given the lead role on enforcement of the Integrated Pollution Control scheme under the Environmental Protection Act 1990. In deciding whether to grant an authorisation for a process which discharges prescribed substances into controlled waters, HMIP must consult the NRA. Other water discharges are the responsibility of the NRA (for controlled waters) and the relevant sewerage undertaker (for discharges to sewers).

(d) *Radio-active emissions*: HMIP operates the authorisation procedures under the Radioactive Substances Act 1993. These cover the registration of 6,000 premises and the authorisation of over 1,000 waste disposal processes.

National Rivers Authority (NRA)

With the Water Act 1989, the organisation of the water authorities was radically changed. The water authorities which provided services to customers were privatised and a new regulatory agency, the National Rivers Authority (NRA), was established. **3–010**

Before the privatisation, the same water authorities extracted and supplied water, used it for discharges and protected it from pollution. The government sought to avoid the "poacher-gamekeeper" conflict by giving the NRA responsibility for preventing pollution and controlling abstraction. Newly created private water service companies were made responsible for water supply, sewerage systems and sewage treatment. Further, through privatisation, the water industry could improve facilities through access to private sector funds.

The NRA is responsible for water environment which includes all rivers, lakes, reservoirs, estuaries, coastal waters up to three miles from the shoreline, and water stored naturally under the ground, which the Water Resources Act 1991 defines as "controlled waters". Its responsibilities with regard to controlled waters are as follows:

- River quality and quality of inland and coastal waters;
- Land drainage and flood control;
- Management of water resources;
- Fisheries;
- Navigation;
- Licensing the abstraction of water;

- Independently monitoring river, water quality and discharges from sewage treatment plants;
- Enforcement of new water quality objectives;

It controls pollution of controlled waters by:

- Issuing discharge consents;
- Monitoring water quality;
- Taking enforcement action where necessary;

It identifies whether local water quality meets prescribed standards and, if not, determines the most immediate and practical way to bring about improvement. It monitors quality by taking samples periodically at points over the country.

NRA also interacts with HMIP when HMIP decides whether to grant authorisation of discharge of prescribed substances into aquatic environment. In respect of authorisation procedures involved in integrated pollution control, the NRA may:

(a) Certify that a release will result in or contribute to a failure to achieve a statutory water quality objective under the Water Industry Act 1991, which incorporates E.C. water quality objectives (thus HMIP cannot grant the authorisation);
(b) Dictate conditions it thinks appropriate for authorisations;
(c) Require HMIP to vary conditions of an authorisation.

Chapter Four

ENVIRONMENTAL PROTECTION ACT 1990

OVERVIEW OF ACT

The Environmental Protection Act 1990 (EPA 1990), was born of a need for an effective, integrated system of pollution control. To a large extent, the previous pollution control laws were poorly co-ordinated and enforced, and left without adequate resources: 4–001

> "In the course of our review we have come across many instances where adverse effects in one part of a system have resulted from measures for environmental protection elsewhere .... From this stems a need for pollution control authorities to have broad areas of responsibility and appropriate powers of enforcement....
> Environmental control policy generally, should be accorded the priority and resources adequate for their integration in the national decision-making process.[1]

Whether the Environmental Protection Act 1990 achieves this objective remains to be seen. Bryan Gould, the Labour Party's then environment spokesman, certainly expressed his doubts in the Environmental Protection Bill's Second Reading debate when he described the legislation as:

> " ... little more than a rag-bag of measures drawn from disparate sources, many of which have been dusted down and brought to life again simply to be cobbled together to give it a lick of green paint and the impression of action and cohesion."[2]

Whilst not the panacea for all ills in the old system, the Environmental Protection Act 1990 does provide a cross-media approach to

[1] "Tackling Pollution—Experience and Prospects," The Royal Commission on Environmental Pollution's Tenth report, February 1984, Cmnd. 9149, Chapter IV.
[2] *Hansard*, H.C. Vol. 165, col. 50, January 15, 1990.

pollution control as well as the equipment for enforcing authorities with stronger powers.

Framework of the Environmental Protection Act 1990

4–002 The Environmental Protection Act 1990 marks the beginning of a new generation of environmental legislation in the United Kingdom. It seeks to provide an integrated approach to pollution control, under which systems are looked at as a whole when applying environmental regulations.

The Act introduces tighter environmental controls and stiffer penalties. Government's commitment to new standards of rigorous enforcement is shown by the strengthening of the powers of Her Majesty's Inspectorate of Pollution (HMIP) and local authorities.

As far as accountability is concerned, the Act ensures that for the first time, the potential exists for the public to have a right of access to much of the information compiled by the inspectors, on industry's compliance with environmental standards.[3] There is further discussion on public registers in Chapter 7.

In addition to remedying problems with the old control regime, the Environmental Protection Act 1990 has its own ambitions. The following excerpts from the Environmental Protection Act 1990's Statement of Purpose, list some of those aspirations:

- to control pollution arising from certain industrial and other processes;
- to re-enact the provisions of the Control of Pollution Act 1974 (COPA 1974) relating to waste on land;
- to restate the law defining statutory nuisances and improve the summary procedures for dealing with them;
- to provide for the termination of the existing controls over offensive trades or businesses;
- to provide for the extension of the Clean Air Acts to prescribed gases;
- to amend the law relating to litter and create further obligations imposing or to keep public places clear of litter and clean;
- to establish further the controls over the import, export, use, supply and storage of prescribed substances and articles, and the import or export of prescribed descriptions of waste;
- to obtain information about potentially hazardous substances; and,
- to amend the law relating to the control of hazardous substances on, over and under land.[4]

[3]*The Common Inheritance: Britain's Environmental Strategy* (1990), Cm. 1200. p. 139.

[4]Tromans S., *The Environmental Protection Act 1990: Text and Commentary* (1st ed., 1991) pp. 43–6 – 43–7.

Walk through the Sections

In Part I (sections 1–28,) the Environmental Protection Act 1990 establishes two separate systems of Pollution Control: Integrated Pollution Control (IPC) and Local Authority Air Pollution Control (LAAPC). It regulates waste management and licensing in Part II (sections 29–78). Part III controls statutory nuisances (sections 79–88) while Part IV (sections 86–99) applies to litter. Part V (sections 100–105) amends the Radioactive Substances Act. Genetically Modified Organisms are regulated under Part VI (sections 106–127). Finally, Part VII (sections 128–139) provides for mainly institutional changes to nature conservation in the UK and countryside matters in Wales. **4–003**

INTEGRATED POLLUTION CONTROL AND LOCAL AUTHORITY AIR POLLUTION CONTROL

Under Part I of the Act, there are two separate pollution control regimes: Integrated Pollution Control (IPC) and local authority air pollution control (LAAPC). Each establish similar systems requiring authorisation for prescribed processes capable of causing harm to the environment. They also share similar regulations for enforcement, publicity and offences. The distinction between them lies in their responsibilities and their personnel—IPC controls releases into all environmental media of air, land and water, whereas local authority air pollution control only regulates releases into air. Integrated Pollution Control is enforced by HMIP in England and Wales. Local authority air pollution control is enforced by the local authorities. **4–004**

Integrated Pollution Control covers the most heavily polluting processes and those which release prescribed substances into more than one environmental medium. These are the more complex and highly technical processes. It is said that these processes are subject to "central control."

Local authorities are responsible for all processes carried on within their area caused by releases into the air, but not for the other environmental media of land or water. The local authorities are also responsible for dealing with mobile plant.[5]

Schedule 1 of the Environmental Protection (Prescribed Processes and Substances) Regulations 1991[6] lays out in detail which processes are covered under IPC (Part A processes) and which are

[5]Environmental Protection Act 1990, s.4.

[6]To be known as the "Prescribed Processes Regulations"

covered under local authority air pollution control (Part B processes).

The European Commission is finalising plans to introduce a European Community system of Integrated Pollution Control which would be similar to the system introduced in Part I of the Environmental Protection Act 1990.

Integrated Pollution Control

4–005 Although the decision to monitor the discharges and emissions of industrial operations now seems an obvious choice of pollution control, it was not conceived until the Environmental Protection Act 1990. The Act envisages that over 200 types of processes would be prescribed, involving at least 5,000 individual operations in the United Kingdom. Integrated Pollution Control regulates "the most polluting industrial processes." All processes falling within Part A of the Prescribed Processes Regulations need to apply for an authorisation to operate within a graduated time scale set out in Schedule 3 to the Prescribed Processes Regulations which covers specified periods between April 1991 and January 1995.

The Integrated Pollution Control system seeks to achieve the following goals:

- to prevent pollution at source;
- to minimise the risk of harm to human health and the environment;
- to encourage and apply the most advanced technical solutions, while recognising the integrated nature of the environment and the need to achieve the "Best Practicable Option" (BPO) for the environment as a whole given discharges and emissions to more than one medium;
- to apply a "critical loads" approach by assessing the levels of pollutants which local environments can tolerate without significant damage, in order to focus protection on the most vulnerable environment;
- to ensure that the polluter pays for the necessary controls;
- to contain the burden on industry, in particular by providing for a "one stop shop" on pollution control for the potentially most seriously polluting processes;
- to provide the means to fulfill international obligations relating to environmental protection;
- to prevent problems arising through regular assessment of plant design and waste management and by ensuring the currency of authorisations.

Local authority air pollution control

4–006 Local authority air pollution control operates under the same authorisations scheme as IPC, although the local authority's function is limited to the control of atmospheric emissions.[7] It is estimated that around 20,000 processes are subject to Local Authority Air Pollution Control. It applies to Part B processes under the Prescribed Processes Regulations which have been divided into three blocks.

ENFORCING AUTHORITIES FOR PART I OF THE ENVIRONMENTAL PROTECTION ACT 1990

The provisions of Part I of the Environmental Protection Act 1990, are enforced by Her Majesty's Inspectorate of Pollution (HMIP) and the local authorities. Her Majesty's Inspectorate on Pollution was formed in 1987 from a newly created Water Pollution Inspectorate and three previous inspectorates: the Industrial Air Pollution Inspectorate, the Hazardous Waste Inspectorate, and the Radiochemical Inspectorate.[8] It was created to develop a coherent approach to the control of emissions and discharges to air, water or land, and to give advice to other pollution control authorities. **4–007**

Her Majesty's Inspectorate of Pollution's authority extends to discharges into water under the IPC system but not to final disposal on land. (That is the function of the waste regulation authorities, under Part II of the Act).[9]

Local Authorities

Within Greater London, the local authorities for the purpose of the Environmental Protection Act 1990 are: the London borough councils, the Common Council of the City of London, the sub-treasurer of the Inner Temple, and the Under Treasurer of the Middle Temple. Outside Greater London, the local authorities are the district councils and the council of the Isles of Scilly. The port health authority is the local authority for any port health district.[10] In Scotland, they are the islands or district councils.[11] **4–008**

[7]Environmental Protection Act 1990, s.4(3).

[8]HMIP: discussed in depth above in Section 4.4.

[9]There is an area of waste disposal that HMIP does regulate. Where the prescribed process involves the keeping of waste on land short of final disposal, the Secretary of State has under s.33(3) the ability to exempt the necessity for a waste management licence otherwise required under s. 33(1). The Government has stated that it will use this power to ensure that any process that is the subject of an IPC authorisation shall not be required to have a waste management licence in addition.

[10]Environmental Protection Act 1990, s.4(12).

[11]Environmental Protection Act 1990, s.4(11).

Authorisation Enforcement—Inspectors

4–009 To enforce the authorisation procedures under the Environmental Protection Act, both HMIP and local authorities use inspectors who have a range of powers.[12]

Inspectors can enter premises at any reasonable time when there is an immediate risk of serious pollution, *e.g.* from a fractured pipe or a leaking tank. They can make an examination and investigation, dismantle an article to test it, require records or information from relevant persons, and require any person to give facilities and assistance on premises where a prescribed process is believed to be carried on. If there is reason to believe imminent danger of serious harm is at hand, inspectors have the power to seize the article or substance and cause it to be rendered harmless.

Definitions

4–010 The Secretary of State has determined which processes are most likely to have a polluting effect on the environment and thus require authorisations. They are listed in the Prescribed Processes Regulations, Schedule 1. Determinations have been based upon the harm caused to the environment, the process characteristics, the area in which the process is carried on, and other processes of which the review is a part. The Secretary of State can, at any time, prescribe different standard requirements for measurement of substances and prescribe other standards or requirements for any aspect of a process.[13] Different standards can be set for different parts of the country.

"Prescribed Processes"

4–011 A "Prescribed Process" is any activity carried on in the United Kingdom, whether on premises or by means of mobile plant, which is capable of causing pollution to the environment.[14] The general categories for prescribed processes are listed in the Prescribed Processes Regulations. The "process" comprises all operations from receipt of raw materials to dispatch of products and waste.[15]

Schedule 2 to the Prescribed Processes Regulations provides various rules that distinguish the different categories. It is crucial to identify the correct category for a particular process. That decision will dictate when an application for authorisation should be made,

[12] Environmental Protection Act 1990, s.17.
[13] Environmental Protection Act 1990, s.3.
[14] Environmental Protection Act 1990, s.1(5).
[15] "Secretary of State's Guidance on Environmental Protection Act 1990", G.G.4 (91) Introduction, p. 1.

to whom, and how many authorisations should be sought. The more relevant interpretational guidelines are:

Rule 3—Where a process comprises two or more "sub-processes" which are described in the same section of Schedule 1 and those processes are operated by the same person at the same location, this is a single process which needs one authorisation. If any of the "sub-processes" falls within Part A of the Section, all will be subject to IPC control; **4–012**

Rule 4—Where a process could be covered by more than one description in Schedule 1, it should be treated as falling within the one which most aptly fits the process;

Rule 7—Where, because of use of different fuels or materials, or because of disposal of different wastes at different times, a process (using the same plant or machinery) sometimes falls within Part A and sometimes within Part B, the process should sometimes be treated as a Part A process. Similarly, where a process sometimes falls within either Part A or Part B but otherwise is not covered by a description in Schedule 1, the process should be treated as a Part A or Part B process (as appropriate);

Rule 9—A number of descriptions of processes in Schedule 1 include a reference to "related" processes. These references should be interpreted as references to processes carried on by the same person and at the same location.[16]

A "single process" covers each individual observed process undertaken by the same person (the authorisation holder which represents the company) at the same location. Thus three Part B processes operated by the same person at the same location would constitute one process for local authority control and require one authorisation. If two Part B processes and one Part A are were operated by the same person at the same location, they are treated as one process subject to central control. If these processes are operated by separate persons at the same location, then they are regarded as one Part B process controlled locally and one Part A process for central control.[17]

Where operators are unclear whether their process falls to HMIP or local authority control they should approach the authority they consider is most likely to be responsible. If the local authority is unsure whether a process should come under its control, it will discuss interpretation with the relevant office of HMIP.[18] **4–013**

There are exceptions to the general principle that processes listed

[16] "Secretary of State's Guidance on Environmental Protection Act 1990", G.G.1. (91) para. 11

[17] *Integrated Pollution Control: Guide*, p. 11.

[18] "Secretary of State's Guidance on Environmental Protection Act 1990", G.G.1 (91) para. 13.

in Schedule 1 of the Regulations need authorisation. Regulation 4 excludes processes which:

- will not, or are unlikely to, release into the air any substance prescribed in Schedule 4, or will release substances only in quantities which are so trivial that they can cause insignificant harm, or no harm at all;
- are undertaken at a working museum to demonstrate an industrial process of historic interest;
- are undertaken for educational purposes in a school;
- are engines being operated on or within an aircraft, hovercraft, mechanically propelled road vehicle, railway locomotive or ship or other vessel in order to propel such aircraft, hovercraft etc.; and
- are carried out as a domestic activity in connection with a private dwelling.[19]

The exceptions for processes releasing substances in "trivial quantity with insignificant capacity to do harm" are intended to cover cases where the process has such a low pollution potential as to be inconsequential. Such processes will commonly operate at an extremely small scale or infrequently. An example might be a university laboratory undertaking occasional or small-scale experiments, which would strictly fall within one of the definitions of process in the schedule.

"Prescribed Substances"

4–014 A prescribed substance is any substance designated as such in regulations made under Environmental Protection Act 1990, sections 2(5) and 2(7) which has the potential of causing harm to the environment. In some instances, there are minimum concentrations or quantities below which substances are not prescribed. The prescribed substances are incorporated into many of the definitions of the prescribed processes in Schedule 1 of the Environmental Protection (Prescribed Processes and Substances) Regulations 1991. The Lists of prescribed substances can be found in either Schedules 4, 5 or 6 of the Prescribed Processes and Substances Regulations, depending upon which medium they effect.

"Contamination"

4–015 Contamination is not defined in the Environmental Protection Act 1990. However contamination is the presence of substances capable of causing pollution to the environment. No judgment is passed as to whether the substances have caused, or are liable to cause damage or harm. This distinction becomes important when discussing con-

[19] "Secretary of State's Guidance on Environmental Protection Act 1990", G.G.4 (91) D.E.T. 1381, para.7; The Environmental Protection (Prescribed Processes and Substances) Regulations 1991, reg. 4.

taminated land, since "contaminated land" may or may not be polluted. It is polluted land which has its real value reduced by the presence of pollution.

"Pollution"

Pollution is not directly defined in the Environmental Protection Act 1990. The Act defines "pollution of the environment" below, but with regard to "pollution" alone, a well-known definition used in other contexts is: **4–016**

> "Pollution is the introduction by man into the environment of substances or energy liable to cause hazards to human health, harm to living resources and ecological sources, damages to structures or humanity or interference with legitimate uses of the environment."[20]

In practice the word pollution is used to describe the act of polluting and the consequences.

"Pollution of the Environment"

The phrase "pollution of the environment" means pollution due to the release (into any environmental medium) from any process of substances which are capable of causing harm to man or any other living organisms supported by the environment.[21] **4–017**

"Harm"

The word "harm" covers not only harm to the health of living organisms or other interference with the ecological system of which they form a part, but it also covers offence caused to any human senses and harm to property.[22] Health has been protected for decades, but the EPA 1990 introduces protection to human senses and property. This is interconnected to pollution because if it causes such harm it is considered a form of pollution. **4–018**

Authorisations

An "authorisation" is the authority granted by HMIP or a local authority to run a prescribed process according to certain conditions imposed by the enforcing authority. The listed prescribed processes may not be operated without an authorisation after the date specified in Schedule 3 to the Prescribed Processes Regulations for that process. **4–019**

The enforcing authorities are under a duty to ensure that in the authorisation procedure certain criteria are met, which include:

(a) In carrying on a prescribed process, the "Best Available

[20]Holdgate M. W., *A Perspective of Environmental Pollution*, (1979)
[21]Environmental Protection Act 1990, s. 1(3).
[22]Environmental Protection Act 1990, s. 1(3)(4).

Techniques Not Entailing Excessive Cost" (BATNEEC) must be used;

(b) A release cannot breach European Community or international obligations that the United Kingdom is bound to follow relating to environmental protection; and

(c) When a process is likely to involve releases into more than one medium, the "Best Practicable Environmental Option" (BPEO) must be achieved.[23]

Conditions

4–020 Authorisations are usually issued with conditions attached to them. Conditions apply to the very basic structure of the discharge, such as when the operator is required to limit the concentration or characteristics of a released substance. The Secretary of State's Guidance on Authorisations contains a list of specimen conditions that the enforcing authorities may find appropriate to include in authorisations.[25]

The Department of Environment believes that conditions relating to the composition of a substance should be used sparingly. "Operators should, in most cases, be allowed the freedom to use what raw materials and to operate their process at whatever rate they wish".[26] The enforcing authorities cannot grant an application if they consider that the applicant will be unable to carry on a process without being in breach of conditions which would be normally included in the authorisation.

The enforcing authorities can seek additional information and specify the timescale within which it must be provided.[27] They may discuss a proposal with the applicant before a formal application is made. In these informal discussions the inspectors can give an indication of what they are looking for and how likely the application would be to receive approval. This can give the operator a chance to discuss points before hand so the application will have a better chance of success, although it is not guaranteed.

Her Majesty's Inspectorate on Pollution and the Department of the Environment (DoE) have produced the following documents and internal instructions which give specific information on authorisations and are available publicly:

- "Application Form for an Authorisation under IPC and Guidance to Applicants for Authorisation";
- "Determining Applications made under IPC";

[23]Environmental Protection Act 1990, s. 7(2), (7).
[24]Environmental Protection Act 1990, s. 7(8).
[25]"Secretary of State's Guidance on Environmental Protection Act 1990", G.G.2. (91), Appendix 2.
[26]"Secretary of State's Guidance and EPA 1990," G.G.2 (91), para.69.
[27]Environmental Protection Act 1990, Sched. 1, paras. 1 (3), 1 (4).

- "Powers and Duties of Inspectors";
- "Enforcement and Prohibition Notices";
- "Variation Notices";
- "National Security and Commercial Confidentiality";
- "HMIP Integrated Pollution Control Fees and Charges Scheme (England and Wales)."

"BEST AVAILABLE TECHNIQUE NOT ENTAILING EXCESSIVE COST", "BEST PRACTICAL ENVIRONMENTAL OPTION", "BEST PRACTICAL MEANS"

Best Available Technique Not Entailing Excessive Cost

In every authorisation, there is implied a general condition that the **4–021**
process must be carried out using the "Best Available Technique Not Entailing Excessive Cost" (BATNEEC) for:

(a) Preventing the release of substances prescribed for air, land or water into that medium, or where not practicable, reducing to a minimum and rendering harmless any such substances; and

(b) Rendering harmless any other substances which might cause harm if released into air, land or water.[28]

In simple terms, this means bringing plant and equipment up to pollution control standards. The CBI originally estimated that for small and medium size companies the application of BATNEEC will cost up to £40–£50 million pounds for each of the next ten years.[29] For operators, it is more cost effective and less disruptive, to design effective controls over operating procedures into a plant, rather than face remedial action later. Thus, the research on the BATNEEC requirements is usually conducted at the design of plant phase for new operations.

The enforcing authorities determine what is BATNEEC for individual process applications. In making their decisions inspectors look too at configuration, size and other individual characteristics of the process. The Secretary of State has created guidance notes that comment on the BATNEEC standard for a large number of prescribed processes. There are approximately 200 guid-

[28]Environmental Protection Act 1990, s.7(4). This would include substances not on the prescribed substance list but which could cause harm, such as certain metals, substances with excessive acidity or too much organic matter, or solids in water. (Timothy Graham - Principal Pollution Inspector).

[29]Downs J., *"Who Pays What" in Integrated Pollution Management*, (1991), p. 10.

ance notes. They are not legal documents and the contents are not prescriptive.

Since BATNEEC does not actually prohibit pollution but instead prevents or seeks to minimize it through pollution controls, a particular process could emit prescribed and other kind of substances which will cause harm to the environment. For substances which are not prescribed but could cause harm, there is a requirement that BATNEEC is to be used to render any release harmless (but not to prevent release altogether). The Environmental Protection Act 1990 seeks to balance the need to try to minimise harm with the constraints of feasibility and cost of prevention.

A criticism levelled by Professor Michael Purdue, author of a published study on IPC, is that the level of the damage caused to the environment is not expressly brought into the BATNEEC equation:

> "As long as BATNEEC is being employed it does not matter that the emissions will actually cause or be highly likely to cause substantial damage."[30]

The control is on the technique used and not the actual damage caused. Thus there is a potential unfairness in a case where an expensive BATNEEC standard is imposed on a process "likely" to cause pollution, but which in actuality does not cause any pollution.

Where a process is designated for control by HMIP and is likely to involve the release of substances into more than one environmental medium, the conditions must not only achieve the BATNEEC principle, but the "Best Practicable Environmental Option" (BPEO), as well, discussed later in this Chapter at para. 4–023.

INTERPRETATION OF BATNEEC

4–022 The DoE has defined the individual components of the BATNEEC acronym in its publication "Integrated Pollution Control: A Practical Guide" as follows:-

"Technique"—includes not only technology, but also hardware and operational factors. This includes how the concept and design of the process and its components interrelated to make the whole. It also includes operational details such as staff numbers, working methods, training, supervision, and the organisation of the process.

"Available"—should be taken to mean procurable by any operator of the process. The standard requires general accessibility rather than that the technology be in general use. If there is a monopoly

[30] Purdue M., "Integrated Pollution Control" in *Modern Law Review*, (1990) 54 M.L.R. 534.

supplier, the technique is available, provided that any operator can procure it from that supplier.

"Best"—should be taken to mean most effective in preventing, minimising or rendering harmless polluting emissions. Under this definition, there may be more than one set of techniques that achieve the same degree of effectiveness. The effectiveness of the technology must have been demonstrated to meet this criterion. "Best" may also implicate use of a particular piece of hardware or may be applied in terms of emission standards.

The enforcing authorities are under a "duty to follow developments in technology and techniques for preventing or reducing pollution of the environment."[31] This obligation includes checking sources in the local library, so it can be implied that the "best" standard means that it is "best available technique worldwide."[32]

"Not Entailing Excessive Cost"—(NEEC) can vary depending on whether it is applied to new or existing processes. For new processes the presumption will be that the best available techniques will be used. Therefore, there may be less of a focus on the excessiveness of the cost. That presumption can be modified by economic considerations where it can be shown that the cost of applying the best available technique would be excessive in relation to the nature of the industry and the protection to be achieved.[33] The particular emissions involved will be relevant for this test. A certain amount of additional expense that would be excessive in other contexts may be required if the emissions in question are particularly dangerous.

For existing processes full and immediate application of the BATNEEC standard immediately may impose a heavy burden of expenditure on the operator. Therefore the guidance notes give stages at which particular controls must be introduced.[34]

Best Practical Environmental Option (BPEO)

Where the prescribed process is likely to involve the release of substances into more than one environmental medium (air, land, or water), an additional requirement is applied. The operator will need to use BATNEEC to minimise pollution caused to the environment as a whole—not just the receiving medium—having regard to the "Best Practicable Environmental Option" (BPEO) available for the "substances released." Since this applies only to substances released into more than one medium, this requirement does not apply to local authority air pollution control. Stephen Tromans, Editor of *Current Law* annotations to the Environmental Protection Act **4–023**

[31] Environmental Protection Act 1990, s.4(9).

[32] HC Standing Committee H, col. 203, Jan 30, 1990.

[33] *Integrated Pollution Control: A Practical Guide*, p. 17.

[34] "Secretary of State's Guidance on EPA 1990," G.G.S. (91), para. 25

1990, has devised the following approach to the relationship between BATNEEC and BPEO:

(a) identify the substances that may be released;
(b) decide what is the best practicable environmental option in relation to such substances;
(c) "having regard" to the BPEO so identified, identify the BATNEEC that will minimise the pollution which may be caused to the environment as a whole, focusing here on the carrying on of the process rather than simply on the substances.[35]

BPEO looks to the substances; BATNEEC looks to the techniques. BPEO is a check to see if particular pollution controls such as BATNEEC would conflict with the achievement of BPEO[36] Reading the application of BPEO as such, it appears that the crucial concept is that the BPEO analysis looks to see how the substances interact in other media and then checks to see if this matches BATNEEC requirements.

BPEO is not defined in the Environmental Protection Act 1990, but the concept was discussed in the 12th Report of the Royal Commission on Environmental Pollution called "Best Practicable Environmental Option," presented to Parliament in February 1988:

> "There are many possible approaches to the task of identifying a BPEO. A structured but adaptable approach that emphasises imaginative and critical thought and seeks to identify and evaluate as complete a set as possible of the feasible options is more likely to produce a satisfactory outcome. The BPEO concept can be applied to any project or activity that may affect the environment, for example, building a road, a factory, a power station, a marina; disposing of waste; erecting power lines; growing crops; or rearing livestock . . . The extent and detail of a BPEO exercise will depend on the extent, complexity and potential environmental impact of the project . . . the report of the study may range from simple annotated checklist through to an informative summary of several pages, and in particularly complex cases may be a substantial document."[37]

For each case, HMIP will verifying what is the BPEO. To achieve this result, HMIP consults other agencies such as the NRA and other statutory consultees.

[35]Tromans, *Environmental Protection Act 1990: Text and Commentary* (1993), p. 43–82.

[36]Royal Commission on Environmental Pollution, 12th Report, "Best Practicable Environmental Option", Cm. 310, para 1.4.

[37]*ibid.* paras. 2.17–2.18.

Best Practical Means (BPM)

Under previous legislation, operators of scheduled processes were under a general duty to employ the "Best Practicable Means" (BPM) to prevent the emission of "noxious or offensive substances" and "to render harmless or offensive" any residual emissions. Even though the standard has changed to BATNEEC for authorisations under Part I of the Environmental Protection Act 1990, BPM is still the current standard under Part III of the Environmental Protection Act 1990 which deals with statutory nuisances. It is important to note that these standards are not identical, if in the unlikely event one is trying to meet both for a particular plant. **4–024**

Best Practical Means uses best "practical" means which seems a less onerous task than getting the best technique available. Therefore, guidance on BATNEEC contained in the process guidance notes should not be regarded as being automatically applicable in determining the BPM for similar processes in relation to the statutory nuisance controls under Part III. For example, the BATNEEC process guidance note on the manufacture of timber and wood-based products explains the standards for large prescribed operations. These standards may be excessively costly, and consequently not the BPM, for a small, non-prescribed process.[38]

GUIDANCE NOTES

In order to give industry guidance on what is BATNEEC for a particular process, "guidance notes" on individual processes have been produced for many of the industry sectors. Others will be produced as the authorisation application deadlines expire. **4–025**

About 200 individual process notes are being produced containing, information about the characteristics of each process and why it is prescribed. The notes will give information on particular features that the enforcing authorities will take into account in processing authorisation applications and implementing enforcement procedures. They cover requirements for upgrading existing processes as well as standards for new plant. They are intended to be available at least six months before processes described are scheduled to come under control.[39]

The notes will, where appropriate, provide an emission standard that must be achieved where appropriate. They may also describe a

[38] "Secretary of State's Guidance on Environmental Protection Act 1990," G.G.1 (91), para. 94.

[39] See the ENDS Report for published and forthcoming guidance notes.

particular technique or range of techniques such as the requirement to use specific hardware. However, BATNEEC notes will usually be expressed in general terms so as not to constrain the development of improved techniques nor to restrict unduly the operator's choice in achieving a given standard.

The guidance notes are to be reviewed and updated as necessary, at least every four years. Since advances in technology may move faster than the revisions, the notes are described as being based on the state of knowledge and understanding of processes at the time of publication. Prior to publication of each set of the notes, there will be a period of consultation with interested bodies.

New Processes

4–026 For new processes, it is expected that plants will be designed to achieve the standards in the appropriate guidance notes. The notes also set deadlines for bringing existing plant, which has been switched to a new process, up to the standard required for new plant and give guidance as to what constitutes a "substantial change."[40]

Existing Processes

4–027 In relation to existing processes, the Chief Inspector will be concerned with establishing timescales for upgrading. To apply the BATNEEC standard immediately may impose high expenditure on the operator. The process guidance notes provide a timetable for bringing existing processes up to the BATNEEC standard and interim improvements that can be made while upgrading. However, it may of course in some cases be more cost effective for the operator to upgrade the process to the full standards required by the relevant process guidance note in one renovation rather than in stages.[41]

The first authorisation for an existing process will specify the interim conditions to be achieved before the process can be fully upgraded in accordance with the relevant process guidance note. Any authorisation issued during this initial period is given on the basis that the BATNEEC objective for that process is secured by compliance with relevant legislation existing at the time of the authorisation:

(a) in a case where a process was subject to registration under the Alkali Works Regulation Act 1906 and the Health and Safety at Work, etc., Act 1974, the requirements (or what would have been the requirements) under the 1906 and 1974 Acts;

[40] "Substantial Change" is discussed below.

[41] "Secretary of State's Guidance on Environmental Protection Act 1990," G.G.2 (91), para. 25.

(b) in any other case, what would have been the requirements (where appropriate) under the Clean Air Act 1993 and the statutory nuisance provisions of Part III of the Environmental Protection Act (subject to considerations of the BPM);
(c) and any interim standards included in the relevant process guidance note.[42]

PROCEDURE

The procedure for obtaining an authorisation is found in the Environmental Protection (Applications, Appeals and Registers) Regulations 1991 (as amended) and Schedule 1 to the Act itself. The application must be made in writing on forms which are available from HMIP and the local authorities. The following information must be provided: **4–028**

- the name, address and telephone number of the applicant;
- the name of the local authority and the address where the prescribed process will be carried on;
- a description of the prescribed process;
- a list of the prescribed processes (and any other substances which might cause harm if released into any environmental medium) which will be used in connection with, or which will result from, the carrying on of the process;
- a description of the techniques for preventing or minimising the release of prescribed substances and rendering harmless any substances which are released;
- details of any proposed release of a substance into any environmental medium and an assessment of the environmental consequences;
- the matters upon which the applicant relies to establish its compliance with BATNEEC and any limits or requirements prescribed by the Secretary of State;
- where a process releases substances in to more than one environmental medium, a BPEO assessment will be required;
- proposals for monitoring the release of substances;
- any additional information the applicant wishes the enforcing authority to take into account in considering the application.[43]

The enforcing authorities will need to know the precise nature of the process they are being asked to authorise, and how the operator **4–029**

[42] "Secretary of State's Guidance on Environmental Protection Act 1990", G.G.2 (91), para. 24.
[43] *Integrated Pollution Control: A Practical Guide*, para. 6.2.

proposes to deal with pollution from the process. The essential requirement is that the application should be sufficiently detailed to allow the enforcing authorities to examine all stages of the process, from the receipt of raw materials to the despatch of waste and finished products. There should be a description not only of the physical characteristics of the process, including for instance, the proposed height and location of any stacks or vents and the abatement technology, but also of how the process is to be operated. This might include, for example:

> "... a description of the fuel and raw materials to be used, whether the process will be continuous or batch, the maximum production capacity, the arrangements for storing raw materials and waste, the proposed levels of process maintenance, the extent of staff supervision, the qualifications of the workforce, and the contingency arrangements for process breakdown.[44]"

When the technique used is fully in line with the relevant process guidance note, the appraisal can be less detailed, since a full appraisal will have been carried out by the DoE in determining the standard.

The DoE has stated that a detailed environmental impact statement for each process considered, and for all substances involved, is not usually needed. What they do require is an assessment of the main areas in which the process is likely to have impact on the environment and a justification of the process and technique to be used.[45]

There are circumstances, however, where an applicant should include in its application a justification of its proposal in terms of its likely environmental impact. This could be where:

- there are a number of alternative means of minimising emissions to air, each having a different environmental impact;
- the applicant proposes to depart significantly from the advice contained in the Secretary of State's process guidance notes;
- a process is, or will be, located in or near to a sensitive environmental area—for example, in a town centre or close to a Site of Special Scientific Interest;
- a process is, or will be, located in an area with already high air pollution levels, particularly where there is the likelihood of the emissions causing levels to approach or exceed statutory air quality standards.[46]

[44] "Secretary of State's Guidance on Environmental Protection Act 1990," G.G.3 (91), para. 10.

[45] "Secretary of State's Guidance on Environmental Protection Act 1990," G.G.3 (91), para. 16.

[46] "Secretary of State's Guidance on Environmental Protection Act 1990," G.G.3 (91), para. 17.

Mobile Plant

The local authority is responsible for the control of processes which use "mobile plant." "Mobile plant" is defined as "plant which is designed to move or to be moved whether on roads or otherwise."[47] These would include processes such as roadstone coating plant, mobile incinerators or mineral crushing plant. The authority responsible will be the local authority in whose area the operator has its principal place of business. 4–030

Mobile plant are hired out with or without operators. They may or may not be operated as part of another prescribed process. The Secretary of State's Guidance on Part I of the Act[48] sets out approaches to authorising mobile processes in different situations. The person who will be carrying on the process must apply for authorisation. If an equipment hire firm and a party that hired the plant operate the same plant at different times, both will require authorisation to do so.

When to Apply for Authorisations

Existing Processes

The Integrated Pollution Control and local authority air pollution control schemes are applied to existing processes through a rolling programme. The dates set out in the Prescribed Processes Regulations are the dates between which operators of existing processes must apply for authorisation.[49] The dates by which existing processes will need to be updated to the BATNEEC standard are set out in the guidance notes for that process. 4–031

An existing process is one which was being carried on at some time in the 12 months prior to April 1, 1991[50] or was:

(a) under construction,
(b) being commissioned, or
(c) the subject of a construction contract before April 1, 1991.

New Processes

For processes designated for central control, no new process must operate after April 1, 1991 without an authorisation.[51] For processes 4–032

[47] Environmental Protection Act 1990, s.1(6).
[48] G.G.1 (91), para. 60.
[49] The Environmental Protection (Prescribed Processes and Substances) 1991 D.E.T. 1381, Sched. 3.
[50] The dates which apply to processes carrying out in Scotland different from those which are carried on in England.
[51] The Environmental Protection (Prescribed Processes and Substances) Regulations 1991, Sched. 3.

which are designated for local authority control, new processes must apply for authorisation during the time listed in the table in the Environmental Protection (Prescribed Processes and Substances) Regulations 1991, Schedule 3, Part I, paragraph 12. The three time periods listed fall between April 1, 1991 and September 30, 1992. A "new process" is one that does not fit under the definition of an existing process.

For new processes with normal characteristics and guidance notes available, it will be appropriate for applications to be made when full designs have been drawn up, prior to the beginning of construction.

"Complex and novel" processes—staged applications

4–033 For the majority of prescribed processes, the operator will be in a position to submit an application for an authorisation at the design stage, since information about the technology and use of the process will be known at that point. If in the course of construction major changes are made affecting the information, the operator will need to initiate "variation procedures."[52]

However, some processes are so novel and complex that it is impossible for HMIP fully to determine an application at the design stage. In these cases, applicants will need initially to involve the HMIP at the early stages of design and the authorisation procedure may spread over some years up to the start of construction between the design and construction stages. Applicants would need to seek HMIP involvement at the earlier stage of process design. This will ensure options relating to the "Best Practicable Environmental Option" (BPEO) are not closed off prematurely. For this type of process, the DoE has developed the "staged application procedure." Under this procedure, HMIP and the applicant agree on a plan and a timetable for the application and supporting information to be submitted in a number of tranches, as the process plan develops.[53]

With the staged application procedure, each tranche of information is subject to the normal register procedure and commercial confidentiality rules. Because the application will be open to public scrutiny at each stage, objection to the proposal is more likely to emerge at an early stage and the risk of unnecessary expenditure is reduced.[54]

Determination

4–034 Once the application is received, there is a 28 day period for the enforcing authority to confer with consultants and others wishing

[52] *Integrated Pollution Control: A Practical Guide*, para. 6.14–6.16. Discussed below at pp. 31 to 33.

[53] *Integrated Pollution Control: A Practical Guide*, para. 6. 17–6.18.

to make representations. This period begins on the day that notice of application was given or advertisement made.[55]

The enforcing authorities require four months from the date of receipt of the application to make a decision on the application. They can agree upon a longer period with the applicant.[56] There is an exception to this timing for local authorities considering existing processes. The Environmental Protection (Authorisation of Processes) (Determination Periods) Order 1991, (S.I. 1991 No. 513) gives local authorities 12 months to decide first time applications for existing processes (and 18 months in the case of existing small waste oil burners under 0.4MW).[57]

Charge Scheme

The Integrated Pollution Control and local authority air pollution control systems have a charge scheme to recover the cost of administering the authorisation procedures. The scheme does not however cater for cost of environmental damage caused by the authorised processes.[58] **4–035**

To ensure that the fees and charges are sufficient, the amount expended by the authorities are to be reviewed periodically so that the rates can be adjusted. Thus, as enforcing authorities spend more on carrying out their functions, the Secretary of State may raise the charges.[59]

Whilst the operators of prescribed processes are not actually paying for environmental damage within the cost of their applications, they are incurring substantial pollution control costs in the sense that the application of the BATNEEC principle often necessitates the purchase of expensive control equipment.

IPC charges scheme

The Integrated Pollution Control charges scheme is laid out in "Fees and Charges for Integrated Pollution Control 1993–94" and "Fees and Charges for Local Authority Air Pollution Control 1993–94". The payment on a particular process is determined by the number of defined "components" which the process contains. There is a flat rate for the component sums. The definition of components for each of the process categories is set out in Appendix 1 to the IPC Charges Scheme. **4–036**

[54] *Integrated Pollution Control: A Practical Guide*, para. 6.19–6.20.
[55] Environmental Protection Act 1990 Sched. 1, para. (6).
[56] Environmental Protection Act 1990, Sched. 1, para. 5.
[57] However, for new waste oil burners under 0.4MW which are to be operated using waste oil generated by the applicant from this other activities on the same site, the Order specifies a two week period for decision.
[58] Environmental Protection Act 1990, s.8(6), (7).
[59] Environmental Protection Act 1990, s.8(2).

The IPC Charges Scheme operates on the basis of three categories of charges:

(a) An application fee to cover the costs of consideration of each IPC application, which is currently £2,500 per component for processes which have previously been subject to air pollution control and £3,750 per component for processes coming under HIMP regulation for the first time.
(b) A subsistence charge payable annually for each IPC authorisation to cover the on-going costs of inspection, monitoring and enforcement, which is currently £1,540.
(c) A substantial variation fee to cover the costs of considering an application for a subsequent substantial variation of an authorisation, which is currently £1,250.

In the case of a major installation or a novel and complex process, where planning development and commissioning will be spread over a number of years, the operator and HMIP may use a "staged application" procedure.[60] The staged application and supporting information will be submitted in tranches at agreed stages in the progress of the project. In these cases, the standard application fee will not apply. Instead the applicant will be charged on the basis of HMIP's actual time and cost of dealing with the application.

Local Authority Charges Scheme

4–037 The Secretary of State has drawn up a charges scheme for the local authorities under Part I of the Environmental Protection Act 1990. This scheme is to be reviewed annually in consultation with the local authorities and industry representatives.

The fees and charges currently:

- initial application for authorisation; except £965
- where the process is registered under the Alkali Act £580
- where the process comprises one or more waste oil burning appliance under 0.4MWth £100
- substantial changes (sections 10 and 11 of the Act); £620
- annual subsistence charge; £585

The fees are levied per process rather than by the component system used by HMIP

Transfer of an Authorisation

4–038 An authorisation may be transferred when there is a change in the authorised holder.[61] The transferee must give notice of the transfer to the enforcing authority within 21 days of the transfer.[62] The

[60]Discussed above at para. 4–033.
[61]Environmental Protection Act 1990, s.9.
[62]Environmental Protection Act 1990, s.9(2).

authorisation, will be subject to the same conditions and continue after the transfer.[63]

Curiously there is no power given to the enforcing authorities to object to the transfer, even though the capability of the applicant was a condition of the original authorisation. However, the enforcing authority is not without remedy when faced with an environmentally undesirable transferee. If the authority doubts about the ability of the transferee to carry on the process in accordance with the conditions, then it may serve an enforcement notice (section 13) which would force compliance measures, or in extreme cases serve a prohibition notice (section 14) which would suspend the operation of the process or revoke the authorisation (section 12).[64]

Variation of an Authorisation

A holder of an authorisation must notify the enforcing authorities when a "relevant change" is to be made to a process. If the "relevant change" is also a "substantial change," then the operator will need to go through a procedural step similar to the original application. **4–039**

A "relevant change" alters the substances released, or the amounts released or other characteristics. A "substantial change" leads to a considerable change in the substances released or in their amounts or characteristics. Not all relevant changes will be "substantial," but all "substantial" changes will be "relevant."

When does a change cross the threshold from relevant to substantial? The Department of the Environment says that a change is substantial when a process is to be altered to such an extent that it no longer resembles the process which was originally authorised. That radical type of change would justify the level of scrutiny used for an application for a substantial change.[65] In addition DoE advises:

> "In broad terms, local authorities should treat as substantial any change which would involve any alteration in the process technique (including technology)—whether to plant, process, control systems, raw materials, intermediates, finished products or wastes—which has the potential to change significantly the nature (including mass, volume, concentration or environmental impact) of air emissions.[66]

The Chief Inspector's guidance notes on a particular process will include what constitutes a substantial change to that process. Until

[63]Environmental Protection Act 1990, s.9(3).

[64]Tromans S., *The Environmental Protection Act 1990: Text and Commentary* (1st ed. 1991).

[65]"Secretary of State's Guidance on Environmental Protection Act 1990," G.G.1 (91), para. 49.

[66]"Secretary of State's Guidance on Environmental Protection Act 1990," G.G.1 (91), para. 50.

the guidance notes for a particular process are produced, a change will generally be regarded as substantial if it results in an increase in the rates, concentration or absolute quantity of releases of a prescribed substance, unless HMIP can be satisfied that no significant environmental harm will result.

Variation Procedures—By Holders of Authorisations

4–040 The holder of an authorisation will be obliged to notify the enforcing authorities of an intention to make a relevant change to a process if notification of a relevant change is a condition of the authorisation.[67] Where no condition is imposed in the authorisation, the operator does not have to notify the enforcing authorities, but is strongly advised to do so. Otherwise, there is a risk that after carrying out the change, the authority will take the view that the authorisation holder has breached the terms of the authorisation and will take enforcement action.

Thus, in anticipation of a change, the holder can either notify the local authority of the proposal and ask for a determination of whether the change would be considered substantial, or simply request a variation.

Under the first option, the holder can request the enforcing authority to determine whether the change would involve breach of any condition of the authorisation.[68] If there is no breach, the enforcing authority would then determine whether the variation would be considered substantial.[69] If the change is not substantial, the enforcing authority can either require the operator to apply for a variation to the authorisation conditions in a prescribed form,[70] or allow the change to proceed without any further requirements because it deems the conditions of the authorisation to be unaffected.

If the authority determines that the change is substantial, the holder must formally apply as if there were a new application.[71] The application will then be subject to advertisement and consultation procedures and the fee for making a substantial change.[72]

The second option available to the operator is to apply directly for a variation specifying which of the conditions of the authorisation are to be changed.[73] If the change is relevant but not substantial, the Environmental Protection Act 1990, section 11(6) provides a fast-track approach which enables an operator to ask the enforcing authority to make a specified change to an authorisation condition

[67] Environmental Protection Act 1990, s.7(8) (*b*).
[68] Environmental Protection Act 1990, s.11(1) (*b*).
[69] Environmental Protection Act 1990, s.11(2).
[70] Environmental Protection Act 1990, s.11(3) (*b*).
[71] Environmental Protection Act 1990, s.11(4) (*b*).
[72] Environmental Protection Act 1990, s.11(4) (*b*); Sched. 1, para. 7.
[73] Environmental Protection Act 1990, s.11(6).

without going through the notification stages required by section 11(3)(*b*). If the enforcing authority deems the change to be substantial, the holder must apply formally under Environmental Protection Act 1990, s.11(4)(*b*).

If under either procedure an application for variation is refused, the operator can appeal the decision.[74]

Variation Procedures—By the Enforcing Authority

The enforcing authorities have the power to vary the conditions in an authorisation at any time.[75] "They can vary the conditions if it appears to them that the conditions of the authorisation have become inappropriate. This could happen when, for example, the technology for a process changes. The Chief Inspector is under a duty to keep abreast of developments in pollution abatement techniques and technology.[76] Process guidance notes will be updated regularly to reflect changes in knowledge and understanding so the authorities will know when to vary authorisation conditions. **4–041**

Where the enforcing authorities deem it necessary, they will serve a "variation notice" on the operator.[77] This requires the holder to notify the local authority of the action proposed to be taken in order to comply with the authorisation as varied.[78] This would include giving details of additional pollution control equipment to be introduced to meet any emission standards set out in the notice.

If the enforcing authority believes that the action proposed by the holder in consequence of a variation notice will involve a substantial change, the enforcing authority will notify the holder of this opinion.[79] In that case the holder must advertise its actions in accordance with the notice and pay the relevant fee.[80] The enforcing authority will then consider whether the variation notice is acceptable or whether further variation is necessary. If further variation is necessary, the enforcing authority will issue another variation notice to the holder.

There is no requirement to consult or advertise where the change is not substantial. Any variation of the authorisation will appear on the public registers.

[74]Environmental Protection Act 1990, s.15(1) (*c*).
[75]Environmental Protection Act 1990, s.10(1).
[76]*Integrated Pollution Control: A Practical Guide*, para. 3.15.
[77]Environmental Protection Act 1990, s.10(2).
[78]Environmental Protection Act 1990, s.10(4) (*a*).
[79]Environmental Protection Act 1990, s.10(5).
[80]Environmental Protection Act 1990, Sched. 1, para. 6.

Revocation

4–042 The enforcing authority may at any time revoke an authorisation by giving notice in writing to the holder of the authorisation.[81] This is an unconditional grant of power, without any explanatory caveat as to when it is likely to be applied. The Environmental Protection Act 1990, gives one example of the use of revocation. If where the enforcing authority has reason to believe that an authorised process has not been carried on for a period of at least 12 months,[82] it can revoke. A revocation is effective 28 days from the day on which notice is served.[83]

Registers

4–043 The freedom of access to information on the environment that can be seen throughout the Environmental Protection Act 1990, springs from the European Community Directive on Freedom of Information, 90/313. The Directive requires Member States to ensure that public authorities make environmental information available to the public.

In accordance with the Directive, the Environmental Protection Act 1990, requires that Registers containing information on particular applications and authorisations are made available for public inspection at HMIP Regional Headquarters (either Leeds, Bedford, or Bristol) and local authority offices.[84] As a complementary measure, the Environmental Information Regulations 1992[84a] will require disclosure of any information whose disclosure is required by virtue of Directive 90/313 but whose disclosure is not referred to or even prohibited by the Act or the regulations. However, any such disclosure is subject to the exceptions set down in the Directive and Environmental Information Regulations.

The HMIP registers record information relating to IPC processes within their areas. An index to the entire HMIP register is available at HMIP Headquarters in London. Local authorities hold the same information on local authority air pollution control processes in their areas. The "Air Register" of prescribed information (as set out in S.I. 1989 No. 318) relating to application for registration under The Control of Industrial Air Pollution (Registration of Works) Regulations 1989, has been available since April 1, 1989.

Local authorities also keep information on local IPC processes. Although the information is freely available, there has been little or no interest shown in it. Prescribed information related to applica-

[81]Environmental Protection Act 1990, s.12(1).
[82]Environmental Protection Act 1990, s.12(2).
[83]Environmental Protection Act 1990, s.12(3).
[84a](S.I. 1992 No. 3240).
[84]Environmental Protection Act 1990, s.20.

tion for registration/authorisation under the Radioactive Substances Act 1993 (RSA Register), as amended by the Environmental Protection Act 1990, has been available in register format since January 1, 1991.

The Environmental Protection (Applications Appeals and Registers) Regulations 1991, provide details of the information that will be contained in the register. This includes:

- applications—all information submitted with any application for an authorisation made to the enforcing authorities;
- notices and information—any notice to an applicant for additional information and the information furnished in response;
- representations—all information and representations made by the statutory consultees;
- authorisations—a copy of any authorisation granted (including those granted but subject to appeal);
- other notices—all information involved in respect of a variation notice, an enforcement notice, a prohibition notice or a notice of appeal;
- convictions—details of any conviction for an offence relating to the operation of an authorised process;
- monitoring data—all information relating to the monitoring of a prescribed process obtained by the enforcing authority as a result of its own monitoring or furnished to the enforcing authority by virtue of an condition of the authorisation;
- notification—that information has been omitted from the register on the grounds of commercial confidentiality;
- reports—any report by the Chief Inspector relating to an assessment of the environmental consequences arising out of a prescribed process.[85]

Confidentiality

The Act of 1990, allows certain information to be withheld from **4–044**
the register, if inclusion of that information would be contrary to the interests of national security or if publication in the register would prejudice the commercial interests of the business.[86] Any applicant who wants information withheld from the public register needs to have made a request in their application and give reasons why the information should be kept confidential.

In making a decision on confidentiality, the Secretary of State will need to balance competing interests. The principle "freedom of information" predicates the availability of information on applications for authorisation, the requirements for controlling

[85]The Environmental Protection (Applications and Appeals and Registers) Regulations 1991, reg.15.

[86]Environmental Protection Act 1990, s.21,22.

emissions from prescribed processes, and the performance of operators in meeting such requirements. Access to this information assists public procedures, generates confidence in the system and facilitates the public participation, all of which are important to the controls under Part I of the Act. It enables the public to ascertain that adequate pollution control measures are in force.

Yet the principles of national security and free trade must not be put in jeopardy. This latter exception was created by way of recognition that there may be legitimate commercial advantage incorporated in a trade secret, new technology, a particular raw material, or a specific feature which, if made public, would be seriously affected.

The onus is on the applicant to justify a claim of commercial confidentiality. The Government has indicated that it will regard such claims with scepticism. Mr David Trippier, the former Minister for the Environment has stated that "cogent and specific evidence" would be required to substantiate claims.[87] Draft guidance was issued with the DoE News release which stated:

> "Arguments based on general claims, for instance, that disclosure might damage the reputation of the operator and hence his commercial competitiveness are unlikely to be given weight."

A determination of confidentiality lapses after a period of four years.

Local authority functions can be vested in the HMIP in order to transfer control on processes which give rise to national security issues.[88]

ADVERTISEMENT AND PUBLIC COMMENT

4–045 Applications for authorisation and for substantial changes to a process must be advertised in a newspaper circulating in the locality of the site of the process.[89–90] The enforcing authority will consider any representations it receives from the public when determining the application.[91]

The advertisement must contain the following details:

(a) the name of the applicant;
(b) a brief description of the process and where it will take place;
(c) the location of the registers which will have information on the particular authorisation and a statement that access to the registers will be free of charge;

[87] DoE News Release No. 56, January 30, 1990.
[88] Environmental Protection Act 1990, s.4(4).
[89] The Environmental Protection (Applications, Appeals and Registers) Regulations 1991, reg.5.
[90] The requirement does not apply to certain waste oil burners and mobile plant.
[91] Environmental Protection Act 1990, Sched. 1, Part I, para. 5.

(d) an explanation that any person may make representations in writing to the enforcing authority within the period of 28 days beginning with the date of the advertisement.[92]

The advertising schedule is as follows:

- the advertisement must not be placed until at least two weeks has lapsed from the date the application is made (this is to allow local authorities time to check that the application is correct and to place a copy on the public register);
- the deadline for placing the advertisement is taken six weeks from the date when the application is made.[93]

All representations received from the public within 28 days of publication are considered by local authorities in deciding the application. Unlike comments from statutory consultees, local authorities may take into account representations received after the due date if they have not determined the application by this time.[94]

This commentary procedure and the availability of the registers are intended to build public confidence in the system and facilitate public participation. They give the public the ability to determine whether adequate pollution measures are in force and whether there are standards that are in need of attention. Failure by companies to comply, or by authorities to enforce, will be open to public scrutiny. It has been suggested[94A] that vital monitoring information in relation to authorisations has not found its way to the registers in many cases, suggesting that the system of information availability to the public is not working.

Consultation

The enforcing authority is under statutory obligation to consult with various parties with regard to authorisations and variations.[95] The statutory consultees include: 4–046

(a) the Health and Safety Executive (which must be consulted on all applications, except for certain waste oil burners);
(b) the Ministry of Agriculture, Fisheries and Food;
(c) the Secretary of State for Wales;
(d) the Secretary of State for Scotland;
(e) the National Rivers Authority for processes designated for

[92] The Environmental Protection (Applications, Appeals and Registers) Regulations 1991, reg. 5.

[93] "Secretary of State's Guidance on Environmental Protection Act 1990," G.G.3 (91), para. 26(*b*).

[94] "Secretary of State's Guidance on Environmental Protection 1990," G.G.3 (91), para. 26 (*d*).

[94A] "IPC: The First Three Years", Environmental Data Services, 1994.

[95] The Environmental Protection (Applications, Appeals and Registers) Regulations, 1991, reg. 4.

central control which may result in the release of any prescribed substances into "controlled waters";

(f) the sewerage undertaker, or in relation to Scotland the regional or island council, for processes which result in the release of any substances into the sewers;

(g) the Nature Conservancy Council for England, the Countryside Council for Wales and Scottish Natural Heritage for on applications which may involve an emission to air that affects a Site of Special Scientific interest within the their area.[96]

Time Limits for Determining an Application

4–047 Where the application does not contain commercially confidential or nationally sensitive material, the enforcing authority has four months to determine the application.[97] This period is calculated from the date the enforcing authority receives the application. Where an application does contains information which is commercially confidential or which affects national security, the period will be four months from the day those issues have been resolved.

If the enforcing authority fails to determine an application within the four month period allowed, the operator of the process may treat the application as refused. In this case the operator must notify the enforcing authority that it will be treated as such, and then the operator is able to use the appeals procedures.[98]

Enforcement Notices

4–048 If a condition of an authorisation is contravened or the enforcing authority believes it is likely to be contravened, the enforcing authority can serve an enforcement notice upon the operator.[99] This also applies to companies' operation without authorisation. The notice will specify the matters constituting (or likely to constitute) the contravention and require steps to be taken in order to remedy the situation.

Failure to comply with the notice is an offence.[1] For precedent on how to use enforcement notices, the authorities may inquire as to how planning enforcement notices under the Town and Country Planning Legislation have been implemented.

[96] The Environmental Protection (Application, Appeals and Registers) Regulations 1991, reg. 4(1).

[97] Environmental Protection Act 1990, Sched. 1, para. 5.

[98] Environmental Protection Act 1990, Sched. 1, para. 5 (2).

[99] Environmental Protection Act 1990, s.13.

[1] Environmental Protection Act 1990, s.23(1) (*c*).

Prohibition Notice

If the enforcing authority believes that there is an imminent risk of serious pollution from a prescribed process under an authorisation, the authority can serve a prohibition notice on the operator of the process.[2] The notice may suspend that part of the authorisation which covers the operation. In addition, it may impose conditions on any other part of the process.[3] This also applies to companies operating without authorisations. The notice itself will specify the risk, the steps which must be taken to remove it and the time by which they must be taken. 4–049

Appeals

Section 15 of the Environmental Protection Act 1990, gives an operator the right to appeal to the Secretary of State against: 4–050

- the refusal to grant or vary an authorisation;
- the revocation of an authorisation;
- the conditions attached to an authorisation;
- enforcement and prohibition notices; and
- a determination that information is not commercially confidential and must as a consequence be included in the public register.[4]

The Environmental Protection (Applications Appeals Registers) Regulations 1991 give the details of the appeals procedure. The time limits for appeals are:

(a) For appeals against refusal of an authorisation or variation against the conditions attached to an authorisation, within six months of the date of decision complained of;
(b) For appeals against a deemed refusal of an application, within six months from the expiry of the four month period that the enforcing authority has to determine the application (the operator must notify the enforcing authority that he is treating it as if it had been refused, under Environmental Protection Act 1990, Sched. 1, para. 5 (2));
(c) For appeals against revocation of an authorisation, prior to the date on which the revocation takes effect;
(d) For appeals against an enforcement notice, a prohibition notice or a variation notice, within two months of the date of the notice; and
(e) For appeals against a refusal to exclude information from the

[2]Environmental Protection Act 1990, s.14.
[3]*Integrated Pollution Control: A Practical Guide*, 3.23 at p. 9.
[4]Environmental Protection Act 1990, s.15(1).

register on grounds of commercial confidentiality, within 21 days of the refusal.[5]

Where an authorisation is granted for an existing process, it is an offence to operate the process other than in accordance with the conditions of authorisation even if the conditions are the subject of an appeal. Where an authorisation is refused for an existing process and an appeal is lodged, the process may be operated without an authorisation until the appeal has been decided.[6]

4–051 An appeal against a revocation has the effect of suspending that revocation. However, appeals against other notices do not have the effect of suspending those notices or conditions. An appeal against a determination that information is not commercially confidential has the effect of preventing the entry of the information in the register pending the final determination or withdrawal of the appeal.[7]

To lodge an appeal, the operator needs to give notice to the Secretary of State and the enforcing authority. In addition to the notice, the operator must provide the following information:

- a statement of the grounds of the appeal;
- a copy of the relevant application;
- a copy of any relevant authorisations;
- a copy of any relevant correspondence between the appellant and the enforcing authority;
- a copy of any decision or notice by the enforcing authority which is the subject matter of the appeal; and
- a statement indicating whether the appellant wishes the appeal to be determined on the basis of written representations or a hearing.[8]

Appeals can be decided on the basis of written representations or a hearing.

Written representation procedure

4–052 The written representation procedure will only be used if the appellant so requests and the Secretary of State agrees.[9] The Secretary of State is unlikely to object unless a hearing is appropriate because of the importance of the case or the public interest involved.

Where the procedure is adopted following delivery of a notice of appeal to the Secretary of State, the Department will invite a

[5] The Environmental Protection (Applications, Appeals and Registers) Regulations 1991, reg. 10.

[6] "Secretary of State's Guidance on The Environmental Protection Act 1990," G.G.1 (91), para. 18.

[7] Environmental Protection Act 1990, ss.15(8)(9)and 22(5).

[8] The Environmental Protection (Applications, Appeals and Registers) Regulations 1991, reg. 9.

[9] Environmental Protection Act 1990, s.15(5).

response to the notice of appeal from the enforcing authority.[10] The enforcing authority must respond within 28 days from the date the Secretary of State confirms that the appeal is valid. A copy of the enforcing authority's response and any written representation received in response to the notice will be sent to the appellant, who has 14 days to reply.

The exchange of representations usually ends with the appellant's reply unless the Department considers the reply has raised new issues which should to be put to the enforcing authority. The papers will then be passed to an appeals inspector who will may make recommendations to the Secretary of State. The appeals inspector may ask the parties for further information or clarification of their original statements.

Hearing procedure

Where there is to be a hearing the Secretary of State must notify the appellant and the enforcing authority at least 28 days before the date of the hearing.[11] If the hearing is in public, a copy of that notice is advertised in the locality of the process at least 21 days before the hearing is to take place. The hearing takes place in public unless the appeals inspector otherwise orders on the application of either party that commercial confidentiality or national security would be prejudicially affected. **4–053**

Some of the procedures already well-established under planning law, are used as guidance for the system of these environmental appeals.[12]

Hearings are organised by an appeals inspector appointed by the Secretary of State. The appeals inspector will require both the appellant and the enforcing authority to produce not less than 21 days before the hearing, written statements containing the full particulars of their case. Hearings are intended to run informally through round table discussion rather than formal presentation of evidence. There are no formal rules of procedure.

All interested parties who wish to make representations will be given an opportunity to do so. They can to decide to be professionally represented, although this is not compulsory.

There are certain types of appeal which are particularly complex or controversial and require a more formal procedure. In such cases the hearing would be more akin to a public inquiry, including any appropriate pre-hearing procedures.

[10] The Environmental Protection (Applications, Appeals and Registers) Regulations 1991, reg. 12.

[11] The Environmental Protection (Applications, Appeals and Registers) Regulations 1991, reg. 13.

[12] Tromans, *The Environmental Protection Act 1990: Text and Commentary*, (1991) Appendix 4, para. 30.

Determination

4–054 At the conclusion of a hearing, the appeals inspector makes a written report to the Secretary of State containing recommendations. A written report is also provided in respect of written representations. The Secretary of State will consider the report and append his opinion.[13]

Criminal Prosecution

4–055 Section 23 of the Environmental Protection Act creates various criminal offences relating to failure to comply with the statutory duties imposed on operators in Part I of the Environmental Protection Act 1990 including:

- Carrying on a prescribed process without an authorisation;
- Operating a prescribed process without an authorisation or in contravention of the conditions within an authorisation;
- Failing to notify the enforcing authority of a transfer of an authorisation to another person;
- Failing to comply with a requirement of an inspector;
- Failing to furnish information to an enforcing authority when required to do so;
- Making false or misleading statements in relation to an investigation;
- Forging an authorisation;
- Failing to comply with a court order which requires the cause of an offence to be remedied.

The above offences may be prosecuted before a magistrates' court.[14] If the enforcing authority believes that proceedings for the failure to comply with conditions of an enforcement or prohibition notice would be ineffectual in the magistrates' court, the authority may take the proceedings to the High Court.[15].

Penalties

4–056 The Environmental Protection Act 1990 allows a maximum fine of up to £20,000 and/or a maximum two year jail term, in the magistrates' court when a person is convicted of:

(a) Carrying on a prescribed process without an authorisation,
(b) Failing to comply with an enforcement or prohibition notice,
(c) Failing to comply with a court order to take steps to remedy the cause of an offence.[16]

[13]The Environmental Protection (Applications, Appeals and Registers) Regulations 1991, reg. 14.
[14]Environmental Protection Act 1990, s.23(5).
[15]Environmental Protection Act 1990, s.24.
[16]Environmental Protection Act 1990, s.23(2).

Persons guilty of the following offences shall be liable for fines not exceeding the statutory minimum and/or imprisonment for the maximum of two years:

(a) Failing to give notice required for transfer and authorisation without reasonable excuse;
(b) Withholding information upon notice to give information which the authorities reasonably consider they need within the notice period;
(c) Making a false or a misleading statement with regard to a requirement to furnish information under Part I or in order to obtain an authorisation or variation of an authorisation;
(d) Intentionally making a false entry in any record required to be kept as a condition of an authorisation;
(e) Defacing or using a document issued or authorised to be issued under the conditions in an authorisation with the intent to deceive.[17]

The court may instead of, or in addition to, imposing a penalty for breaching an authorisation, or a prohibition or enforcement notice, order the person convicted to take particular steps to remedy the matters that were the subject of the offence.[18] The order will specify the time within which the steps must be taken. In addition, the chief inspector can arrange for reasonable steps to be taken to remedy any harm caused as the result of such an offence. The operator may be required to pay the full costs of such a clean-up action.[19]

WASTE ON LAND

The collection and disposal of waste is a thriving industry which is set to grow both in volume and in complexity. The Environmental Protection Act 1990, reorganises the structure of waste regulation and introduces a tight licensing system for those involved in the handling of waste. The United Kingdom legislation has been greatly influenced by the "framework" Directives issued by the European Commission[20] which has also taken an active interest in specific areas of waste management with initiatives aimed at allocating liability for pollution caused by waste and controlling the land filling of waste. **4–057**

The legislation at national, and increasingly, European level will not only affect those involved professionally in the management of waste but every producer of waste. The increased costs of the dis-

[17]Environmental Protection Act 1990, s.23 (3).
[18]Environmental Protection Act 1990, s.26.
[19]Environmental Protection Act 1990, s.27.
[20]Dir. 75/442; ([1975] O.J. L.194/39) amended by Dir. 91/156 ([1991] O.J. L.78/32).

posal of waste and reduction in the total volume of waste will be met by those who produce it. New economic instruments may be introduced to ensure that the true costs of waste management are met by those who create waste.[21]

WHAT IS "WASTE"?

4–058 Waste includes any substance that is a scrap material, or other unwanted surplus arising from the application of any process, or any substance or article which is required to be disposed of because it is broken, worn out or otherwise spoilt.[22]

The definition is to be construed very widely; anything which is discarded or dealt with as if it were a waste must be presumed to be waste unless it is proved not to be.[23]

What falls into the above categories depends on the subjective view of the person disposing of the material. Therefore material that is the valuable by-product of a process and which may be sold for further processing by another commercial concern can nevertheless be waste in the hands of the original producer.

The Environmental Protection Act 1990 is primarily concerned with "controlled waste" which is defined as; household, industrial and commercial waste. Those expressions are further defined as:

"Household Waste"—waste from domestic property used wholly for purposes of living accommodation including a caravan, a residential home, premises forming part of an educational establishment or a hospital.

"Industrial Waste"—waste from any factory, or from premises used for the provision of public transport services, the supply of public utilities or provision of postal and telecommunication services. Details of what waste falls into this category have been issued in Regulations[24] and it includes waste from contaminated land.

"Commercial Waste"—waste from premises used wholly or mainly for the purposes of a trade, business, or personal recreation or entertainment, where it does not fall into the categories of household or industrial waste.

"Special Waste"—there is a further category of "special waste" which is dangerous, difficult to treat, or requires special provision.[25] Whether waste falls into this category is at the discretion of the

[21] Dir. 75/442; ([1975] O.J. L.194/39) amended by Dir. 91/156 ([1991] O.J. 78/32).

[22] Environmental Protection Act 1990, s.75(2).

[23] Environmental Protection Act 1990, s.75(3). *Cf. R. v. Metropolitan Stipendiary Magistrate, ex p. London Waste Regulatory Authority* [1993] Env. L.R. 417 and *Leigh Land Reclamation v. Walsall Borough Council* [1991] Crim. L.R. 298.

[24] Sched. 3 to the Controlled Waste Regulations 1992, (S.I. 1992 No 588).

[25] Environmental Protection Act 1990, s.62.

Secretary of State. The Secretary of State is empowered to issue regulations to specify how this waste should be dealt with. No regulations have been issued yet under the EPA but there are existing regulations under the Control of Pollution Act 1974.[26] Categories of waste include asbestos, acids and pharmaceutical waste.

The vast majority of all waste produced is therefore going to be covered by the Act. Uncontrolled waste includes waste from agricultural premises, mines and quarries, and most radio-active waste.[27] The development of E.C. policy will undoubtedly question these areas of exclusion from control. It seems likely, for example, that "non-organic" agricultural waste may, before too long, be subject to control.

The framework Directive, as amended, provides for the registration of certain waste management processes, particularly where waste can be processed without adverse environmental impact on site (for example), so exempting such processes from many of the licensing requirements in Part II, described below.

The Secrctary of State may also make regulations applying provisions of the Act to waste that is not controlled within a prescribed geographical area[28] thus being able to bring a previously unregulated area within the ambit of the Act.

ENFORCING AUTHORITIES FOR PART II

Three new authorities are created with separate responsibility for 4 059
regulation, disposal and collection of waste. The separation of these functions is meant to increase efficiency, but also to avoid the potential conflict where previously the same authority dealt with both the operational side of waste disposal and its regulation. Increased regulation and consequently increased resources will have to be supplied by local authorities.

Waste Regulation Authorities

The Waste Regulation Authority has a largely supervisory role. It 4–060
is responsible for framing policies and for the implementation of those policies.[29]

A significant part of its responsibility is the supervision of the

[26] Control of Pollution (Special Waste) Regulations 1980, (S.I. 1980 No. 1709) as amended by (S.I. 1988 No. 1790).
[27] Environmental Protection Act 1990, s.75(5-8).
[28] Environmental Protection Act 1990, s.63.
[29] DoE Circular 10/91

waste management licensing system.[30] Waste Regulation Authorities are increasingly positive in their enforcement of licensed activities despite problems encountered as a result of criminal proceedings particularly where a defendant is, in effect, a "shell company" or unable (allegedly) to afford compliance with an order of the court.

Waste Regulation Authorities have inspectors to enforce licensing requirements. Waste Regulation Authorities are obliged to carry out inspections for these purposes. The inspectors may enter private land for inspection purposes where controlled waste has been deposited on the land or where the waste regulation authority has reason to believe that there may be concentrations or accumulations of noxious gases or liquids. The powers of inspection have teeth; it is a criminal offence to fail to comply with the inspectors' lawful requirements as to entry and inspection.

Waste Disposal Plan

4–061 As part of their management responsibilities waste regulation authorities are required to draw up a waste disposal plan. This plan identifies the current and projected amounts of waste in the area and administers the disposal authorities' policies for disposal and recycling.[31] One of the benefits of the plan is that it is expected to give waste disposal contractors a long term view of the waste that they will have to deal with in their area. The plan will also include policy statements in relation to the issue of licensing by the authority. The plan is required to give a strategic overview which should be useful in determining planning applications for new facilities.[32] A filing date will ensure that these plans are drawn up and filed with the Secretary of State.

Area-based waste disposal plans will be replaced by a national statement of policies and priorities and local plans provided for under the Town and Country Planning Act. Regional planning guidance will be issued, drawn from data and other information from planning authorities and reflective of their interpretation of "national" data.

Waste Regulation Authority

4–062 A model for the proposed waste regulation authorities has been operating in London since 1986. It is funded by a levy, calculated pro rata based on the population in each London Borough Council. If it proves typical, then waste regulation authorities will have a more vigorous approach to prosecuting persons who act in breach of

[30]Discussed below at p. 67.
[31]Environmental Protection Act 1990, s.50.
[32]Waste Management Paper No. 4, para. 3.10.

their licence or who deposit waste without possession of a licence. Successful prosecutions by the LWRA in the year 1989/90 totalled 94; the latest in a trend of increased prosecutions over the last few years.[33]

Liaison and Accountability

The Waste Regulation Authority is obliged (pending the disappearance of waste disposal plans, referred to previously) to consult with the National Rivers Authority or any local authority or other party likely to be affected by any measures it intends to take. The general public should also be provided with an opportunity to make representations. This is partly to ensure that Waste Regulation Authorities act in concert with other bodies having responsibilities in the area, but is also part of a new "consensual" approach. Instead of issuing proposals from above, the waste regulation authority must now consult those involved in disposal or treatment of waste before any proposal is implemented. This is to be welcomed, as clearly those businesses involving waste management are the most directly affected by the proposals of the waste regulation authority.[34] **4–063**

Structure

Waste Regulation Authorities are formed within the county councils except for Greater London, which already has its own, and the metropolitan areas which will either have a specially constituted waste authority or the local district council will be responsible. Although individual county councils have been given this responsibility, it is the government's intention that local regional groups should be formed to ensure more efficient use of local waste disposal facilities.[35] The Secretary of State can require one large regional authority to be formed if the county councils do not do so voluntarily. Other powers given to the Secretary of State over waste regulation authorities include the power to take over the functions of the waste regulation authority where it has failed to discharge its functions or comply with the Secretary of States directions.[36] **4–064**

Waste Disposal Authorities

Waste Disposal Authorities have responsibility for arranging for the disposal of waste. They do not actually carry out the disposal of waste themselves, but must form a Waste Disposal Company or **4–065**

[33]Waste Management, "Changes in Control" by J. Ferguson, Director of the London Waste Regulation Authority.
[34]Environmental Protection Act 1990, s.50.
[35]Environmental Protection Act 1990, s.31.
[36]Environmental Protection Act 1990, s.31.

contract out the work to a private business. Their duties include managing the sites where collected waste will be deposited and also providing refuse amenity sites for the residents of an area to deposit waste.[37]

Local Waste Disposal Companies

4–066 If the waste disposal authority wishes to be involved in the operational side of disposal it must set up a separate company at "arms length" to carry out this role. There are two types of company that can be set up by the waste disposal authority. In the first, all the shares are owned by the waste disposal authority but only one fifth of the board of directors can be members or officers of the local authority.[38] In the second there will be private share ownership as well as local authority ownership and the company would be able to take advantage of private investment without being restricted by the finance rules that apply to local authorities. Whichever type of local authority waste disposal company is set up it is intended that it should compete on a commercial footing with any private contractor.[39]

Recycling of Waste

4–067 There is a scheme of "exchangeable credits" between the waste disposal authority and the waste collection authority to encourage recycling. The amount saved by either authority through the other's recycling activities will be recognised. This scheme is also extended to where a third party saves the waste disposal authority money by collecting waste for recycling. However payments to third parties are not always a policy priority for some authorities. Most credits until now have been paid to the waste collection authorities.[40]

Waste Collection Authorities

4–068 It is the waste collection authority's function to arrange for the collection of waste in its area. The authority is under a duty to collect household waste free of charge, but will only collect commercial waste on request and a reasonable charge may be made for it. Collection of industrial waste will be only be undertaken with the consent of the disposal authority and will again be charged for. The authority can stipulate the type of receptacles it requires for household waste and it is within the discretion of the authority to provide such receptacles and to charge for them. Similarly, the

[37]Environmental Protection Act 1990, s.51.
[38]Local Government and Housing Act 1989, Part 5.
[39]Environmental Protection Act, 1990, s.32.
[40]Environmental Protection Act, 1990, s.52. *Cf.* S.I. 1992 No. 462, as amended.

waste collection authority will supply suitable receptacles for commercial or industrial waste on request but may impose particular requirements for certain types of waste.[41]

Structure of Waste Authorities

Waste collection falls to the local district council or London borough. Both the waste disposal authority and the Waste Regulation Authority are the function of the county council. The poacher/game keeper conflict, where a body had control of both the regulatory and the operational side of waste disposal which had been perceived as a problem, is resolved by keeping the two bodies administratively separate by having separate committees in control and different teams of officers. The sharing of support staff is acceptable but the whole process of separation is subject to the approval of the Secretary of State. **4–069**

WASTE MANAGEMENT LICENSING

A waste management licence is required by anyone in occupation of land who either keeps or disposes of controlled waste. The operator of mobile plant is also required to obtain a licence. A "licensed waste manager" is one in possession of a licence under section 35 of the Environmental Protection Act 1990. Licences are also issued for the treatment or keeping of waste by intermediate holders. The licensing process is now governed in detail by new regulations, supplemented by a revised Waste Management Paper and a Department of the Environment Circular.[42] **4–070**

Conditions

The licensing is controlled by the waste regulation authority subject to the supervision of the Secretary of State. The conditions of the licence can relate not only to controlled waste but to the disposal, treatment or keeping of any other waste. They are likely to regulate the activities which the licence authorises, stipulate precautions to be taken and/or works to be carried out. **4–071**

The approach to the imposition of conditions on licences will be similar to that previously used for licensing under COPA. That legislation imposed conditions in the following areas:

[41] Environmental Protection Act, 1990, s.47.

[42] Waste Management Licensing Regulations 1994 (S.I. 1994 No. 1056). *Cf.* Waste Management Paper No. 4 and DoE Circular 11/94.

- safety precautions;
- site opening hours;
- quantities of waste received;
- type of waste received;
- storage of waste;
- waste containment;
- design and construction of site;
- ground surface liquids;
- litter blowing about site;
- record keeping procedures.

This list is not exhaustive. The waste regulation authority has a wide discretion to impose any condition that it thinks to be appropriate providing it relates to the underlying purpose of the legislation. A fundamental limitation of the former regime in Part I of the Control of Pollution Act was that conditions (and their enforcement) had to be referable to the "deposition" of waste. Consequently there was a limitation on the imposition of conditions for the provision of site fencing, for example. This limitation is now removed under section 35 of the Environmental Protection Act.

It is possible for conditions to relate to adjoining land or be impossible to carry out without the consent of a third party. This situation is not properly addressed by the Environmental Protection Act 1990. The Act does require third parties to grant the holder of a licence such rights in relation to land as will enable the holder to comply with any requirements imposed on him by the licence.[43] Yet there is no intention to impose a blanket duty on a third party who has no interest in the licence to assist a neighbour in satisfying the conditions imposed on by the licence. There is no mechanism within the Act to enforce this duty nor any penalty for failure to comply with it. However, the third party would still presumably be open to an action brought by the licence-holder for breach of statutory duty.

Grant of Licences

4–072 An application for a licence must be made to the local waste regulation authority. This is varied slightly in the case of a mobile plant operator who must make a application to the waste regulation authority in the operator's principal place of business.[44]

If planning permission is required for the land, this must be acquired prior to an application for a licence but if an established use certificate, stating the lawfulness of the use of the site for waste disposal, (pursuant to section 192 of the Town and Country Plan-

[43] Environmental Protection Act 1990, s.35(4).

[44] Environmental Protection Act 1990, s.36(1). *Cf.* the Waste Management Licensing Regulations 1994 (S.I. 1994 No. 1056).

ning Act 1990) is already in force then those activities may be licensed.[45]

In order to obtain a licence the applicant must satisfy the criteria for being a "fit and proper person." There are three tests:

(a) the applicant or any other "relevant person" must not have been convicted of a "relevant offence";
(b) the management of the licensed activities must be in the hands of "technically competent person"; and
(c) the applicant must have adequate financial provision to discharge the obligations arising from the licence.

Relevant Person; Relevant Offence

The applicant or any other "relevant person" must not have been convicted of a "relevant offence." The definition of a "relevant offence" is to be found in the Waste Management Licensing Regulations 1994 which refer to convictions for offences under a variety of Acts, including the Control of Pollution Act, the Control of Pollution (Amendment) Act, and the Water Resources Act.[46] **4–073**

A problem for large commercial operations, however, is likely to be the extent to which conviction of a subsidiary company, or a person within a subsidiary or connected company, will be considered to be a "relevant offence." The successful prosecution of a company at one site could for instance result in the failure of future applications for a licence to manage a new site. It might also cause the revocation of existing licences.

The indications are that weight will be given to the nature, gravity and number of offences committed. Particular factors pointing to the refusal of a licence will be if the offence involved special waste, caused serious pollution or a penalty of imprisonment was imposed. This will be so even where the offence was committed by a "relevant person" rather than the applicant.

The definition of "relevant person" covers the following:

(a) An employee of the applicant or licence holder if the offence was committed in the course of this individual's employment,
(b) A partner in a business if the offence was committed in the course of the business;
(c) A director, manager, or company secretary or other similar officer if the company was convicted at any time while they held a post in it;
(d) A company where the offence was committed at a time when the applicant or licence holder was an officer of that company.[47]

[45] Environmental Protection Act 1990, s.36(2).
[46] reg. 3.
[47] Environmental Protection Act 1990, s.74(7).

A significant number of people could fall within the ambit of this definition of "relevant person." It will involve licence holders in meticulous checks into the career history of any prospective employee. The guidelines that have been issued provide some insight into the way Waste Regulation Authorities will implement these criteria. Nevertheless, consistency of application by different waste regulation authorities will be hard to achieve.

Technically Competent Person

4–074 The management of the licensed activities must be in the hands of a "technically competent person." The requirements are set out in regulations issued by the Secretary of State.[48] They will necessitate the introduction of a system of training and education. Waste Management Industry Training and Advisory Board certificates will provide the badge of technical competence for present purposes. It is planned to introduce these to ensure that there will be sufficient certified managers in place for the new licensing system.[49] There will be provision within the system for certificates to be issued to those who have already gained five years experience within the industry without any further training being necessary. An agreement between the Board and the DoE commenced on the October 1, 1990.[50] It is expected that the funding for the training will be largely found from within related industries but with some government grants to institutions.

Financial Provision

4–075 The applicant must have adequate financial provision to discharge the obligations arising from the licence. Unlike the previous two conditions, the Secretary of State has no power to make regulations in relation to this. However, guidelines are to be found in Waste Management Paper No. 4 on the Licensing of Waste Management Facilities.[51] It seems likely that some type of bonding, insurance, industry or company financial pool will be required. This requirement would favour large companies who would either have a record of no claims on their pollution policies or a substantial capital base to enable them to borrow to provide a bond. It may make it difficult for a new company, with limited financial means, to set up in the field of waste management. This would leave only the local authority waste disposal companies and a very few large private concerns to have control of the entire market. Insurance in this area is not widely available and, without the full scope of a company's liability being obvious, the premiums are likely to be very high. Waste Man-

[48] Waste Management Licensing Regulations 1994 (S.I. 1994 No. 1056).
[49] *Ibid*. reg. 4 and 5.
[50] *Hansard*, H.L. Vol.522, col.290.
[51] (3rd. ed. 1994).

agement Paper No. 4 highlights some of these concerns and sets out the different stages in the sites life for which the provision will need to be made. It will involve detailed analysis of a prospective licencees finances and insurance cover and a combination of insurance and some form of guarantee may well be required.

Even if the three criteria are satisfied and the applicant is judged to be a "fit and proper person" an application for a licence can still be rejected providing the rejection is for the purpose of preventing:

(a) Pollution to the Environment;
(b) Harm to human health;
(c) Serious detriment to the amenities of the locality.

"Pollution of the environment" is defined as pollution of land, sea or air, due to the release of substances resulting from waste and capable (by reason of the quantity or concentrations involved) of causing harm to any living organisms supported by the environment.[52]

"Serious detriment to the amenities of the locality" is intended as a possible reason for a refusal of a licence where planning permission is not relevant. If planning permission is in force in relation to the use to which the land will be put under the licence, then this provision cannot be used to refuse a licence. This question will already have been considered at any early stage of the planning application.

These grounds for refusal are very wide and may present considerable problems to those applying for licences. However a licence cannot be refused where the problems referred to can effectively be controlled by the imposition of conditions. This is an important provision because, in practice, most potential problems could be quite properly dealt with by the imposition of conditions.

There is a duty placed on the waste regulation authority to consult with the National Rivers Authority and the Health and Safety Executive, and to take account of any representations that those two bodies may make. The National Rivers Authority may request that a licence be refused and in the event of a dispute, the matter is to be referred to the Secretary of State who will make a final decision.[53]

If within four months of receipt of an application the waste regulation authority has not granted an application then it shall be deemed to have failed. The period can be extended by agreement with the waste regulation authority. If an application for a grant of a licence is refused, the applicant is able to appeal to the Secretary of State.[54] Appeals are discussed later in this Chapter.

[52]Environmental Protection Act 1990, s.29(3).
[53]Environmental Protection Act 1990, s.36(4).
[54]Environmental Protection Act 1990, s.36(9).

Variation of licences

4–076 The waste regulation authority is able to modify the conditions of the licence provided that in the opinion of the authority, it is unlikely to require unreasonable expense on the part of the licence holder. The waste regulation authority would want to modify a licence in the case of danger to public health or water pollution arising from site activities. The authority is required to vary a licence if it is necessary to prevent pollution to the environment, known to harm human health or a detriment to the amenities of the liability. The Secretary of State has the power to direct a waste regulation authority to vary any licence; it remains to be seen how much the Secretary of State will use these powers to control the industry.

The licence holder is also able to apply to have the licence conditions varied.[55] On variation, there is a similar duty of consultation with other bodies by the waste regulation authority as applies upon the initial consideration of a licence. There is a period of two months after which an undetermined application will be deemed to have failed.

Revocation of licence

4–077 A licence can be either partially or fully revoked, although this power tends to be used rarely. The grounds for full revocation of a licence are:

(a) That the holder is no longer a fit and proper person by reason of a conviction for a "relevant offence."
(b) The continuation of licensed activities would cause pollution to the environment or harm to human health or would be seriously detrimental to the amenities of the locality affected.

The waste regulation authority can therefore revoke if it believes a site to be a danger to public health. The individual waste regulation authority determines what constitutes "seriously detrimental." There are some situations which would clearly merit immediate action, such as if the site was attracting pests, such as rats or flies, which were not being controlled and were spreading to the surrounding area, or if the site was creating methane gas which was threatening ground in the area.

If a site licence is partially revoked, the licensee may no longer be able to carry out the licensed activities. The waste regulation authority can nevertheless impose conditions on the licence which

[55]Environmental Protection Act 1990, s.37.

are binding on the licensee. This enables the waste regulation authority to prevent an operator from having any benefit from the licence whilst leaving the operator with a continuing liability for any conditions which may be imposed by the licence relating, for example, to the maintenance of the site.

Partial revocation, so far as it authorises the carrying on of the activities specified in the licence, may be imposed if the management of the activities is no longer in the hands of a technically competent person.[56]

A licence cannot be revoked either partially or fully if the reasons for revocation could be remedied effectively by the imposition of conditions. However a licence may be revoked where the licence conditions are not complied with following notification by the authority.[57]

Suspension of licence

The waste regulation authority may suspend a licence if: **4–078**

(a) the licence holder is no longer a fit and proper person because the licensed activities are not in the control of a technically competent person;
(b) serious pollution of the environment or serious harm to human health has resulted from the licensed activities or is about to do so; or
(c) the continuance of the licensed activities will lead to serious pollution or harm.

The fact that the licence is suspended does not prevent the licence holder being liable to comply with any directions from the waste regulation authority to deal with or prevent pollution or harm. Should the licence holder fail to do this, the licence holder would be committing a criminal offence.

There is a requirement of "serious harm to human health" for a licence to be suspended but there is only a requirement of "harm to human health" if it is to be revoked. Suspension appears to be designed as the immediate response to a situation, and it is maintained even where an appeal is pending. Revocation, however, is the ultimate sanction but does not normally take effect while an appeal is pending.

Surrender of licences

Under the Control of Pollution Act 1974 licences could be unilaterally surrendered thereby relieving the licence holder of any further **4–079**

[56] Environmental Protection Act 1990, s.38(2).
[57] Environmental Protection Act 1990, s.42(5).

responsibility for the land. However, under the Environmental Protection Act 1990, existing licences cannot be unilaterally surrendered.

A licence may only be surrendered if it is acceptable to the waste regulation authority. This could have significant repercussions for licence holders, since they are no longer necessarily in the position where they can release themselves from their licence and any conditions attached to it. The waste regulation authority will refuse to accept the surrender of the licence if satisfied that the land is likely to cause pollution of the environment or harm to human health.[58] They will decide whether this is the case after inspection. They also have a duty to consult with the National Rivers Authority to establish their agreement to the surrender of the licence.

The application to surrender a licence is deemed to be refused if a period of three months goes by without determination.[59]

Waste Management Paper No. 26 issued by the DoE sets out the basic approach that will be taken by the Waste Regulation Authority to the surrender requirements.[60] When it is considered that the waste in a landfill has sufficiently stabilised a phase of "Completion Monitoring" begins. Strict default criteria for leachate, groundwater, gas and settlement and stability are proposed. An application to surrender will only be accepted when these criteria are met and there is no upward trend in the monitoring data. This monitoring will continue for a minimum of two years if sufficient monitoring data is present but five years if not. The regime imposes a considerable burden on most landfill operations which is leading them to consider the surrender of their licence in the period before the regime comes into force.

Once the surrender of licence has been accepted, the licensee who is also an owner is exempted from the important provisions imposing a liability to pay for the clean-up of polluted land upon the owner.[61]

Transfer of licences

4–080 A licence can be transferred on joint application of the present holder and the proposed new holder. The proposed new holder will only be approved if the waste regulation authority is satisfied that the proposed transferee is a fit and proper person.[62]

[58] Environmental Protection Act 1990, s.39(6).

[59] Environmental Protection Act 1990, s.39(10).

[60] *Cf.* Waste Management Paper No. 26A, "Landfill Completion". *Cf.* Waste Management Paper No. 4 which deals (in Chap. 7) with surrenders otherwise than in relation to landfills.

[61] Environmental Protection Act 1990, s.61.

[62] Environmental Protection Act 1990, s.40.

Fees for licences

There are scales of fees for licences and applications. It is proposed that the fees will cover the estimated cost of the whole of waste regulatory activity.[63] The aim is to produce a national scale of charges which will not necessarily reflect the local variations in the actual cost of waste regulatory activity in that area, but will be standard throughout the country.[64] **4–081**

Supervision of Licensed Activities

The waste regulation authority has a continuing duty of supervision of the licence holder. This is to ensure that pollution of the environment and harm to human health do not occur. It is also to ensure compliance with the conditions attached to the licence.[65] **4–082**

The waste regulation authority has extensive power to carry out remedial work on the land covered by the operator's licence in an emergency and to recover the cost of that work from the licence holder.[66] The permission of a licence holder does not have to be sought before work is carried out while the licence is in force. It is possible for the holder to refuse payment on the grounds that no emergency requiring any work has occurred or that the expenditure was unnecessary. Once a licence has been surrendered the cost can only be recovered from the former licence holder for the amount of work carried out prior to the surrender of the licence.[67]

Appeals

Providing a decision has not been taken on the explicit direction of the Secretary of State, an appeal is allowed in the following situations where: **4–083**

(a) Restrictions are placed on an application for licence;
(b) Conditions are attached to a licence;
(c) The conditions attached to a licence are modified;
(d) A licence is suspended;
(e) A licence is revoked;
(f) An application to surrender is rejected;
(g) An application to transfer is rejected;[68]

[63] Environmental Protection Act 1990, s.41.
[64] *Hansard*, H.L. Vol.522, col.335.
[65] Environmental Protection Act 1990, s.42(1).
[66] Environmental Protection Act 1990, s.42(3).
[67] Environmental Protection Act 1990, s.42(3).
[68] Environmental Protection Act 1990, s.43(1).

In the case of a transfer, it is the proposed transferee who must appeal.

Where a licence has been suspended, a pending appeal does not postpone the suspension. However, where a licence is modified or revoked and an appeal is lodged, the modification or revocation is ineffective unless the authority inserts a statement in the notice of modification or revocation that it shall be effective immediately. The authority then bears the risk of having to pay compensation in the event that it is found to have acted unreasonabley by the Secretary of Sate or the inspector who hears the appeal. The same risk applies if an authority is found to have unreasonably suspended a licence.

Waste Management Papers

4–084 The DoE has issued a series of waste management papers which are intended to act as guidelines to the industry and waste regulation authorities. They include (in Paper No. 4) guidance on licence applications.

CRIMINAL OFFENCES RELATING TO LICENCES

4–085 In respect of any application that relates to a licence, it is a criminal offence to make statements which are either known to be false in a material particular or made recklessly and are false in a material particular.[69]

A "material particular" is an item of information which the authority would have acted in reliance on in such a way that it may affect the outcome of their decision. It does not appear to be necessary that the authority shall have actually relied on the statement or that the material particular actually influenced the decision. Upon conviction on indictment, there is a possible sentence of two years imprisonment.

Unauthorised Disposal of Waste

4–086 It is a criminal offence to deposit controlled waste or knowingly cause or knowingly permit controlled waste to be deposited, unless there is a current waste management licence in force and the deposit is in accordance with the licence.[70] The treatment, keeping, or disposal of controlled waste will also be an offence in similar circumstances. The only exemption at present, is in relation to household

[69]Environmental Protection Act 1990, s.44.
[70]Environmental Protection Act 1990, s.33(1).

waste from domestic property,[71] although Regulations deal with such areas as construction waste, agricultural waste and premises such as factories where waste is stored pending disposal.[72]

There has been criticism of the wording of this clause as the offender who has not actually deposited the waste is only required to have "knowingly caused" or "knowingly permitted" the deposit. The element of knowledge must therefore be proved for an offence to have been committed.

This offence is designed to prevent the situation where a waste producer consigns waste to a contractor knowing or suspecting that the contractor will dispose of the waste unlawfully. The waste producer is instead put in a position where he cannot ignore the consequences of assigning waste to an irresponsible contractor. This should produce a measure of self regulation in the waste management industry, as a waste producer will want to see a relevant licence pertaining to the land where his waste is to be deposited by the contractor. Importation of the requirement of "knowledge" must be seen against the background of the Duty of Care, which is examined later in the present Chapter, at paragraph 4–097 *et seq.*

Treating, Keeping or Disposing of Waste Causing Harm

The Environmental Protection Act 1990 covers a further offence **4–087**
which is the treating, keeping or disposing of controlled waste in a manner likely to cause pollution of the environment or harm to human health.[73] This is a wide offence; it is not linked to the holding of a licence but the offence can be committed by someone holding a current and valid licence. It does not require any state of knowledge; the offence is committed by the disposal of the waste in an incorrect manner. An example of such an offence might be fly-tipping or the disregard of the duty of care through improper packaging of waste.

Contravention of Licence Conditions

An offence is committed regardless of whether the condition relates **4–088**
specifically to the deposit of waste or to an ancillary matter such as the keeping of records referred to previously. This was a loophole under the previous legislation where only contravention of a licence condition relating to the actual handling of waste was an offence.[74] This led to the situation where conditions designed to ensure the safety and security of a waste deposit site could be flouted with impunity.

[71]Environmental Protection Act 1990, s.33(2).
[72]Controlled Waste Regulations 1992 (S.I. 1992 No. 588).
[73]Environmental Protection Act 1990, s(33)1(*c*).
[74]Control of Pollution Act 1974, s.3(1)(*a*).

Failure to Comply with Direction of Authority

4–089 It is an offence to fail to comply with any requirement to take measures to deal with or avert pollution or harm during the suspension of a licence by the waste regulation authority.[75]

Waste in Motor Vehicles

4–090 There are special provisions for the case where waste is carried in or deposited from a motor vehicle. The person who controls or is in a position to control the motor vehicle is treated as "knowingly causing" the waste to be deposited, whether or not that person gave instructions for this to be done.[76] This provision is intended to prevent fly-tipping where the owner of the waste is not known but merely the identity of the vehicle from which it is deposited. There is no need for actual knowledge on the part of the controller of the vehicle. The mere fact that this activity is being carried out makes the controller liable.

Defences

4–091 There are three defences to liability for the above offences:

(a) A person took all reasonable precautions and exercised all due diligence to avoid the commission of the offence;
(b) A person acted under the instructions of his employer and that person neither knew nor had reason to suppose that his actions constituted an offence;
(c) The acts in question were carried out in an emergency and to avoid danger to the public.

It is a matter of fact in each individual case as to whether the third defence is applicable but there is a duty to provide particulars to the waste regulation authority of the incident as soon as reasonably practicable.[77] A road accident where waste is accidentally, but illegally, deposited would be a good example of a situation where the third defence would apply.

Penalties

4–092 The penalties for breach of these provisions are severe, being a maximum of two years imprisonment on conviction on indictment or an unlimited fine. The penalties are increased further where the

[75]Environmental Protection Act 1990, s.38(10).
[76]Environmental Protection Act 1990, s.33(5).
[77]Environmental Protection Act 1990, s.33(7)(c).

waste is "special waste" to a maximum term of imprisonment of five years.[78]

POWERS OF AUTHORITIES TO REMEDY POLLUTION

4–093 The Control of Pollution Act 1974, was criticised for not having enough powers of enforcement. As a result of that criticism, the Environmental Protection Act 1990 has various powers that enable the waste regulation authority to become involved in the clean-up of deposits of waste. This can occur with or without the permission of the owner or occupier, and if appropriate, very shortly after the owner or occupier is required to take remedial action themselves.

Power to Require Removal of Unlawfully Deposited Waste

4–094 The occupier of land where waste has been unlawfully deposited can be required by either the waste regulation authority or the waste collection authority to remove the waste within a period of 21 days, or to take steps with a view to eliminating or reducing the consequences of the deposit of the waste. If the occupier fails to comply with a notice setting out what is required, then the relevant authority has the power to deal with the waste itself and recover any expenses reasonably incurred in doing so.[79]

This provision is aimed primarily at waste that has been fly-tipped or otherwise unlawfully deposited. This could affect a licence holder who is prima facie the occupier of a site where waste has been deposited in contravention of the licence because, for instance, it is of a type not authorised by the licence for that particular site.

An occupier served with a notice has a period of 21 days to appeal against that notice. An appeal can be made on the basis that the occupier was an "innocent occupier" who neither deposited nor knowingly caused or permitted the deposit of the waste. A material defect in the notice would also provide grounds for an appeal. Failure to comply with the notice is a criminal offence punishable by a fine.

There are additional powers for both the Waste Regulation Authority and the Waste Collection Authority to act immediately to remove the waste if it appears to the authority that immediate action must be taken in order to remove or prevent pollution or harm to human health. The authority has similar powers if there is

[78]Environmental Protection Act 1990, s.33(8) and (9).
[79]Environmental Protection Act 1990, s.59(6).

no occupier of the land or the occupier neither made nor permitted the deposit of the waste.[80] When the authority acts immediately, it will have recourse against whoever was responsible for depositing the waste in respect of its expense of removal, treatment and clean-up. The primary burden will fall on the site occupier unless this individual can prove innocence in regard to depositing or knowingly causing or permitting the deposit of the waste. In that case the authority will have the right to recover its costs against the actual depositor of the waste.[81]

The authority has the ability to deal with all waste that has been illegally deposited without first having to establish to whom the waste belongs and who is responsible for it.

Duty of Waste Regulation Authority to Inspect Land Believed to be Causing Harm

4–095 The section with the potential for having the biggest impact on landowners is section 61 of the Environmental Protection Act 1990 which is not (at September 1994) in force. Although the title to section 61 reads "Duty of waste regulation authorities as respects closed landfills," the wording of the section actually extends beyond closed landfills to land in a state which could cause harm to humans and the environment. In addition to used landfill sites it will be applicable to other sites that have handled controlled wastes where noxious liquid is discharged from the site.

Section 61 of the Environmental Protection Act 1990 imposes a duty on the local waste regulation authorities to monitor and clean up sites where, by reason of "relevant matters,"[82] there is a danger of "pollution of the environment or harm to human health" within their areas. The waste regulation authority is entitled to recover the cost or part of the cost incurred in doing so from "the person who is for the time being the owner of the land."[83]

Thus, the local waste regulation authorities are under a duty to inspect land in their area which may cause problems, clean up any polluted land and send the bill to the "owner" of the land. These costs may be astronomical. In the United States, the government estimates the average clean-up cost per site which poses a threat to be $47 million. Not surprisingly, all owners, potential owners and

[80] Environmental Protection Act 1990, s.59(7).

[81] Environmental Protection Act 1990, s.59(8).

[82] "Relevant matters" are noxious gases or liquids caused by deposits of controlled waste which have accumulated and are now emitted or discharged from the land. This section covers gases produced by microbiological processes within the waste or chemical compounds arising from reactions within the waste. Tromans, *The Environmental Protection Act 1990: Text and Commentary*, (2nd ed. 1993), p. 43–177.

[83] Environmental Protection Act 1990, s.61(8).

parties acting with a certain degree of involvement in property are looking very carefully at how this section will be applied.

The focus upon the reimbursement by the owner is a move toward strict liability for owners of polluted land and a move away from the "polluter pays principle." The owner could be an innocent purchaser who happens to purchase a polluted piece of property or a lessor who is not causing the pollution.

"Owner" is not defined in the Environmental Protection Act 1990 and thus will need to be defined judicially to determine whether it includes various involved parties such as mortgagees and lenders. However, the owner has been given a wide definition elsewhere in United Kingdom legislation.

> "The person other than a mortgagee not in possession, who is for the time being entitled to dispose of the fee simple of the land, and includes also a person holding or entitled to the rents and profits of the land under a lease or agreement."[84]

If the definition of owner under the section 61(8) comes to the United Kingdom's courts for interpretation, and the court adopts the wide approach, the net of liability would encompass owners and lessors, disregarding any lack of involvement in the polluting activities. Thus a lessor is concerned to ensure that its tenant is using the land in an environmentally safe manner. The lessor can ask for contractual guarantees to this effect.

The type of land on which the waste regulation authority is to **4–096**
fulfil its duty is yet to be seen. The land must be in a state where pollution of the environment or harm to health is likely to be caused. This language encompasses the immediate problem of build up of dangerous gases, such as methane, on landfill sites and the pollution of groundwater sources by escaping leachate. But it is also wide enough to catch almost any kind of existing pollution the Authority already has information about. Closed landfill sites will be priority under this section.

The duty extends to land adjoining the original site which may be polluted. In this instance, it is not clear whether the owner of the original site or the adjacent owner will be required to reimburse the waste regulation authority for the cost of cleaning up the land.

The duty does not apply to sites for which a site licence is in force or to sites where the waste regulation authority has accepted the surrender of a site licence.[85] It follows that a purchaser should insist that the vendor surrenders his licence to the waste regulation authority pursuant to section 39 of the Environmental Protection Act 1990, before the purchase is effected. If the waste regulation authority is satisfied that the condition of the land is unlikely to cause pollution or harm then it shall accept the surrender of the

[84] Agricultural Statistics Act 1979, s.6(1).
[85] Environmental Protection Act 1990, s.39.

licence and issue a "certificate of completion." The purchaser should seriously consider insisting on the grant of this certificate as a condition precedent to the completion of the transaction.

DUTY OF CARE WITH REGARD TO WASTE MANAGEMENT

4–097 The Duty of Care in respect of transfers of waste came into effect in April 1992. Under this Duty, all parties to a transfer of controlled waste must make sure that waste is not mishandled. Their responsibility lies in checking the next party to the transfer and keeping alert that others along the line are acting in compliance with their own Duty of Care.

In order to comply with the duty parties to the transfer of waste must take all reasonable measures to:

(a) Prevent any other person from unlawfully disposing of, treating or storing controlled waste;
(b) Prevent the escape of waste from both their own control or that of any other person;
(c) Ensure that waste is only transferred to an authorised person or to a person authorised for transport purposes;
(d) Ensure that there is a written description accompanying any transferred waste that is sufficient to enable any person who is receiving the waste to comply with their Duty of Care and to enable them to handle the waste properly.[86]

The Duty of Care is essentially self-regulating, as compliance is secured mainly by waste holders checking on each other in connection with transfers of waste.

Everyone in the chain is responsible for checking the next person and keeping their eyes open for any suspicious behaviour elsewhere in the chain:

> "Every waste holder should be alert for any evidence that suggests that the duty of care is not being observed or that illegal waste handling is taking place."[87]

Section 34 Environmental Protection Act 1990 does not give an enforcement function to any particular authority. However the Secretary of State may, in the future, appoint an enforcing authority if necessary.

The DoE has assessed the cost of implementing the Duty of Care. It is not meant to be burdensome for individual waste producers, as

[86] Environmental Protection Act 1991, s.34.
[87] DoE Environmental Protection Act 1990, "Waste Management—The Duty of Care Code of Practice (1991)," s.5(5).

they will simply need to introduce new procedures into their waste management practices. The DoE estimated that this will work out at £11.5 to £16 per year for an average company.

Code of Practice

The Secretary of State has issued a Code of Practice to provide guidance on how to discharge the duties imposed upon them. The Code sets out a step by step guide for dealing with waste. **4–098**

It is not an offence to breach the Code of Practice itself, but rather to breach the Duty of Care. Compliance with the Code does not amount to compliance with the Duty of Care; however compliance with the Code is admissible as evidence in court.[88]

Parties to Whom the Duty of Care Applies

The Duty of Care applies to importers, producers, carriers, those who keep, those who treat, and those who dispose of controlled waste. There is an exception for occupiers of domestic property in respect of household waste. The parties to a transfer of waste are expected to take measures that are applicable to them in their capacity and that are reasonable in the circumstances. Reasonable measures in the capacity of one party will require different measures from that of another party. For instance, as discussed in the Code of Practice, the producer of waste will need to: **4–099**

(a) Identify its waste in a transfer note,
(b) Correctly package the waste, keeping in mind its content and destination; and
(c) Transfer the waste to an authorised carrier.

However, a carrier of waste will not have the same responsibilities as the producer under the Duty of Care. A carrier may need to:

(a) Adequately package waste under the carriers' control, since it cannot rely exclusively upon how it is packaged or handed over by the previous holder;
(b) Visually inspect the waste to make sure it appears to match the description given by the producer;
(c) Create a new description, if certain types of alteration of the waste has occurred; and
(d) Check the waste management licence of the waste manager.

The Department of Environment has indicated that local authorities, as waste producers themselves, are subject to the Duty of Care in the same way as any private company. The Crown is also bound by the Act.[89]

[88] DoE Circular 19/91.
[89] *Ibid.*

Issues for producers of waste

4–100 The above previous section lists the general responsibilities attributed both to producers of waste and others under the Duty of Care. This section explores the responsibilities of producers in more detail. Producers are potentially more vulnerable to breaches of duty. They are unlikely to be in the waste management business and may have less understanding of their obligations. The discussion is however pertinent to other parties in the waste disposal chain who have similar responsibilities.

Is it waste?

4–101 The first step for a producer is to determine whether the substance that is being discarded fits within the definition of "waste." The relevant definition is set out in section 75 of the Environmental Protection Act, discussed at paragraph 4–058. It describes waste in general as any substance which is required to be disposed of because it is "broken, worn out or otherwise spoilt." This definition is itself open for questions including whether an item is waste if it still has value to others (as scrap material may) or if it has a further use (such as for some waste oils that are recycled for industrial use).

The Code of Practice defines waste practically from the point of view of the person producing or discarding it. If any of the following questions can be answered by the producer in the affirmative, the substance at issue probably is waste:

(a) Is it what would ordinarily be described as waste?
(b) Is it a scrap material, surplus to the business purposes of the producer?
(c) Is it an effluent or other unwanted surplus substance?
(d) Does it need to be disposed of as broken, worn out, contaminated or otherwise spoiled?
(e) Is it being discarded or dealt with as if it were waste?

Applying these criteria, scrap material, even though it has a value to others, is surplus to the business requirements of the producer, and would be regarded as waste. As for waste oil that is recycled to be used for other businesses, although it can be sold and is useful to others, if it would ordinarily be described as waste from the point of view of the producer, it would therefore also be considered waste.

Waste Transfer Documentation

4–102 Waste that is transferred must be accompanied by a transfer note which is to be completed, signed and kept by the parties to the transfer.[90] The note must state the quantity of waste, how it is

[90]See Annex to DoE Circular 19/91.

packed (loose or in a container), the time and place of transfer and, if in a container, the type of container used. There must also be a description of the waste either separately or in the transfer note.[91]

The parties to the transfer must keep records of the transfer note and a description of the waste for two years.[92] The Code of Practice adds that each individual transfer does not need to be separately documented where there are multiple transfers of the same type of waste between the same two parties in a year.

Often waste management companies will provide their clients with pre-printed transfer notes for completion. They may ask for guarantees beyond the scope of the legislation, such as a warranty from producers that they will be liable for any damage caused by the waste. Acceptance of the transfer note as part of the contract between the parties, will escalate the burden placed on the producer.

Waste managers may offer to keep records for their clients of the transfer notes and waste description. This practice also is at odds with the Duty of Care. The Regulations specify that both the "transferor and the transferee shall each keep the written description of the waste and the transfer note" for two years after the transfer. The transferor must therefore keep its own records. From a practical point of view, if a question arises and the waste regulation authority needs to view the records, a producer may not want its waste manager to be in possession of the only copies.[93]

Transfer of waste to an authorised carrier

Waste may only be handed on to authorised persons or to persons authorised for transport purposes. Usually waste is transferred to a waste carrier who transports it, or directly to a waste manager who stores waste or who processes it in some intermediate way. For certain carriers, the producer is not required to check registration: **4–103**

(a) charities and voluntary organisations;
(b) waste collection authorities collecting any waste themselves (though an authority's contractors are not exempt);
(c) British Rail, when carrying waste by rail; and
(d) ship operators where waste is to be disposed of under licence at sea.[94]

On transfer to a carrier other than these exceptions above, the producer must inspect the carrier's certificate of registration, or a copy certificate provided by the waste regulation authority, (certified under the Control of Pollution (Amendment) Act 1989,

[91] Environmental Protection (Duty of Care) Regulations 1991, (S.I. 1991 No. 2839), reg. 2.
[92] *Ibid.*
[93] *Ibid.* reg. 4.
[94] DoE Environmental Protection Act 1991; Waste Management (The Duty of Care) Code of Practice, para. 3.6.

and the Controlled Waste (Registration of Carriers and Seizure of Vehicles) Regulations 1991).

Where waste is sent to a waste manager for disposal or treatment, the Code suggests that the waste holder should physically check the waste management licence (or disposal licence, if issued before April 1993) and ensure that it permits the type and quantity of waste at issue to be dealt with.

In the case of repeated transfers it is not necessary to carry out this procedure for every transfer of waste. The Code suggests that the licence, registration or evidence of exemption should be seen and checked at least once a year.

CONTROL OF POLLUTION (AMENDMENT) ACT 1989

4–104 This Act deals with the specific problem of fly-tipping by regulating the transport of waste. It came fully into effect in April 1992.[95]

A person is guilty of an offence if that person transports controlled waste in the course of business or with a view to profit without being registered. Transport within the same premises or in the course of import or export of controlled waste is not included in the offence.

It will be a defence to show that the waste was being transported in an emergency or that it could not have been known that it was controlled waste being transported. It is also a defence that a person was acting under instructions from their employer. On conviction a person will be liable to a fine.

Regulations for the registration of carriers came into force on the October 14, 1991.[96] Certain bodies such as the waste regulation authority are exempt from registration. Application must be made to the waste regulation authority and this may be refused if the applicant has been convicted of a prescribed offence and the waste regulation authority considers it undesirable that the applicant be authorised to transport waste. There is an appeal procedure for applicants who have been refused registration.

There is also provision for the seizure of a vehicle used in the commission of an offence if the waste regulation authority is unable to ascertain who was using the vehicle at the time. The waste regulation authority may also eventually dispose of the vehicle and its contents after taking specified steps to locate the owner.

[95]S.I. 1991 No. 1618.
[96]S.I. 1991 No. 1624.

EUROPEAN COMMUNITY LEGISLATION ON WASTE

European Community law and policy on waste is an area increasingly targeted for action.[97] Initiatives deal with hazardous wastes and their transport,[98] landfilling of waste and the apportionment of liability where damage has been caused by waste. 4–105

Council Resolution of May 7, 1990 on Waste Policy

This Resolution lists the aims of the European Council. General principles are set out including an emphasis on reduction of waste and recycling of waste. There are proposals for bringing the criteria for products within the concept of BATNEEC[99] and a community wide Eco-label award which scheme was adopted in 1992.[1] A need for community-wide data on the volume and type of waste produced is recognised. 4–106

The Resolution also recommends that the quantity of waste consigned to landfill should be reduced where appropriate and appears to favour incineration and a more environmentally sound method of waste disposal. This aim is reflected in the draft Directive on the Landfill of Waste.

It is eventually intended that all the policies proposed in the resolution should be implemented through further detailed Directives.

Draft Directive on Civil Liability for Damage Caused by Waste

The first draft Directive on civil liability for damage caused by waste was published in September 1989. The present draft was issued in July 1991 and incorporated significant amendments made by the European Parliament. Although the Directive only deals with one aspect of environmental impairment, it is considered important as it is expected to set the stage for future Directives covering other types of environmental damage.[2] 4–107

Parties Liable

The Directive imposes liability on the producer of the waste in the event of damage to people or property or impairment to the environment caused by waste. A stated objective of the Directive 4–108

[97] Haigh, *Manual of Environmental Policy: the E.C. and Britain*, Chap. 4.

[98] Unusually, the transfrontier shipment of hazardous waste is subject to E.C. regulation (259/93), rather than a directive, the normal vehicle for implementation of E.C. policy.

[99] *Cf.* pp. 24 and 25 *ante*.

[1] Regulation 880/92 Eco-label.

is to apply the "polluter pays principle" and to prevent disparities among laws of Member States leading to artificial patterns of investment thus distorting competition.[3]

A "producer" may include an importer or the operator of a waste disposal centre. The person having actual control of the waste at the time of a polluting incident will be liable if that person is unable to identify the producer. In certain circumstances the person responsible for the installation, establishment or undertaking where the waste was lawfully transferred may be liable, on the basis that this person falls within the definition of "having actual control of the waste."

The producer will only escape liability if in the "absence of fault," damage to the environment is caused intentionally by a third party—for example in the case of deliberate vandalism or if the damage or impairment resulted from "force majeure" an overwhelming event outside the control of the producer.

The eliminator of the waste may attract liability by virtue of having control of waste. This person is given special protection in the proposal, providing that there is an absence of fault. This individual, who carries out disposal or recovery operations, and must prove that the producer of waste deceived him over the character of the consignment of waste which caused the damage.

Damage and impairment to the environment caused by Waste

4–109 The damage caused by "waste" covers all types of waste generated by economic activity, but does not include nuclear waste or pollution caused by oil at sea. "Impairment to the environment" is defined as significant physical, chemical or biological deterioration of the environment. This is a very wide definition and has been criticised by International Chamber of Commerce for being too broad. The ICC also expressed concern about the concept of "damage to the environment" being contained in a Directive whose purpose was to deal with damage caused by waste.[4]

Strict liability

4–110 The Directive proposes "strict liability" for producers of waste where damage is caused by waste to a person or property or where there is "impairment to the environment."[5] The House of Lords Select Committee which considered the Directive stated in its summary that:

> "strict civil liability should apply to those who carry out dangerous or potentially dangerous activities which give rise to

[3] House of Lords, European Community's Select Committee, 25th report, "Paying for Pollution," Part I, para. I.

[4] Draft Statement, November 21, 1989.

[5] Draft Directive on Civil Liability for damage caused by Waste, Art. 3.

environmental damage. It is appropriate to apply a strict liability regime to waste management."[6]

There are legitimate concerns that while the strict liability system may be economically efficient in addressing environmental problems it would not necessarily attribute the cost directly to the polluter. There are also circumstances where the producer of waste may be liable although he did not have effective control over it.[7] This is almost inevitable when waste passes through a number of hands before its final disposal. Even the most rigourous vetting of assignees by a producer of waste could not ensure that a polluting incident does not occur.

This liability is joint and several, meaning that when more than one party is found liable the liability is shared, although each party can be held responsible for the whole amount at issue.

An important provision states that liability will not be retrospective.[8] This means liability only applies to damage caused by incidents occurring after the date on which the Directive is adopted. Therefore it would not cover land with existing pollution upon it, such as that which was used as a landfill site at one point in time. This remains a major problem which has not yet been addressed at EC level.

A question arises if the pollution is "continuing," so that it both pre-dates and succeeds the date the Directive is adopted. Will the clean-up costs relate to cleaning up the entire contamination or just that which could be attributed to damage after the adoption of the Directive? Because of the impracticality of determining when certain pollution occurred in this situation, one would think that the liability would include cleaning up the entire damage. However, this will need to be tested in the courts.

It is not possible to "contract-out" of the liability imposed by the Directive, no contractual clause can successfully seek to exclude these provisions of the Directive.

Insurance

The European Parliament in the July 1991 draft recommended a system of compulsory insurance. This was rejected by the Commission in the first instance because discussions with insurers suggested that no such suitable insurance would be made available without the insurers having a much clearer idea of the potential risks. The amended proposal requires companies to name their insurers for civil liability purposes in their published accounts. Whether the insurers are willing to produce an affordable policy that would cover these liabilities remains to be seen. **4–111**

[6]House of Lords Select Committee on the European Community's Report, October 16, 1990, Summary of Conclusions, p. 37.

[7]Draft Directive on Civil Liability for damage caused by waste, Art. 2.2(*b*) (i).

[8]*Ibid.*, Art. 13.

Absent or bankrupt polluter

4–112 The Commission is studying possible compensation arrangements where the polluter is either unknown or unable to pay.[9] In its submission to the Select Committee on the European Communities the Confederation of British Industry stated "The current availability of cover for gradual pollution is being rapidly eroded and is unlikely to be generally available under a strict liability regime."[10]

In the United States there is a contingency fund, known as Superfund, which is expected to cover situations where the polluter cannot be identified or is unable to pay. The European Commission has in the past rejected this idea, but in a recent Green Policy Paper which set out alternatives for a civil liability for pollution system, the fund (a "joint compensation fund") idea was included as a genuine alternative.

Common interest group actions

4–113 Common interest groups are able to join in proceedings for damage caused by waste that have already been brought by other parties, subject to conditions defined within national legislation. The draft Directive envisages court actions brought by common interest groups or individuals who may "seek only the prohibition or cessation of the act giving rise to the injury to the environment."[11] In some European jurisdictions, it is possible to bring such actions.

Draft Directive on the Landfill of Waste

4–114 This Directive is a direct result of the Council Resolution of May 7, 1990. Its intention (as originally stated) is to "ensure that Member States adopt a homogeneous policy relating to landfills and that standards are harmonised throughout the Community."[12]

The general tenor of the Explanatory Memorandum appears to be hostile to the concept of landfilling of waste in general, preferring alternative methods of waste disposal, particularly incineration: "another objective that should be considered is the need to minimise landfilling of waste."

Use of landfill as a method of disposal varies throughout the Community. However landfill forms a very significant part of United Kingdom waste disposal. About 90 per cent. controlled waste arising in the United Kingdom went into landfill in 1990. Therefore, this Directive is likely to have a major effect on the United Kingdom waste disposal industry.

[9] *Ibid.*, Art. 11.
[10] *Ibid.*, Art. 3, at p. 84, qq. 297, 311 and 316.
[11] *Cf.* pp. 5 and 6, *ante*.
[12] COM(91) 102, [1991] O.J. C190 and COM(93) 275, [1993] O.J. C21.

Classification of waste in the Directive is by origin. Waste is either:

(a) "municipal" meaning domestic as well as commercial or trade refuse similar to domestic refuse; or
(b) "industrial" meaning waste arising from manufacturing or industrial activity.

Waste is further described as hazardous, non-hazardous or inert.

There are provisions for a permit system and technical standards to determine whether waste is acceptable for landfill or to which class of landfill the waste ought to be consigned.

There is also a proposal for strict civil liability to be placed upon the operator in respect of damage or impairment caused by the land-filled waste. The operator would also have to provide a financial guarantee covering the estimated cost of closure procedures and after care operations to the landfill site. It is envisaged that these costs will be passed on to the polluter in the price to be charged for the disposal of waste in the landfill. In view of present problems occurring in landfill sites which have only materialised a significant number of years after closure of the site, insurance is likely to be very difficult to obtain in respect of these risks.

In addition to a financial guarantee by the operator, the draft Directive proposes a "Landfill Aftercare Fund." This would cater for the normal aftercare costs of closed landfills and damage to the environment not recoverable from the insurance or financial guarantee of operators.

The House of Commons Environment Committee in its seventh **4–115**
report criticised the draft Directive for dealing with this one issue of landfills in isolation from other aspects of waste disposal. This criticism was supported by the Government in its response to the report:

> "in particular we see a need to stress the desirability of considering landfill as a part of the European Community approach to waste disposal as a whole."[13]

In June 1991 the Department of the Environment submitted an Explanatory Memorandum on the draft Directive. In it the DoE stated that a new directive should not "add significantly to the responsibilities of waste regulation authorities currently being brought forward." It also expresses concern about the implications of the proposals for a Landfill Aftercare Fund and the financial guarantees. It concludes that:

> "landfill operators may incur some additional costs to meet the proposed higher standards"

[13]DoE: The Government's Response to the Seventh report from the House of Commons Select Committee on the environment, February 1992, Chapter 2.

The Commons seventh report recommended that the findings of the DoE's insurance working group are submitted to the Commission for consideration.

It can seen that, while discussions are obviously continuing on the final draft, there are a number of areas of concern to the waste management industry. In particular, the financial implications could be huge if standards are adopted which will entail extensive categorisation of waste before landfilling.

The Council of the E.C. has adopted a common position in relation to the long-debated Landfill Directive. Echoing the "hierarchical" approach landfill is to be seen as a final option in the waste management process. Accordingly the philosophy is likely to be based on measures minimising environmental impacts from landfill. Some categories of waste will not be regarded as suitable for acceptance for landfill except through the medium of "monolandfill". There are indications that co-disposal may be practised only subject to restrictions. More particularly, any "legal" practise of co-disposal may continue without restriction of time but subject to supervision by relevant authorities in a member state in circumstances where the environment is not endangered. Failure to comply with such a restriction will require cessation of the practice five years following the entry into force of the Directive. This provision will be observed with interest, particularly in view of the Environmental Protection Act provisions on the surrender of licences. It seems likely that this "concession" (if concession it be) will not apply to new co-disposal operations. Another issue with a resonance with the Environmental Protection Act is the requirement for financial guarantees in resepect of landfills. The Waste Management Licensing Regulations clearly stipulate that guarantees are applicable to sites operating on or after May 1, 1994. The proposed Directive refers to *any* landfill, no matter what its age although a period of 10 years is allowed for introduction of such facilities for financial guarantees.

STATUTORY NUISANCES

4–116 Statutory Nuisance is deals with in Part III of the Environmental Protection Act 1990. Statutory nuisances are adverse environmental conditions that have been specifically identified and legislated against by statute. They have developed out of the common law concepts of public and private nuisance.[14] Those responsible for a statutory nuisance who do not abate it after being formally notified are committing a criminal offence.

[14]See discussion of common law nuisances in Chapter six, para. 6–002, below.

The Environmental Protection Act 1990 introduces little new law in this area but does consolidate existing legislation from a wide variety of sources.

The following are statutory nuisances providing they are prejudicial to health or a nuisance.

(a) Any premises ("premises" are given a very wide definition, including land and vessels). This particular section only covers the physical state of the premises;
(b) Smoke emitted from premises: exemptions are made (*inter alia*) for smoke from the chimney of a private dwelling within a smoke control area, and dark smoke from trade or industrial premises or a boiler or industrial plant;
(c) Fumes or gases emitted from premises;
(d) Any dust, steam, smell or other effluvia arising on industrial, trade or business premises;
(e) Any accumulation or deposit;
(f) Any animal kept in a place or in such a manner as to be prejudicial to health or a nuisance;
(g) Noise emitted from premises;
(h) Noise emitted from or caused by a vehicle, machinery or equipment in a street;
(i) Any other matter declared by any enactment to be a statutory nuisance.

The local authority is under a duty to inspect its area to detect any statutory nuisances.[15]

ENFORCEMENT PROVISIONS

Where a local authority is satisfied that a statutory nuisance exists **4–117** or is likely to occur or re-occur it is required to serve an abatement notice either prohibiting or restricting the adverse environmental conditions or stipulating steps to be taken to modify its effect. A person served with an abatement notice may appeal to the magistrates court within 21 days of the date of service. The local authority itself can be the subject of a complaint to the magistrates court alleging a statutory nuisance.

Failure to comply with an abatement notice is a criminal offence. If the offence takes place on an industrial trade or business premises there is maximum fine of £20,000 but otherwise the maximum fine is £2,000 together with a further fine based on the period of time the offence continues after conviction.[16]

[15]Environmental Protection Act 1990, s.79.
[16]Environmental Protection Act 1990, s.80(5), (6).

The local authority has extensive power to take steps to abate the nuisance if an abatement notice has not been complied with. It can then recover its costs from the person responsible. If the local authority considers that criminal proceedings in the magistrates court would not be an adequate remedy it may take proceedings in the High Court to obtain an injunction. The nature of these proceedings means that it is likely to be a last resort on the part of a local authority.[17]

An individual is also able to bring an action in the magistrates' court on the basis that he has been aggrieved by a statutory nuisance. Proceedings by way of a complaint against a local authority were referred to above. The court can then make an order that has a similar effect to an abatement notice and it is a criminal offence to contravene such an order.

DEFENCES

4–118 There is a general defence of "reasonable excuse" which is an objective test of reasonableness usually connoting that the circumstances surrounding the alleged statutory nuisance were beyond the control of the person concerned.

Where the statutory nuisance arises on trade or business premises it will be a defence to show that best practical means were used to prevent or counteract the effect of the nuisance.[18]

This defence is not available where the local authority is seeking an injunction or where the statutory nuisance is caused by smoke emitted from premises (unless from a chimney) or where fumes or gases are emitted from premises[19].

LITTER

4–119 The litter provisions, Part IV of the Environmental Protection Act 1990, are apocryphally said to have been inspired by Margaret Thatcher's shame at having to drive with visiting dignitaries through London's debris-strewn streets. Part IV of the Act, a revision of the Litter Act of 1983, provides more stringent sanctions for non-compliance and stricter enforcement measures than existed under the previous legislation.

[17]Environment Protection Act 1990, s.81.
[18]Environmental Protection Act 1990, s.80(7).
[19]*Ibid.* s.80(8). BPM discussed further in s. 3.

Reliable statistics on litter are hard to find. It is thought that smokers are responsible for a third of all litter by dropping cigarette butts, packets and matches. Although the nature of litter has changed over the years, it is by definition caused by individuals throwing waste onto the ground instead of into a bin.[20]

The Environmental Protection Act 1990 has launched a two-pronged attack on litter. A new duty is imposed duty on various authorities to keep public land and highways free from litter. The Government estimates that this new duty will add some £50 million to spending on street cleaning by local authorities in England. There is also a newly created ability for individuals to apply for a litter abatement order against authorities that are not keeping their areas clean.

Duty to keep land and highways free from litter

The Act imposes a duty to keep designated "relevant land,"[21] trunk roads,[22] and relevant highways[23] free from litter on local authorities, principal litter authorities,[24] Crown authorities, designated statutory undertakers,[25] educational institutions and the occupiers of any relevant land within a "litter control area" of a local authority.[26] **4–120**

The principal litter authorities may designate land within their area a "litter control area."[27] They will do so when the condition of the land is, and will continue to be, a detriment to amenities of the locality.[28] The type of land at issue would be car parks, beaches, shopping precincts, and industrial estates. The Act does not provide for appeal against such a designation, although persons affected by the order will have the opportunity to make representations in respect of the designation.[29]

"This Common Inheritance: Britain's Environmental Strategy," (1990), Cm. 1200 p. 197

[21]"Relevant land" is land that is open to the air (or partially covered to make it apply to bus stations and sports stadiums) and under the direct control of one of the authorities.

[22]"Trunk road" means a highway or a proposed highway, which is a trunk road by virtue of s.10(1) or s. 19 of the 1980 Act or by virtue of an order or direction under s.10 of the 1980 Act or under any other enactment (s.239(1)).

[23]"Highway" means the whole or part of a highway other than a ferry or bridge, Highways Act 1980, s.5.

[24]In England and Wales the following are "principle litter authorities":

[25]"Statutory undertakers" are those bodies authorised to carry out transport-related functions, such as British Rail and the London Regional Transport.

[26]Environmental Protection Act 1990, s.89.

[27]Environmental Protection Act 1990, s.90(3).

[28]Environmental Protection Act 1990, s.90(4).

[29]Environmental Protection Act 1990, s.90(6).

Code of practice

4–121 To help explain the duty to keep relevant land free from litter, the Secretary of State has issued a code of practice to provide guidance and to set acceptable standards of cleanliness.[30]

The code divides "relevant land" into 11 categories of which the most important are the two road categories, and the four general zones. These four general zones are ranked according to land usage and volume of traffic. The code assigns to each category a standard of cleanliness. This is not for example, how frequently the area is to be cleaned or swept; instead it is a measure of the cleanliness to be achieved in the area.

Aggrieved individuals and Litter Abatement Orders

4–122 Individuals aggrieved at the state of litter in a "relevant area", may take their complaint to the magistrates' court (or, in Scotland, to the Sheriff), having given five days notice to the responsible party.[31] Where the magistrate thinks the complaint is justified, a litter abatement order will be issued which will require the offending area to be cleaned by the responsible party within a specified time. Non-compliance is an offence, and the penalty is a maximum of £1,000, with a further fine of £50 for each subsequent day that the Litter Abatement Order is ignored.

Litter abatement notice

4–123 Certain principal litter authorities can issue litter abatement notices, for any "relevant land" (including that of a Litter control area but not their own land or highway land) to be cleared of litter within a specified time period, and subsequently kept clear.[32] Non-compliance can mean that the recipient of the notice is liable to summary conviction, with the same penalty as for a Litter Abatement Order.

If a person on whom a litter abatement notice is served fails to comply with the requirement imposed by the notice, the authority may enter the land, clear the litter and recover from that person the expenses attributable to having done so.

Street litter control notices

4–124 Where there is street litter, certain principal litter authorities can issue street litter control notices on premises with a frontage to a

[30]Environmental Protection Act 1990, s.89(7)
[31]Environmental Protection Act 1990, s.91(1)
[32]Environmental Protection Act 1990, s.92

street in the vicinity of the particular problem.[33] This could be to remedy recurrent litter problems posed by businesses whose clientele generate litter, such as fast-food chains. The conditions for the issue of these notices are:

(a) recurrent defacement by litter of a street in the vicinity of the frontage;
(b) that any open land which forms part of the premises and is by the frontage, is in such a state as would be "detrimental to the amenities of the locality" without the notice; or
(c) that the activities within the premises produce litter which defaces nearby streets.[34]

The notice will impose requirements necessary to keep the specified areas free from litter, such as the emptying of rubbish bins. The person on whom the Street Litter Control Notice is to be served—21 days' notice must be given beforehand by the council—can make comments to the council about the notice which should be taken into account. The notice can be appealed to the magistrates' court, which can uphold alter or quash the notice. Failure to comply with the notice is an offence, and can lead to a maximum fine of £1,000.

Littering by individuals

Littering by individuals is dealt with in section 87 of the Environmental Protection Act. Not only does this section raise the maximum penalty for littering to £1,000—but it also extends to all district and borough councils, and National Parks, the authority to issue fixed penalty notices for littering (similar to parking tickets). The penalty is £10. Non-payment of this (within 14 days) can lead to prosecution for littering in the magistrates' court.[35] **4–125**

MISCELLANEOUS SECTIONS

This section examines some of the more topical sections of the Environmental Protection Act 1990, such as directors' liability, contaminated land registers, genetically modified organisations and radioactive substances. **4–126**

[33] Environmental Protection Act 1990, s.93.
[34] *Ibid.*, subs. (2)
[35] Environmental Protection Act, s.88.

Directors' and Officers' Liability

4–127 '. . .until more directors have sweated it out in the box, business will not take its responsibilities to the environment and health and safety seriously[36]."

When an offence committed by a body corporate is proved to have been committed with a consent or connivance of, or because of the neglect of any director, manager, secretary or similar officer of that body, the officer will be personally liable as well as the body corporate itself.[37] If corporate affairs are managed by corporate members, any acts or defaults of a member in connection with the member's functions of management can generate personal liability.

Section 157 of the Environmental Protection Act 1990 which covers personal liability, follows a trend of legislation that holds corporate management personally responsible for negligent acts of the corporation. The Water Resources Act 1991 has a similar provision.

It is not sufficient for directors and officers, in response to this legislation, simply to purchase Directors and Officer's liability insurance (D. & O. policies). First, such policies do not underwrite costs and fines involved in a criminal prosecution, because that is regarded as contrary to public policy. Secondly, most policies only cover civil claims for negligence, so that a finding of wilful neglect or default is not covered.

The better response is to establish procedures which will pre-empt environmental problems. This would entail auditing the company's existing procedures to environmental issues that need attention. Once these issues are known, a programme can be constructed to monitor in-house systems and establish whether they are running in an environmentally sound manner and complying with relevant law.

It is important to have a clear delegation of responsibility for monitoring the systems. It is crucial to set up education on environmental issues for employees. This should include practical advice on legal aspects. "Flippant memos on environmental matters don't seem very amusing in the context of a court hearing following a serious incident."[38]

Contaminated Land Registers

4–128 One of the most controversial sections of the Environmental Protection Act 1990, is section 143 which places a duty on local authorit-

[36]Paul Smith, In-house, "Directors' Liability for the Environment," November 1990, p. 31.
[37]Environmental Protection Act 1990, s.157(*a*).
[38]*Op. Cit.* n. 36.

ies to compile and maintain registers of land which has been put to a contaminative use. A contaminative use is "any use of land which may cause it to be contaminated with noxious substances."[39]

Contamination is not synonymous with pollution but is seen as a precursor to it. The Royal Commission on Environmental Pollution has stated that today's contamination may be tomorrow's pollution when "substances accumulates in the environment to what are harmful concentrations, or as knowledge is gained of hitherto unsuspected effects."[40]

The controversy centres upon the ability of such registers actually to provide useful information about land whilst not doing unjustifiable damage to its value. The register is permitted to contain information on land which "could possibly be polluted" because of the use or past history of the land. It will not render judgement on the actual state of the land.

By way of example of the potential extension of registration, Birmingham City Council expected 30 per cent of the area of the city to be included in the registers.[41]

Potential problems with the register

The Government has recognised the possibility that a register entry indicating possible contamination may cause the value of a site to fall or, in an extreme case, may make the land unsaleable. Register entries could also give rise to public alarm whether or not there is reasonable cause.[42] **4–129**

Consultation Paper justifies its position by saying that risks are inherent in any attempt to identify land which may be contaminated and that the potential for alarm will always be present. It points out that most of the information allowed in the registers is already public knowledge and could easily be discovered upon investigation of the site. The government took the view that it was better for everyone concerned to be aware of possible contamination so that appropriate investigations could be carried out on a basis of knowledge.

The difficulty with this analysis is that it assumes everyone using the register will understand the bases upon which it has been assembled. Unfortunately, this will most likely not be the case. The stigma arising from inclusion included on the "contaminative uses register" may be enough drastically to lower market values, even though cleanup has taken place.

[39]Environmental Protection Act 1990, s.143(6).
[40]Royal Commission on Environmental Pollution: "Tackling Pollution Tenth Report Experience and Prospects." Cmnd.9194. HMSO, para. 1.12.
[41]Ryden Planning Occasional Paper: "Contaminated Land—Implications of the Environmental Protection Act 1990."
[42]DoE consultation "Public registers of land which maybe contaminated paper, May 1991, s. 4.1.

As a result of such concerns and their effect in particular on land prices in an already depressed market, it was announced that the Registers would not be implemented as initially envisaged.

History

4–130 Section 143 is the brainchild of studies and reports on contaminated land. In 1988 the Conveyancing Standing Committee of the Law Commission studied a proposal to reverse the principle of *caveat emptor.*[43] The proposal itself was ultimately rejected, although the idea that more information should be publicly available on the contamination of land was endorsed. The Committee suggested creating public registers of information on contaminated land in its report entitled "Let the buyer be well informed."[44]

Subsequently, in 1988, the DoE put together a working party on Registers of Contaminated Land which determined that while land records existed for different purposes, there was no integrated source of information on contamination. In creating a register which records contaminative uses, the public would be alerted to the possibility of contamination.

At best registers would only provide an inkling of the possibility that there might be a problem. The DoE Working Party on Registers of Contaminated Land decided that, even if the pointers given by the register were not conclusive, they were better than nothing, since registers showing actual contamination of land were not a practical possibility. It placed the average cost of investigation into actual contamination at not less than £15,000 per hectare. The cost of providing the registers with extensive information on the status of the land would therefore be prohibitively expensive.

Implications for Landowners

4–131 There will be consequences for property owners if the land is included on a contaminative uses register. The value of a site may be reduced even if the contamination exists in low levels, would be inexpensive to cleanup or is not causing damage.

Clean-up costs could exceed the site value so that negative site values may be a possibility. It may be difficult to obtain a loan to purchase land on the register. It may be difficult to conclude a property transaction as conditional deals will include "walkaway" clauses relating to the transfer of liability from one party to another.

All professional property advisors will need to make a check of

[43] "Let the buyer be well informed." Recommendations from Conveyancing Standing Committee of the Law Commission. Law Commission, 1989.

[44] This comes from a May 1991, DoE Consultation Paper on Contaminated Land and quotes from a report of the Law Commission Standing Committee on Conveyancing.

the registers as part of their standard procedures when advising clients.

GENETICALLY MODIFIED ORGANISMS

Genetic modification is the transfer of genes between different organisms in order to develop new varieties of life. In the last twenty years the concept has greatly expanded and now offers the prospect of improvements in medicine, industry and agriculture. For example, genetic modification has been used in the production of human insulin or growth hormone. Genetic modification is also used to clean up oil spills, control pests by biological means, and to replace the need for fertiliser. **4–132**

Genetic modification carries with it risks to the environment:

> "the risks that genetic engineering may entail, and the associated ethical considerations, have been debated since the technology came into the existence in the early 1970s. There can rarely have been new technology which has attracted so much intense discussion of its potential risks from such an early point in its development. To some extent this reflects the nature of the science. There is a natural apprehension stemming from the belief that scientists are now manipulating something as fundamental as life itself."[45]

Genetically modified organisms could change the composition of species' communities thus affecting the established inter-relationships between predators, competitors, parasites and pathogens. Some organisms could pose a threat to human health. At their most extreme, new organisms could conceivably affect weather patterns, the nitrogen cycle or regenerative soil processes.[46]

To reduce the risk of harm to people and the environment, Part VI of the Environmental Protection Act seeks to impose precautionary controls on genetically modified organisms. The purpose of this Part of the Act is to prevent or minimise "any damage to the environment which may arise from the escape or release from human control of genetically modified organisms."[47] The Act prohibits the importation, acquisition, release and marketing of genetically modified organisms without carrying out a risk assessment of possible damage to the environment,[48] notifying the Secretary of State of the **4–133**

[45] Royal Commission on Environmental Pollution, 13th Report, "The Release of Genetically Engineered Organisms to the Environment," para. 1.3.

[46] Royal Commission on Environmental Pollution, 13th Report, "The Release of Genetically Engineered Organisms to the Environment", para. 1.2, 4.2.

[47] Environmental Protection Act 1990, 106(1)

[48] Environmental Protection Act 1990, s.108.

keeping of genetically modified organisms and, in certain cases to be prescribed obtaining consent from the Secretary of State.[49]

There is a duty of care on those who import, acquire, keep, release and/or market genetically modified organisms. This includes responsibility for identifying risks of damage to the environment that could be or have been caused by the genetically modified organisms, using the "best possible techniques not entailing excessive cost" (BATNEEC) for preventing any damage to the environment being caused by their keeping or release. (Environmental Protection Act, section 109). The Secretary of State may serve a prohibition notice on any person he has reason to believe is endangering the environment by breaches of this duty. (Environmental Protection Act, section 110).

A public register will be set up containing information on matters under Part VI. (Environmental Protection Act sections 112 and 123). There are two E.C. Directives on genetically modified organisms. One deals with the contained use of genetically modified organisms and the other deals with deliberate releases into the environment and the marketing of products containing genetically modified organisms.[50] The Directives required to enact local legislation by October 1991, and the Environmental Protection Act 1990, Part VI came into force during that month.

RADIOACTIVE SUBSTANCES

4–134 Integrated Pollution Control does not cover the keeping, use or disposal of radioactive substances. These substances are controlled under the Radioactive Substances Act 1993. If a process must be registered both under the Radioactive Substances Act and the Environmental Protection Act, and there is a conflict between the requirements of a registration or authorisation under the Radioactive Substances Act and an authorisation under IPC, the requirements of the Radioactive Substances Act take precedence.[51]

[49]Environmental Protection Act 1990, s.111.

[50]These are Dir. 90/219 ([1990] O.J. L117) and Dir. 90/220 ([1990] O.J. L117 p. 15), respectively.

[51]3 p. 12, 3.41.

Chapter Five

PROTECTION OF THE WATER ENVIRONMENT

The "Water Environment" encompasses a broad range of terms and uses including lakes, rivers, sewage (treatment and disposal), sea water, bathing water, drinking water, fisheries, flood defence, land drainage, navigation, recreational activities and conservation. This chapter considers how pollution of the water environment is dealt with by legislation, control, and by regulatory agencies. **5–001**

The chapter initially focuses on the history of water pollution control, recent legislation and the agencies that regulate water pollution. The current system of water pollution control is examined through analysis of water-related offences, discharge consents, pollution control registers, and powers to prevent and remedy pollution. The analysis includes reference to Water Protection Zones and Nitrate Sensitive Areas. The control of discharges to the sewerage system are explained together with trade effluent consents, which are required to discharge trade effluent into the public sewers. Finally, there is a discussion of trends in water prosecution cases and a look at relevant European Community legislation.

HISTORY OF WATER POLLUTION CONTROL

Control of pollution in the United Kingdom watercourses is over a century old. In 1876 the Rivers Pollution Prevention Act was enacted. There followed a series of Acts leading up to the Water Consolidation (Consequential Provisions) Act 1991. **5–002**

Various Acts have in particular reflected advances in the concept of control:

- Salmon and Fresh Water Fisheries Act 1974
- Water Act 1974
- Rivers (Prevention of Pollution) Act 1960

- Water Resources Act 1963;
- Water Act 1973;
- Control of Pollution Act 1974 (Part II);
- Land Drainage Act 1976;
- Environmental Protection Act 1990.

Of these, three in particular have shaped the current legislation.

The Water Act of 1973 reorganised the water industry in England and Wales into 10 regional water authorities based upon river catchments. The new water authorities took over the responsibilities previously held by more than 1600 separate local authorities, water undertakers, and river authorities.

Subsequently, these water authorities have themselves been converted into 10 regional water undertakers, and then restructured again through privatisation under the Water Act 1989. The provisions relating to statutory water service companies in the Water Act 1989 were re-enacted in the Water Industry Act 1991.

The Control of Pollution Act 1974 (COPA 1974), Part II, shaped current water pollution control although certain provisions were not brought into force until 1986 and beyond. It no longer survives but has left its mark in the following areas:

(a) **Pollution prevention measures**—It ensured that, subject to a few exceptions, the release of poisonous, noxious or other polluting matter was prohibited;
(b) **Remedial measures**—It enabled water authorities to carry out operations to prevent the pollution of water or, where pollution had already occurred, to remedy its effects and to recover costs of doing so from those responsible.
(c) **Public participation**—Controls over discharges into water were opened up to the public through provision for public advertisement, private prosecutions, third party representations and public enquiry.

5–003 The third of the formative Acts was the Water Act 1989, which largely came into effect in September 1989, and further strengthened the framework constructed by the Control of Pollution Act 1974 for water pollution control. It also, as indicated above, re-organised the water authorities. When it was largely repealed by the Water Consolidation (Consequential Provisions) Act 1991, the changes it had brought to pollution control were nevertheless, in substance, retained. The main features of both Acts include:

(a) A separation of water supply, sewage treatment and disposal functions from river management, pollution control and other regulatory duties;
(b) The establishment of the independent National Rivers Authority (NRA) to improve water quality standards, to control pollution by the water industry as well as other

sources, and to manage the availability and licensing of water resources;

(c) Statutory provisions for the classification of water courses and the setting of statutory water quality standards by the Secretary of State;

(d) The establishment of a Drinking Water Inspectorate to support the Secretary of State; and

(e) The establishment of a Director General of Water Services to protect customer interests by ensuring that water companies provide a satisfactory service.

Although it retained the fundamental pollution controls established by the Control of Pollution Act, the Water Act 1989 also gave certain powers to the NRA to prevent or remedy water pollution. For example, where the NRA believed that a potential pollutant could enter "controlled" waters, it was empowered to carry out preventative work, or to remove the pollutant and restore the area to its previous condition. The Authority was entitled to recover its costs from those responsible for the actual or potential pollution; this entitlement is now incorporated into the Water Resources Act 1991, s.161.

In addition, the Water Act 1989 contained pre-emptive powers:

(a) The Secretary of State was given power to establish "water protection zones" which prohibit or restrict certain activities in areas where those activities are likely to cause water pollution (now found in the Water Resources Act 1991, s.93);

(b) The Secretary of State for the Environment was given power to designate "Nitrate Sensitive Areas". In order to prevent or control the entry of nitrate into controlled waters, in designated areas, the Minister may serve an order which prohibits or restricts certain agricultural activities (now found in the Water Resources Act 1991, s.94).

RECENT DEVELOPMENTS IN WATER POLLUTION CONTROL

Water legislation was consolidated by the Water Consolidation Consequential Provisions Act 1991. This Act developed, and to a large extent repealed, an earlier overhaul of the legislation which had been incorporated into the Water Act 1989. **It will be implemented gradually by statutory instruments**. The consolidating legislation came into effect in December 1991. It merged provisions from **5–004** existing legislation, originating from no less than 27 Acts, into four new Acts:

- Water Industry Act 1991;
- Water Resources Act 1991;
- Statutory Water Companies Act 1991;
- Land Drainage Act 1991 (as amended by the Land Development Act 1994).

The new legislation did not change the substance of the law, but it removed some of the inconsistencies.[1] What did it achieve? It has helped to clarify the provisions, simplify some of the text, and eradicate ambiguities in the existing legislation.

Most of the material relevant to pollution control in the consolidating legislation is contained in Part III of the Water Resources Act 1991 (WRA 1991). It should be stressed again that the Environmental Protection Act 1990 (EPA 1990) brought about Integrated Pollution Control which protects the three environmental media, air, water and land together. The Environmental Protection Act 1990 applies to the most polluting industrial processes as prescribed by the Secretary of State.[2] Provisions on the structure of the NRA are located in Part I and Schedule 1 of the Water Resources Act 1991. Sewerage services are provided for in the Water Industry Act 1991, Part V. The Water Industry Act 1991 sets up water provided for companies to replace the water authorities, which are regulated by the Statutory Water Companies Act.

These Acts also provide the means to implement further legislation which may come down from the European Community. This would be done in the form of statutory instruments. Relevant statutory instruments are listed in Appendix 1.[3] Relevant European Community Directives which affect the water environment are listed in Appendix 2.[4]

Agencies of Water Pollution Control

5–005 The organisation of the water authorities was radically changed by the Water Act 1989. They were privatised and became water companies providing water supply and sewerage services. In addition, the NRA was set up.

Before privatisation, the water authorities extracted and supplied water, granted water discharge consents and protected watercourses from pollution. The government sought to avoid the "poacher-gamekeeper" conflict by passing responsibility for prevention of pollution and control of abstraction to the NRA The new water com-

[1] Consolidation of Legislation Relating to Water, Cm. 1483, 1991.
[2] Discussed above in Chapter 4.
[3] Water Services Association: NRA Waterfacts 1991, p. 11.
[4] Water Services Association: NRA Waterfacts 1991, p. 13.

panies took responsibility for water supply, sewerage systems and sewage treatment.

National Rivers Authority

The NRA is an independent statutory body set up originally under the Water Act 1989. It has over 7,000 employees and is charged with determining whether water quality meets prescribed standards and, if not, identifying the most immediate and practical way in which to generate improvements. 5–006

The Authority is funded in part by the Government and in part by income from the issuance of fishing licences, discharge consents, and income generated by recreation, conservation, navigation, and water resource, as well as flood defence levy.[5] In 1992–93 the NRA planned to expend £72,350,000 in pollution control with its income forecasted was to be £37,450,000.[6] The income for pollution control comes from charges for discharge consents and monitoring.

The NRA is responsible for monitoring pollution in the following ways:

(a) by ensuring that discharge consents are complied with;
(b) by ensuring that environmental quality standards set out by the Secretary of State are achieved; and
(c) by taking enforcement action, where necessary.

Sewerage Undertakers

The Water Act 1989 established private water companies and appointed sewerage undertakers. Sewerage undertakers have a quasi-governmental role with regard to pollution control; they are responsible for applying and monitoring the system of trade effluent consents.[7] 5–007

In general, the sewerage undertaker is responsible for sewerage services within its region which include providing systems for sewerage and sewage disposal within their area and to provide public sewers for properties.

HMIP

Her Majesty's Inspectorate of Pollution (HMIP) is responsible for control of the discharge of effluents from prescribed processes into any part of the water environment. Although the NRA has responsibility for regulating controlled waters, HMIP has been given the lead role in implementing IPC under the Environmental Protection 5–008

[5]NRA Corporate Plan 1991–1992, p. 88.
[6]NRA Corporate Plan 1991–1992, p. 89.
[7]Discussed below in Chapter five, para. 5–029.

Act 1990.[8] In deciding whether to grant an authorisation, however, HMIP must consult with the NRA.[9] Reference has been made previously to a merger of functions with the advent of the new Environment Agency.

The relationship between HMIP and the NRA regarding the authorisation procedure is organised on the bases that the NRA may:

(a) certify that a release will result in or contribute to a failure to achieve environmental quality standards[10] and/or identified uses of the receiving waters (so that HMIP cannot grant an authorisation)
(b) dictate conditions it thinks appropriate for authorisations;
(c) require HMIP to vary conditions of an authorisation.

WATER POLLUTION CONTROL

5–009 The NRA's statutory responsibilities for pollution control of coastal waters, lakes, rivers, ponds and ground water, is set out in Part III of the Water Resources Act 1991.

Chapter I of the Water Resources Act 1991 establishes the power, through regulations, to create environmental quality standards.[11] Chapter II establishes the offences of polluting controlled waters and discharging effluent in violation of notices or regulations.[12] In order to prevent pollution, Chapter III authorises the Secretary of State to make regulations prohibiting persons from having control of polluting matter unless steps have been taken to prevent the entry of the matter into controlled waters.[13] The chapter also creates powers for Water Protection Zones and Nitrate Sensitive Areas to be established.[14]

Definitions

5–010 As with any legislation, it is important to understand certain key terms. The Water Resources Act 1991 does not offer a specific definition of water pollution. In practical terms, pollution can be broadly defined as a discernible deterioration in water quality. What is regarded as pollution will vary with the amount and type of the

[8]Discussed above in Chapter 3.
[9]EPA 1990, s. 28.
[10]an environmental quality standard is that concentration of a substance which must not be exceeded if a specified use of the aquatic environment is to be maintained.
[11]WRA 1991, s. 83.
[12]WRA 1991, ss. 85, 86, 87.
[13]WRA 1991, s. 92.
[14]WRA 1991, ss. 93, 94.

potential pollutant and the receiving waters in question. Substances are considered harmful when their concentration reaches a certain level, which could be minimal for the most dangerous substances. For fresh waters and surface waters, different standards may be applied to a drinking water source as opposed to a recreational lake.

Water pollution can be generated in a variety of sources, including sewage, chemical and agricultural accidents, waste sites, and in particular agricultural and industrial discharges. Agricultural inputs constitute a significant percentage of all water pollution.

The definition of "controlled waters" is found in the Water Resources Act 1991, s.104. It includes inland and coastal waters, but more specifically it includes:

(a) relevant territorial seas waters—within three miles of the baselines from which the territorial limits are measured;
(b) coastal waters—any stretch of water which extends to the land from the same baselines up to the limit of the highest tide or, in the case of relevant rivers or watercourses, the freshwater limit of the river or watercourse;
(c) inland waters—rivers, streams, underground streams, canals, lakes and reservoirs;
(d) ground waters—any waters contained in underground strata.

"Trade effluent" is defined in section 221 of the Water Resources Act 1991 as including any effluent from trade premises other than domestic sewage or surface water. "Sewage effluent" is also defined in section 221 as including any effluent, other than surface water, from a sewer or sewerage works.

Offences

Under Section 85 of the Water Resources Act 1991, an offence is committed if a person "causes or knowingly permits" : **5–011**

(a) **[General pollution offence]**—any poisonous, noxious or polluting matter or any solid waste matter to enter any controlled waters;
(b) **[Specific offence of polluting from drains or sewers in breach of prohibition notice]**—any matter, *other than* trade effluent or sewage effluent, to enter controlled waters by being discharged from a drain or sewer in contravention of a prohibition notice or regulations;
(c) **[Specific offence of polluting without a discharge consent in place]**—any trade effluent or sewage effluent to be discharged into any controlled waters, or from a pipe into the sea outside the seaward limit of controlled waters;
(d) **[Specific offence of discharging trade or sewage effluent in violation of prohibition notice]**—any trade effluent or sewage effluent to be discharged in contravention of a pro-

hibition notice or regulations from a building or any fixed plant onto or into any land or any lakes or ponds which are not inland waters[15];

(e) **[Specific offence of damage caused by the addition of factors to the initial discharge]**—any matter whatever to enter any inland water so as to impede (either directly or in combination with other matter which he or another person causes or permits to enter those waters) the proper flow of the waters in a manner likely to lead to a substantial aggravation of the consequences of such pollution. This could occur, for instance, when solid matter is dumped upstream slowing the flow, causing a legitimate discharge to be less diluted and therefore causing pollution;

(f) **[General offence of breaching conditions of a discharge consent]**—acts in contravention of a water discharge consent.

Two of these offences will in particular concern industry. The first is the general prohibition against "causing or knowingly permitting any poisonous, noxious or polluting matter or any solid waste to enter controlled waters."[16] The discharge does not need to be toxic itself to be polluting matter. The test is whether the matter in question resulted in a deterioration of water quality, as measured by sample analysis.

The second is the threat of conviction for contravening "the conditions of any consent" for discharge of effluent into controlled water.[17] This offence applies to violations of discharge consents and requires specific proof of contravention. The general pollution offence under section 85(1) catches trade and sewage effluent discharge cases where the burden of proof argues against the use of the second offence. Accidental or irregular escapes of trade or sewage effluent are examples of such cases. It would be unlikely that the prosecutor would have an actual sample of the discharge, taken on the day of the accident or escape, with which to prove a breach. However, the general offence only requires the entry of polluting matter into controlled waters and an accident would consequently be caught by it.

Under the second offence, section 85(6), the prosecutor could take a sample of discharge effluent on a given day and prosecute the discharger if the amounts of certain substances exceed the amounts allowed in a consent. In this case, pollution need not actually occur for a violation to be successfully prosecuted.

A particular incident could be found to violate both sections—if,

[15] A lake or pond that is not an "inland water" could be a temporary gathering of water in a particular place, such as the water around a tank overflow, a reservoir, or a large, naturally occurring puddle.

[16] WRA 1991, s. 85(1).

[17] WRA 1991, s. 85(6).

for example, it is an illegal discharge of trade or sewage effluent and it causes pollution.

Obviously, there must be detection before there can be prosecution. An accident may come to the attention of the NRA from complaints in the locality or from unusual readings at one of the NRA's key monitoring sites. However, breaches of consents are more difficult to identify. The NRA can require a consent holder to self-monitor and report to the NRA as a condition of consent. There is also compliance monitoring checking of consent holders, which the NRA performs without advance notice. If a sample is taken in order to prosecute, the analysis result will only be admissible in evidence if the sample was divided into three parts and the occupier of the land given one part of the sample.[18] **5–012**

The prosecution must satisfy the court that the defendant "causes or knowingly permits" one of the offences. The phrase appeared, in respect of pollution, long before the Water Act 1989 and the Water Resources Act 1991.

"Causing" generally requires a positive act or failure to act rather than mere passive on-looking on the part of the defendant.[19] "Knowingly permit" can be used when the defendant has been passive[20]. Liability may, however, arise when pollutants escape through natural causes even in the absence of negligence.[21]

Penalties

Upon contravention of section 85 of the Water Resources Act 1991, or the conditions of a discharge consent, a discharger (an individual or a company) will be guilty of an offence and liable on summary conviction to imprisonment for a term up to three months or to a fine of up to £20,000 (or to both) in the magistrates' court. On conviction on indictment, there can be a prison sentence of up to two years.[22] Upon transfer or appeal from the magistrates court to the Crown Court[23], the fines are unlimited. **5–013**

The application of these penalties differs between cases and between courts.[24] Briefly, from cases already heard, it seems the courts will, in respect of accidents, give weight to the defendant's culpability, willingness to accept responsibility, and willingness to take measures to prevent recurrence. They will also have regard to the amount of damage actually caused and any clean-up measures taken. In respect of violation of discharge consents, the courts,

[18]WRA 1991, s. 209.
[19]*Price v. Cromack* [1975] 1 W.L.R. 988.
[20]*Ibid.*
[21]*Alphacell Ltd v. Woodward* [1972] A.C. 824; [1972] 2 W.L.R. 1320.
[22]WRA 1991, s. 85 (6)
[23]Magistrates Court Act 1980, s. 108.
[24]The trends that can be established from judgments and penalties given by the courts are discussed below in Chapter five, para. 5–034 *et seq.*

again, seem to have regard for the degree of culpability of the defendant, the degree of resultant pollution, mitigating circumstances, and whether remedial action has been taken.

Defences

5–014 Sections 88 and 89 of the Water Resources Act 1991 set out defences to the water pollution offences. It is a defence to have made the particular discharge in accordance with:

(a) A consent given by the NRA or an equivalent under Part II of the Control of Pollution Act 1974;
(b) An authorisation for a prescribed process granted by HMIP under Part I of the Environmental Protection Act 1990;
(c) A waste management licence or disposal licence;
(d) A licence granted under Part II of the Food and Environmental Protection Act 1985;
(e) A discharge for works purposes consent under the Water Resources Act 1991, section 163 or the Water Industry Act 1991, section 165;
(f) Any local statutory provision or statutory order which expressly confers power to discharge effluent into water; or
(g) Any prescribed enactment, which would be a discharge that is made in accordance with another Act in force.

There is an emergency defence in section 89(1) where the discharge was made in an emergency in order to avoid danger to life or health; *and* the person takes all reasonable steps to minimise the extent of the discharge and its polluting effects; *and* the discharger notifies the NRA with the particulars of the discharge soon after the entry occurs.[25]

Sewerage undertaker's defence

5–015 Sewerage undertakers are responsible for obtaining discharge consents from the NRA to discharge their treated sewage into controlled waters.[26] Before treatment, the sewerage undertakers issue a separate consent, a trade effluent consent, to all parties which bring sewage for treatment to their works.[27] The sewerage undertakers must be certain, through the trade effluent consents, what is in the sewage effluent they are treating because they need to know how to treat the sewage and they specify the content when applying for their discharge consents.

If they breach their discharge consent with the NRA, or cause a pollution incident, it is the sewerage undertaker that is held responsible. However there is a defence available if the pollution is caused by an illegal discharge into the sewer which could not

[25] WRA 1991, s. 89(1).
[26] Sewerage undertakers are discussed above in Chapter five, para. 5–007.
[27] Trade effluent consents are discussed below in Chapter five, para. 5–029.

reasonably have been prevented by the sewerage undertaker.[28] In that case, the discharger to the sewer commits an offence under the Water Resources Act 1991, section 85 and under the Water Industry Act.

Discharge Consents for discharges into Controlled Water.

To make discharges of trade or sewage effluent into controlled waters, the discharger has to apply to the NRA for consent. This requirement applies not only to industrial discharges but sewage effluent as well. Sewage effluent is usually discharged by the sewerage undertaker into controlled waters after it has been treated in accordance with the consent. **5–016**

Schedule 10 of the Water Resources Act 1991 sets out the procedure for obtaining a discharge consent. The NRA can give a consent unconditionally, subject the consent to conditions, or refuse the consent.[29] An application will be deemed to be refused if it is not given within a period of four months beginning with the day on which the application is received.[30] A longer period may be agreed in writing between the NRA and the applicant.[31]

Conditions

The NRA will usually attach conditions to the consent. The conditions applied will depend on a number of factors including the nature of the water, the uses of the receiving waters and the environmental quality standards the discharge must meet.[32] **5–017**

The use of environmental quality standards for particularly dangerous substances sets the United Kingdom apart from much of the European Community. Other member states use uniform emission standards for the control of discharges. The NRA believes that the use of uniform emission standards alone is likely to result in discharge standards which are either too lax where applied to receiving waters with a low dilution, or too stringent where there is generous dilution. By using environmental quality standards, both extremes are avoided—environmental damage on the one hand and expensive overtreatment on the other. Typically, tighter conditions are attached to effluents discharged to smaller watercourses or tributaries where substances are less easily diluted.

Conditions can relate to a range of different aspects relating to the discharge: **5–018**

(a) Environmental standards for the receiving water into which the discharges may be made. The NRA looks to standards

[28] WRA 1991, s. 87(2).
[29] WRA 1991, Sched. 10, para. 2.
[30] WRA 1991, Sched. 10, para. 2(3).
[31] WRA 1991, Sched. 10, para. 2(3).
[32] Environmental quality standards are discussed below.

set for the receiving waters given in environmental quality standards and other sources depending on the type of water at issue, *i.e.* Inland Fisheries Advisory Council standards for certain waters used for fishing.

(b) The design and construction of any outlets for the discharges;

(c) The nature of substances at issue including the origin, temperature, volume and rate of the discharge and period during which the discharges may be made. This also could include the incorporation of any relevant European Community standards for emissions of certain substances;

(d) The steps to be taken in relation to the discharges by way of treatment to minimise the polluting effects of the discharges in any controlled waters;

(e) The provision of facilities for taking samples and in particular the provision, maintenance and use of manholes, inspection chambers, observation wells, and bore holes;

(f) The provision, maintenance and testing of meters for measuring or recording the volume and rate of the discharges and apparatus for determining the nature, composition and temperature of the discharges;

(g) The keeping of records of the nature, origin, composition, temperature, volume and rate of discharges and, in particular, of readings of meters and other recording apparatus provided in accordance with any other condition attached to the consent; and

(h) The making of returns and the giving of other information to other authorities about the nature, origin, composition, temperature, volume and rate of the discharges.[33]

For industrial discharges, conditions for specific substances will usually be given in absolute numerical limits. Any amount discharged in excess of the limit will be a breach of the consent.

Sewage discharges by the sewerage undertakers are subject to look-up table consents which allow for a five per ent failure rate. The NRA is reviewing these "inherited" consents to include an absolute numerical limit.

Consents which have already been granted under the Water Act 1989, the Control of Pollution Act 1974 or earlier legislation are translated into valid consents for the purposes of the Water Resources Act 1991. They may be varied or revoked in the future under Schedule 10 to the Water Resources Act 1991.

Notice and Public Comment

5–019 There are notice procedures which give the public an opportunity to comment on or object to an application for a discharge consent.

[33] WRA 1991, Sched. 10, para. 2(5).

The NRA must publish notice of the application, at least once in each of two successive weeks, in a newspaper circulating in the locality of the facility which will make the discharge and in any locality which the NRA believes may be affected by the proposed discharge.[34] There is also a requirement to publish a copy of that notice in an edition of the *London Gazette* no earlier than the day after the publication of the last of the newspaper notices.[35]

The NRA has a duty to consider any written representations or objections to a consent which are made six weeks from the day of the publication of the notice.[36]

Where the NRA proposes to give consent to an application notwithstanding objections, it has a duty to serve notice of the proposal on every person who has made representations or objections.[37]

If the NRA considers that the discharge will have "no appreciable effect" on the receiving water, the NRA can dispense with the notice requirement.[38]

NRA Application requests

If it appears to the NRA that a person is discharging effluent or other matter in violation of the Water Resources Act 1991, section 85(3) (knowingly permitting trade effluent to enter controlled water) and/or section 86 (control of unconsented discharges), the NRA can serve a prohibition notice compelling the discharger, in turn, to apply for a consent. That does not preclude prosecution for causing pollution of the controlled waters under section 85 if pollution has occurred. **5–020**

Review, Revocation and Variation

The NRA is under a duty to review consents and the conditions applied to the consents "from time to time".[39] "From time to time" has not been defined by the statute and the NRA is not required to give notice of review to the consent holder. **5–021**

The NRA has established key monitoring sites to make sure water quality meets United Kingdom and European Community water quality standards. From these sites, the NRA gathers information on pollution and traces the source. If a problem exists within the confines of a consent, the NRA will vary the consent and may still prosecute for the general pollution violation of causing pollution to waterways under section 85 of the Water Resources Act 1991.

[34] WRA 1991, Sched. 10, para. 1(4)(*a*).
[35] WRA 1991, Sched. 10, para. 1(4)(*b*).
[36] WRA 1991, Sched. 10, para. 5(5).
[37] WRA 1991, Sched. 10, para. 3(2).
[38] WRA 1991, Sched. 10, para. 1(5).
[39] WRA 1991, Sched. 10, para. 2.6(1).

Upon review the NRA can:

(a) Revoke the consent;
(b) Modify conditions attached to the consent; or
(c) In the case of an unconditional consent, provide that it shall be subject to such conditions as may be specified in the notice.[40]

The variation option can be used in situations where the legislation changes as scientific standards change or when there is a substance for which a European Community or a British standard has been newly adopted. The option also can be used when a consent is reviewed and the NRA finds that damage to the environment is occurring.

If upon reviewing the consent there has been no discharge during a period of 12 months, the NRA can revoke a consent by notice given to the owner or occupier of land where the discharges were made.[41]

There is no provision for public participation in relation to a variation or revocation.

A variation or revocation cannot take place within two years, without the agreement of the discharger.[42] This appears to give a discharger the ability to pollute for up to two years if the consent was granted on January 1, 1993, and the United Kingdom adds new substances to its list of particularly dangerous substances[43] which took effect on the January 2, 1993. However, in order to comply with an E.C. obligation or an international agreement for the protection of health, or flora and fauna dependent upon the water environment, the Secretary of State has power to direct the NRA to revoke or modify a consent, or subject it to conditions, before the two year period has expired.[44] In this case the NRA will have to pay compensation for loss or damage sustained by any person as a result of NRA's compliance with the E.C. or international obligation.[45]

Appeals

5–022 An applicant or discharger has a right of appeal to the Secretary of State where the NRA has:

(a) Refused a consent;
(b) Attached an unreasonable condition;
(c) Revoked or varied a consent;
(d) Specified a period in relation to a discharge consent, without

40 WRA 1991, Sched. 10, para. 6(2).
41 WRA 1991, Sched. 10, para. 6(3).
42 WRA 1991, Sched. 10, para. 7.
43 Particularly dangerous substances designation is discussed below in Chapter five, para. 5–041 *et seq*.
44 WRA 1991, Sched. 10, para. 6(4).
45 WRA 1991, Sched. 10, para. 6(5).

the agreement of the person who proposes to make the discharge, during which no notice may be served in order to revoke or modify the consent.[46]

Charges

In July 1991 the NRA introduced a scheme for recovering in part the cost of administering consent applications and monitoring compliance. The scheme was effected on July 1, 1991 to March 31, 1994 and is set out in the National Rivers Authority Applications and Discharges Charges Scheme. It enables the NRA to recover most of the cost of running the system and monitoring discharges. **5–023**

There are two charges that the discharger has to pay. The first is an application charge. The fee for this is either the Standard Application Charge (which is currently £350) or a Reduced Application Charge (currently £50). A Reduced Application Charge applies where the effluent involved is one of the following:

(a) sewage effluent where the proposed volume is five cubic metres or less per day;
(b) trade effluent from cooling or heat exchange where the proposed volume is 10 cubic metres or less per day;
(c) surface water not containing trade effluent.

The second charge is an annual charge which is the product of four factors related to the consent. These factors are each given a number which is multiplied against the other factors to produce the annual charge. The factors are as follows:

(a) **The Volume Factor**—relates to the maximum daily volume of discharge permitted by the consent. The factor scale is graduated ranging from 0.4 to 14.0 for the range of discharge from 5 to 150,000 cubic metres of discharge per day.
(b) **The Contents Factor**—relates to the band into which the contents of the discharge falls.
(c) **The Receiving Water Factor**—is the type of water that is discharged into. Groundwater and land have a factor of 0.5; coastal waters have a factor of 0.8; surface waters have a factor of 1.0; and estuarial waters have a factor of 1.5. The different types of water are defined in the Scheme.
(d) **The Financial Factor**—is set annually. The financial factor was £324.00 until March 31, 1993.

Each NRA regional office has a helpline to deal with enquiries about charges for discharges.[47] It is estimated that about £42 million will be recovered through these charges for the year 1993/94. In that same year it is forecast that the expenditure for pollution control will be £78,450,000.[48]

[46]WRA 1991, s. 91.
[47]September 1991, 2 E.L.B. 8, p. 96.

Pollution Control Registers

5–024 Pollution Control Registers have been open to the public since July 31, 1985 and will continue to be maintained under the Water Resources Act 1991 by the NRA.[49] The Register is held on computer and fully indexed by place name, national grid reference, applicant name and river name. The Register is open to anyone for inspection.

The Register contains the following information:

(a) Applications for consent;
(b) Consents issued and the conditions attached to them;
(c) Samples of water or effluent taken by the NRA for the purposes of any of the water pollution provisions of the Water Resources Act;
(d) Information produced by analyses of those samples;
(e) Information on samples of water or effluent taken by any other person and acquired by the NRA under an arrangement with that person.[50]

The Register receives a substantial number of enquiries, frequently from both environmental groups and individuals.

Powers to Prevent and Remedy Pollution

5–025 Where the NRA considers that polluting matter is in danger of entering or has entered "controlled" waters, it has the power to take preventative action, or to remove the pollution. The NRA is entitled to require the person who has custody or control of polluting matter to take action to prevent pollution or restore the area to its condition before the discharge.[51]

Other pre-emptive powers used to prevent water pollution include:

(a) The Secretary of State may make regulations prescribing storage facility standards which must be met by persons using specified substances. Regulations are being made under this provision to set standards for silage installations, farm slurry stores and agricultural oil installations. Farm waste pollution incidents account for 12 per cent of all reported water pollution incidents[52];
(b) The power for the Secretary of State to establish at the request of the NRA, water protection zones in which activities likely to cause water pollution will be prohibited or restricted;

[48] NRA Corporate Plan 1991-1992, p. 89.

[49] NRA, "Environmental Water Quality: General Information, Useful Addresses and Suggested Reading List", WQ7–1088–7RH2, May 1990.

[50] WRA 1991, s. 190.

[51] WRA 1991, s. 92.

[52] NRA News Release, January 21, 1992.

(c) The power for designating Nitrate Sensitive Areas for the purpose of preventing or controlling the entry of Nitrate into controlled waters.[53]

These powers are designed to be preventative. In contrast, section 161 is available to cover clean-up operations after accidental acts of pollution, although it can also be used where there has been a breach of the conditions of a consent. The section allows the NRA, where there is polluting matter in controlled water, to carry out works and operations to remove and dispose of the matter, remedy or mitigate any pollution, and restore the water, flora and fauna to its previous state.

The NRA is entitled to recover the expenses incurred in remedial action from any person who:

(a) Causes or knowingly permits polluting matter to be present where it might enter controlled waters;
(b) Caused or knowingly permitted the matter in question to be present in any controlled waters.[54]

Section 161 is particularly important in that it may represent a greater deterrent to polluters than the worry of £20,000 fines in the Magistrates' Court. Clean-up costs can run into millions of pounds.

Section 161 is a civil remedy. Procedurally, the NRA needs to mount a further set of proceedings in addition to its criminal prosecution under section 85. In this way, the judicial system could be burdened with largely duplicitous court cases. This presents a rationale for a separate environmental court that could hear all environmental claims and award both civil damages and criminal penalties.

Water Protection Zones

Under section 93 of the Water Resources Act 1991, the Secretary of State may designate water protection zones which will prohibit or restrict certain activities within the zone. The zones are to be created to prevent or control the entry of poisonous, noxious or polluting matter into controlled waters.[55] **5–026**

As yet no water protection zones have been designated under the Act: consideration is being given to the first designation, allowing protection of a river important as a source of drinking water. There are existing non-statutory, internal-NRA guidelines on issues such as aquifers (water bearing strata) which concern zones drawn around springs, wells and boreholes. These guidelines (often referred to as

[53] NRA, "Environmental Water Quality: General Information, Useful Addresses and Suggested Reading List", WQ7–1088–7RH2, May 1990, p. 8.

[54] WRA 1991, s. 161.

[55] The procedures for creating Water Protection Zones are contained in Sched. 11 to the WRA 1991.

source protection policies) could become the basis for water protection zones as a need to enforce the guidelines becomes evident.

Nitrate Sensitive Areas

5–027 Section 94 of the Water Resources Act 1991 affords the Secretary of State the power to designate Nitrate Sensitive Areas in which there will be a concentrated effort to reduce nitrate from agriculture.

High concentrations of nitrate in drinking water can endanger human health. Agriculture is the main source of nitrate in ground water; it comes from the overuse of fertilizer both organic and inorganic in excess of the uptake by plants. Farming activities such as ploughing can increase the leaching rates. The speed with which nitrate reaches underground water sources varies, but it can take a long time, particularly for deep aquifers. Thus today's levels may reflect several decades of past activity.

To control the problem of nitrate in water, the government has designated an increasing number of Nitrate Sensitive Areas in England. In these areas farmers have been given free advice on ways to reduce the risk of nitrate leaching into water. Under the plan, payments have been made to those farmers in Nitrate Sensitive Areas who have voluntarily undertaken to observe restrictions on their agricultural practices—such as switching from arable to grassland cultivation.

In later designations, the NRA has launched an intensive advisory campaign in which farmers have received free advice on reducing nitrate leaching.

The first results of the two schemes were reported at a conference in April 1992. According to Michael Madden, Under Secretary on Environmental Policy at the Ministry of Agriculture, Fisheries and Food (MAFF) a "significant minority" of farmers were still applying excessive fertiliser and many farmers in both schemes were not taking the nitrogen content of manures and sewage sludge into account when calculating how much artificial fertiliser to apply. Thus the schemes will need much more input from the farmers if they are to succeed. At the time of writing the Royal Commission on Environmental Pollution is initiating an investigation of soil protection.

THE SEWERAGE SYSTEM

5–028 In England and Wales 96 per cent of all property is connected to sewerage systems and 83 per cent of all sewage is treated at some coastal and estuarine treatment works. The ten water companies in England and Wales are responsible for the operation of about 6,500 sewage treatment works, most of which discharge effluent into rivers. When discharging into controlled waters, the water service company needs to obtain a discharge consent from the NRA.[56]

In 1986, 23 per cent of sewage treatment works were failing to meet their discharge consent conditions. By 1988 this figure had fallen to 17 per cent. Failure to comply is thought to be because treatment plants were inadequate to deal with the loads which had increased since the installation of the plants.

The European Community Urban Waste Water Treatment Directive [57] lays down minimum standards for treatment of municipal wastewater and the disposal of sewage sludge. It requires secondary treatment of municipal wastewater as a minimum, except in coastal areas designated as less sensitive where secondary treatment would not be required. The Directive bans sewage sludge dumping at sea by December 31, 1998.

Trade Effluent consents for discharges into sewers.

The requirement for trade effluent consents applies to any trade premise which discharges trade effluent into the public sewer.[58] The discharger must apply to the sewerage undertaker for a consent at least two months before discharge of effluent begins by serving a notice which contains the following information in respect of the proposed discharge: **5–029**

(a) The nature or composition of the trade effluent;
(b) The maximum quantity of trade effluent which it is proposed to discharge on any one day; and
(c) The highest rate at which it is proposed to discharge the trade effluent.[59]

If the sewerage undertaker is served with a notice from the discharger indicating that the discharge contains "special category" effluent, the undertaker must refer the following questions to the Secretary of State:

(a) Whether the discharges should be prohibited; and
(b) If they are not prohibited, whether any requirements should be imposed as to the conditions on which they are allowed.[60]

Trade effluent will be a "special category" effluent if it:

(a) Contains substances in concentrations prescribed by regulations made under the Water Industry Act; or
(b) Derives from any prescribed process, or from a process involving the use of prescribed substances, or the use of

[56] Discharge consents are discussed above in Chapter five, pp. 76 and 77.
[57] 91/271.
[58] Water Industry Act 1991, s. 119(1).
[59] Water Industry Act 1991, s. 119(2).
[60] Water Industry Act 1991, s. 120(1).

such substances in excess of a prescribed amount, before the determination date of that prescribed process.[61]

The definition of a "prescribed process" is to be found in section 1 of the Environmental Protection Act 1990. As for the "determination date", trade effluent will no longer be considered a special category effluent if it is produced in any prescribed process after an authorisation is granted.[62]

Conditions

5–030 In response to an application for consent, a sewerage undertaker can impose such conditions as are thought fit after taking into account:

(a) the sewers into which the trade effluent may be discharged;
(b) the nature or composition of the trade effluent which may be discharged;
(c) the maximum quantity of trade effluent which may be discharged on any one day, either generally or into a particular sewer; and
(d) the highest rate at which trade effluent may be discharged.[63]

The sewerage undertaker can in any event attach particular conditions to a consent for discharge of trade effluent from any premises specifying:

(a) the periods of the day during which effluent may be discharged;
(b) the exclusion of condensing water from the discharge;
(c) the elimination or reduction of constituents of the trade effluent that the sewerage undertaker believes would affect other segments of the sewerage system;
(d) the temperature, acidity or alkalinity of the trade effluent when it is discharged into the sewer;
(e) the payment to the undertaker of charges for reception and disposal of the effluent;
(f) the provision and maintenance of an inspection chamber which will allow samples to be taken, at any time, of what is passing into the sewer from the trade premises;
(g) the provision, testing and maintenance of meters required to measure the volume and rate of discharge of trade effluent being discharged from the trade premises into the sewer;
(h) the provision, testing and maintenance of apparatus for determining the nature and composition of any trade effluent being discharged from the premises into the sewer;
(i) the keeping of records of the volume, rate of discharge, nature and composition of any trade effluent being dis-

[61] Water Industry Act 1991, s. 138(1).
[62] Water Industry Act 1991, s. 138(3),(4).
[63] Water Industry Act 1991, s. 121(1).

charged and, in particular, the keeping of records in compliance with any other condition attached to the consent; and

(j) the making of returns and giving of other information to the sewerage undertaker concerning the volume, rate of discharge, nature and composition of any trade effluent discharged from the trade premises into the sewer.[64]

Appeals

If a sewerage undertaker has refused an application, imposed a condition with which the applicant disagrees, or has not given consent within the two month period beginning from the day after service of the notice containing the application, the applicant can appeal to the Director General of Water Services, who oversees the sewerage undertakers.[65] **5–031**

If a discharge has been designated as "special category effluent", the two month period for giving consent begins to run from the day after the Secretary of State serves notice on the sewerage undertaker of the determination on the reference.[66]

Variation

A sewerage undertaker may give a direction varying the conditions which have been attached to any of its trade effluent consents.[67] There are limits on this power. No direction can be given within two years from the date of the consent or, where a previous direction has been given, within two years from that direction.[68] **5–032**

In line with the similar provision for discharge consents, conditions can be varied before the two year period expires if the sewerage undertaker considers it necessary in order to provide proper protection for persons likely to be affected by the discharge.[69] The sewerage undertaker will be liable to pay compensation to the owner and occupier of the premises unless the change in circumstances has occurred since the beginning of the two year period and the undertaker could not reasonably have foreseen this change at the beginning of the period.[70]

Charges

The charge for a trade effluent discharge consent is either a minimum charge determined by the sewerage undertaker, a charge per cubic metre, or per 1,000 gallons based upon a formula. The formula takes into account, where applicable, a reception and conveyance **5–033**

[64] Water Industry Act 1991, s. 121.
[65] Water Industry Act 1991, s. 122.
[66] Water Industry Act 1991, s. 123(1).
[67] Water Industry Act 1991, s. 124(1).
[68] Water Industry Act 1991, s. 124(2).
[69] Water Industry Act 1991, s. 125(1).
[70] Water Industry Act 1991, s. 125(2).

charge per cubic metre, a treatment charge for the type of material that is being treated, and a disposal charge for sea outfalls.

TRENDS FROM UK CASES

5–034 The NRA brought a total of 334 prosecutions for water pollution offences in England and Wales during its first year of operation from September 1, 1989 to August 31, 1990.[71] By its second year, the number had risen to 959.

The NRA has commented on its own performance:

> "As well as enforcing strict standards of environmental control, the NRA has worked tirelessly in its first two years to raise environmental awareness within industry, farming and among the general public by, amongst other things, promoting good practice to minimise the risk of pollution. What we are aiming to do is to seek improvements in the water environment by changing people's behaviour. Where prosecution has been necessary, the NRA has proved itself to be a watchdog with razor sharp teeth."[72]

It was a relatively easy task to increase dramatically the number of prosecutions for water pollution offences (one of the stated goals of the government in creating the NRA). The number of pollution incidents prosecuted between 1976 and 1990 were:

1976	5	1981	11	1986	33
1977	5	1982	5	1987	30
1978	9	1983	6	1988	59
1979	9	1984	18	1989	51
1980	5	1985	21	1990	370[73]

Because of the strict liability nature of the offence, most prosecutions are successful.[74] Thus far cases of imprisonment here or in other areas of environmental enforcement are rare.

Although the 1991 figure represents a dramatic increase in pro-

[71] May 1991, 2 E.L.B. 5, p. 65; *Hansard*, H.C., February 27, 1991, Col. 534; *Hansard*, H.C., March 25, 1991, Col. 340.
[72] NRA (Southern Region) Press Release No. 348, October 28, 1991.
[73] July/August 1990, 1 E.L.B. 7, p. 75.
[74] Strict liability is discussed above in Chapter 2, para. 2–003. *Cf.* the more recent enforcement statistics outlined at para. 5–034 *et seq.*

secutions from the previous year, and especially the year before that, the statistic alone may be misleading. There is some criticism that the NRA is not doing enough. For example, in the *Greenpeace v. Albright and Wilson*, the NRA did not prosecute the company for exceeding the legal pollution limits set in their discharge consent. During the above case, Albright and Wilson admitted that they had violated discharge limits and had informed the NRA who did not prosecute.[75]

From the cases brought to court, certain trends can be identified. Most of the cases go to the magistrates court which has had its maximum fine raised through recent legislation to £20,000. The majority of prosecutions are for an accidental breach of a consent rather than consistent breaches of a consent.[76] Some of the more serious offences are taken to the Crown Court where the fine is unlimited:

> "Larger fines will make polluters more aware of their liabilities and should encourage a more reasonable attitude and perhaps avoid decisions being taken on economic grounds with cynical disregard for the environmental consequences."[77]

The Crown Court can additionally impose costs and make a Compensation Order in respect of the clean-up costs for any damage caused by the incident. There may be an emerging trend of willingness to take prosecutions to Crown Court.

Fines

Since the Water Act 1989 was passed, the courts have awarded fines between £100 and £1 million; a fine of £1,000 is not uncommon. Before the increase in maximum penalty before a magistrates' court was introduced by the Environmental Protection Act 1990, the average fine was estimated to be £250. 5–035

The case which most emphatically illustrates the extent to which the courts are willing to use fines as a deterrent is the *Shell case*.[78] In February 1990, Shell were fined £1 million for polluting the Mersey Estuary. On August 19, 1989 a 12 inch bore pipeline carrying oil from the Tranmere oil jetty to Shell's Stanlow oil refinery split. The hole in the pipeline was caused through corrosion by seawater. When Shell officials were told of the leak, they flushed out the corroded pipeline in an attempt to clear the blockage and preserve the 16 year old pipeline. The flushing was also intended to force water beyond the fracture to prevent further oil pollution when the pipe was covered at high tide.

[75] *Greenpeace Business*, No. 3, October 1991, p. 2.
[76] Greenpeace report, "Poison in the System," (1988).
[77] March 1990, 1 E.L.B. 3, p. 25.
[78] *National Rivers Authority v Shell (UK)* [1990] Water Law 40.

The leak was detected at 3.20pm. By 5.30pm there was a 10 mile slick on the Mersey and oil was still leaking into the river the following morning. The slick affected sea birds and pumps used to draw water from the river to cool Fiddlers Ferry power station.

In imposing a fine of £1 million, the highest ever in a United Kingdom water pollution case, the Judge clearly did not accept defence claims that there had been no human error. Shell were also required to pay £100,000 to install a monitoring system capable of detecting the substantial corrosion that had caused the leak. The incident cost Shell a further £1.4 million in operational losses and clean-up charges.

The Judge stated:

> "The only penalty I can impose is a fine. The defendants have enormous resources and could pay any fine, even of several million pounds, without being deeply affected thereby."

He added that Shell had an outstanding record in the field of conservation and are generous in their support of the arts and other worthwhile causes, and indicated "Were it not for those matters, which are very much to their credit, the penalty would have been substantially greater."

Typically, the amount of the fine relates to the behaviour and attitude of the polluters in addition to how much damage has been caused by the polluting incident. The more willing a company is to admit to the problem, alert the authorities, and put in place practices which will prevent a recurrence, the better they seem to fare in court. Serious, persistent or unrepentant polluters attract heavier penalties.

The following sections discuss various factors which the courts take into account in determining a water pollution case.

TYPE OF POLLUTION AS DAMAGE

5–036 By definition, a discharge does not need to be toxic to cause pollution but rather to result in a deterioration in water quality. One of the factors looked at in determining the fine seems to be the damage caused.

In March 1991, the drinks company, Appletise, flushed thousands of litres of apple juice down storm drains. As a result, hundreds of fish died in a stretch of the River Wear. The company was fined £10,000 for causing apple juice to enter the Valley Burn and the River Wear and a further £1,000 for causing apple juice to enter a sewer. Costs of £2,767 were also imposed. The company also agreed to pay a total of £16,263 in compensation to Northumbrian Water and the NRA in respect of the fish which were killed.

It was not the type of pollutant that caused a heavy fine to be issued, but the damage to the environment.

Warning systems

Most water pollution incidents seem to be accidents. In many of the cases warning systems could have caught the problem. The fact that a warning system is installed by the polluter after the event may help to mitigate an offence. **5–037**

In February 1991 fuel oil leaked from a supply pipe at the British Steel Llanwern steel plant into an estuary of the River Severn. Two valves failed and 250 tonnes of oil escaped. The leak was not discovered for one and a half hours. Twenty tonnes of oil made its way through a surface water drain and into the estuary of the River Severn. In the Cardiff Crown Court on July 31, 1991 the company pleaded guilty to the offence under the Water Act 1989.

A fine of £200,000 was imposed. The Judge indicated that the fine would have been greater if there had been any wilful default on the company's part. The Judge also noted the company's cooperative attitude after discovering the leak. They had paid the £68,000 clean-up costs incurred by the NRA and other organisations and financed a £28,000 study by the British Ornithological Trust into the longer term effects on birds in the estuary. The Judge took into account that preventative measures had now been put in place including a television observation system and spillage containment facilities.[79]

Machinery used

Often the courts treat polluters more leniently if they pro-actively take measures to ensure pollution incidents do not recur. **5–038**

T.E. Bayston, an electroplating company, allowed sewage effluent contaminated with cyanide and zinc to be discharged into a sewer as the result of a fault in a treatment tank. It was submitted on behalf of the company that the quantities were small and there was no danger to the public. The firm, based in that area for 45 years, commissioned £21,000 worth of new equipment for its waste treatment system to ensure illegal leakage did not occur again.

The court fined the company £1000 only and imposed costs of £125.[80] This result may have been due to the fact that the damage was minimal, but the court did specifically note the company commissioned equipment which could prevent incidents from occurring in the future.

[79]October 1991, 2 E.L.B. 9, p. 108.
[80]May 1991, 2 E.L.B. 5, p. 58.

Private suit

5–039 The first private prosecution against a company was brought by Greenpeace against Albright and Wilson in the Whitehaven magistrates court in July 1991. The prosecution suit was for discharging illegal levels of heavy metals into the Irish Sea in contravention of the Water Act 1989.

Greenpeace said that it took on the case because Albright and Wilson were a large source of heavy metal pollution in the North Sea and the NRA had caught Albright and Wilson exceeding their consents on numerous occasions without ever prosecuting. The magistrates court found Albright and Wilson guilty and the company was fined £2,000, the maximum the magistrates' court could impose at that time, and £20,000, for Greenpeace prosecution costs.

Albright and Wilson had argued the sample taken by Greenpeace at the end of the pipe could give false readings. They submitted that if a sample has been taken from the NRA sampling point inside the Marchon factory, the results would have been different.

The magistrates did not accept this argument. In their view, it was the composition of the effluent at the end of the pipe which was significant. They were also unimpressed by Albright's reliance on a technical point in circumstances where pollution was admitted. The court was concerned by the unwillingness of Albright and Wilson to admit that they had breached their consent. It was a stance which did not endear the company to the Magistrates.

Albright and Wilson made a tactical decision to defend the case strongly at a high cost. Greenpeace estimates that their internal costs could have run over £150,000.[81] They may want to discourage Greenpeace from spending the time and effort to prosecute cases beyond the NRA.[82] More recently unsuccessful private prosecutions by Greenpeace have failed through analytical problems with substantial costs being awarded against Greenpeace.

EUROPEAN COMMUNITY WATER ISSUES

5–040 As it has with other environmental issues, the E.C. has promulgated many directives over the years regulating the water environment. Most of the environmental quality standards that are currently used in the United Kingdom are derived from E.C. legislation, but the NRA is developing its proposals for statutory water quality standards relevant to the specific uses of water. It will be taking a more

[81] *Greenpeace Business*, No.3, October 1991.
[82] October 1991, 2 E.L.B. 9, p. 107.

proactive role in E.C. legislation in the years to come. There have been very few E.C. Directive standards that the NRA does not agree with.

The scope of Directives on water pollution issues range from global issues such as oil pollution at sea to specifics such as the lindane discharge limit values.[83] The following is a sample of some of the more topical directives together with an indication of how they have been put into practice in the United Kingdom.

Pollution caused by certain dangerous substances discharged into the water environment.

The Dangerous Substance in Water Directive 76/464 is a framework Directive passed with the aim of reducing or eliminating the discharge of specified dangerous substances to water. The Directive (76/464) distinguishes between particularly dangerous (List I or black list) compounds and less dangerous (list II or grey list) compounds, on the basis of the substances' toxicity, persistence and bioaccumulation. **5–041**

List I substances are controlled by uniform limit values, which place an absolute limit on the maximum concentration that is permisable in a discharge to the aquatic environment, and environmental quality standards, which is that concentration of a substance that must not be exceeded if a specified use of the aquatic environment is to be maintained.[84] These values and standards are set on a Community wide basis and published in "daughter Directives".

The discharge of List II substances into the aquatic environment is meant to be limited based upon environmental quality standards set by the Member States.

European Community environmental quality standards are incorporated into United Kingdom legislation via statutory instruments.[85]

In 1978, 129 priority substances were earmarked for analysis as potential List I substances. The list has been extended to 132.

For the water industry, the main impact of the legislation is an increased monitoring requirement for effluents and receiving waters to ensure that the environmental quality standards are not exceeded. This demands analytical equipment and skilled staff to achieve the necessary detection limits. In addition, inventories have to be compiled of the discharges of List I and List II compounds and pollution reduction programmes have to be prepared.[86]

[83] See Appendix 2 for list of E.C. Directives.

[84] Agg and Zabel, "E.C. Directive on the Control of Dangerous Substances (76/464): Its Impact on the British Water Industry" (1989) 3 J.IWEM, p. 436.

[85] WRA 1991, ss. 82, 83.

[86] *Ibid.*, n. 84, at p. 438.

Control of List I Compounds

5–042 It is up to the Member States to determine whether List I consents will be based on uniform emission standards or environmental quality standards. The United Kingdom is the only country to use environmental quality standards as the basis for List I consents.

In practice there may be less difference between the two tests as far as the United Kingdom is concerned. The NRA sets the environmental quality standards with consideration of the uniform emission standards, so the focus is not only upon the receiving waters.

The Dangerous Substances Directive has been the foundation for the following List I "daughter Directives,":

- 82/176 on discharges of mercury by the chlor-alkali electrolysis industry;
- 83/513 on discharges of cadmium;
- 84/156 on discharges of mercury by sectors other than the chlor-alkali electrolysis industry;
- 84/491 on discharges of hexachlorocyclohexane (HCH);
- 86/280 on limit values and quality objectives for discharges of certain dangerous substances included in List I of the Annex to Directive 76/464;
- 88/347 amending 86/280 on limit values and quality objectives for discharges of certain dangerous substances included in List I of the Annex to Directive 76/464.
- 90/415 on limit values for certain other list I substances, including 1,2 Dichloroethane.

These Directives apply to all discharges directly into surface water with different standards sometimes set for discharges to rivers, estuaries and coastal waters[87]. Groundwater is dealt with separately by virtue of Directive 80/68.

Potential List I substances for which a specific directive does not yet exist are to be treated as List II substances until a directive is in place.

Control of List II Compounds

5–043 For List II substances, Member States are required to set national environmental quality standards. The Commission proposed chromium, copper, inorganic lead, nickel, arsenic and zinc as priority List II substances.[88] The United Kingdom has set environmental quality standards for all these List II metals.

The Commission has intentions to set E.C.-based standards for at least one List II substance, in the Draft Chromium Directive, but no progress has been made on this proposal. When this is adopted,

[87]Details of the standards are given in the DoE Circular 11/91, National Environmental Quality Standards for Dangerous Substances in Water.

[88]*Ibid.*

the Member States would set their national environmental quality standards from the European Community objective.

Groundwater

Seventy per cent of E.C. drinking water and approximately 30 per cent of the United Kingdom's drinking water is extracted from underground sources. In order to protect exploitable groundwater sources, which are very difficult to restore once polluted, discharges of dangerous substances to groundwater are regulated. **5–044**

The framework Directive is found in 80/68 ([1980] O.J. L20) Directive on the protection of groundwater against pollution caused by certain dangerous substances. The Directive lists families and groups of dangerous substances, using the List I and List II approach. Those substances within the limited groups and families which exhibit certain specified characteristics are classed on the appropriate list.

For groundwater, List I substances are to be prevented from entering groundwater, while List II substances should be limited, by a consent system.

Drinking water

The Drinking Water Directive 80/778 ([1980] O.J. L229) lays down over 60 criteria relating to the quality of water provided for human consumption, except for natural mineral water or medicinal water. Britain issued the statutory standards of wholesomeness for drinking water in the Water Supply (Water Quality) Amendment Regulations 1991 (S.I. 1991 No. 1837). **5–045**

The Surface Water Drinking Directive 75/440 ([1975] O.J. L194) regulates the quality of inland water used for abstraction for the drinking water supply. The Directive lays down the quality of the surface water required for the water to be suitable for the abstraction to drinking water depending on the water treatment applied.

Chapter Six

MORE POLLUTION CONTROLS

There is a body of law on pollution control which remains alongside the new legislation. This includes the common law[1] which deals with private nuisance, public nuisance, the rule in *Rylands* v. *Fletcher*, negligence and trespass. This chapter explains the common law as well as other controls including the Control of Pollution Act 1974 and Clean Air Act 1993 which restrict noise and atmospheric pollution respectively, the Town and Country Planning (Assessment of Environmental Effects) Regulations 1988, which require certain development projects to undergo environmental assessment before planning permission is considered, and emission limits which set authorisations and environmental quality standards for controlling various hazardous substances. **6–001**

Also included is a discussion of United Kingdom and European Community laws which have been established as a result of various disasters and occurrences, illumination on how these laws are enforced, and an explanation of public registers which attempt to disclose pollution control information to all interested parties.

COMMON LAW

A claim can be made under common law against a person who causes pollution if damage has been suffered. Different types of claims are available, depending on the circumstances. The level of ultimate effectiveness of a claim also varies. Relatively few common law claims over pollution are brought for a number of reasons. Because damage must be suffered, the common law cannot be used to deal with contaminated land in situations where the problem is one of potential damage. Additionally, the ever-increasing scope of regulatory control by Parliament has created statutes that more specifically address these issues. **6–002**

[1] *Cf.* An outline of some aspects of the common law in Chapters 2 and 3.

Private Nuisance

6–003 An action in private nuisance can be brought where there is unlawful interference with the use and enjoyment of land or some right which relates to the land. This can take the form of some sort of encroachment onto the land[2] or actual physical damage to it. For instance, physical damage could occur where a building falls into disrepair and collapses onto adjacent land[3] or flood water collects on a neighbouring property and damages it.[4]

The polluting impact of chemicals on groundwaters was examined earlier in the *Cambridge Water* case.[5] The decision emphasises the ever closer relationship between the law of nuisance and strict liability.

Various rules apply to private nuisance claims:-

Unreasonable interference

6–004 The nuisance must be unreasonable to be actionable. In one case, noise both day and night, and air pollution from a depot, was held to be an actionable nuisance.[6] In addition to assessing the circumstances of the case to determine unreasonable interference, the court will look at two other factors—the nature of the locality and whether the incident was continuous.

Assessing the nature of the locality[7] may complicate efforts to prove nuisance by pollution in a heavily industrialised area. An industrialised area may already be considered polluted, therefore a higher level of pollution would be required to satisfy the test of unreasonableness. However, when actual physical damage is caused to property, the locality ceases to be a relevant consideration.[8]

As well as being unreasonable, the interference must generally be continuous or recurrent. Therefore, an isolated incident of pollution may not be actionable.[9]

Liability may nevertheless arise under the rule in *Rylands v. Fletcher*. The rule states that the person who introduces harmful substance to the land is answerable for all the damage caused by that action. Under this rule, an individual who uses chemicals which accidentally spill on the land will be liable for the damage if the harm or damage was reasonably foreseeable for as long as the chemicals remain in his control.[10].

[2] *Davey v. Harrow Corporation* [1958] 1 Q.B. 60.
[3] *Wringe v. Cohen* [1940] 1 K.B. 229.
[4] *Sedleigh-Denfield* v. *O'Callaghan* [1940] A.C. 880
[5] Chapter 2, para. 2–002 and Chapter 3, para. 3–005.
[6] *Halsey v. Esso Petroleum Co. Ltd* [1961] 1 W.L.R. 683.
[7] *Sturges v. Bridgeman* (1879) 11 Ch. D. 852.
[8] *St Helens Smelting Co. v. Tipping* (1865) 11 H.L.C. 642
[9] *S.C.M. (United Kingdom) Ltd v. Whittal (W.J.) & Son Ltd* [1971] 1 Q.B. 337.
[10] *Cambridge Water Co. v. Eastern Counties Leather PLC* [1994] 2 W.L.R. 53, H.L.

Liability

Primary liability will fall on the creator of the nuisance, whether or not the creator of the nuisance occupies the land.[11] The occupier may also incur liability if the occupier permits or gives consent to a nuisance whether or not the occupier is the creator of the nuisance.[12] **6–005**

If an owner or occupier has knowledge of a nuisance on the land and fails to take reasonable steps to abate it, that person may be liable.[13] This instance occurs if the landowner is aware of the contamination before purchasing the land or, after becoming aware of it, fails to abate it when a nuisance arises. Yet liability does not automatically attach to the landowner; the landowner will have to have acted unreasonably.

An unreasonable action is one that goes outside the normal "give and take" relationship expected between neighbours. (Irrespective of the polluter's activities and the lack of knowledge of the present owner, primary liability will always attach to the present owner). The area of the common law relating to contaminated land has been superseded by section 61 of the Environmental Protection Act 1990 (EPA 1990) which imposes strict liability for the clean-up costs of contaminated land on the owner.[14]

Defences

It is theoretically possible to acquire the right to commit a private nuisance by prescription, with acquiescence by those affected or acceptance of the nuisance over a number of years. This right to commit a private nuisance by prescription is therefore unlikely to apply to polluting accidents which occur at one point in time or to continuous pollution which is not likely to have been agreed to. **6–006**

The time scale for a defence of prescription will be re-started following a change in ownership of the affected land.[15]

An important defence to an action in nuisance is that of "statutory authority." Statutory authority exists when a body is authorised to conduct certain operations by statute and the nuisance is caused by the inevitable result of carrying out what they were obliged or empowered to do. In such cases, there will be no liability unless negligence can be proved.[16]

If a positive duty has been imposed by statute, then the protection is even greater. Even if provision has been made in the statute allowing a claim in nuisance, there can be no liability in relation

[11] *Hall v. Beckenham Corporation* [1949] 1 K.B. 716.

[12] *Tetley v. Chitty* [1986] 1 All E.R. 663; *Page Motors Ltd v. Epsom & Ewell Borough Council* (1980) 78 L.G.R. 505.

[13] *Sedleigh-Denfield v. O'Callaghan* [1940] A.C. 880.

[14] As at September 1994, not yet in force.

[15] *Bliss v. Hall* (1838) 4 Bing N.C. 1983.

[16] *Department of Transport v. North West Water Authority* [1984] A.C. 336.

to the positive duty. It has been held that authority to acquire land and build a refinery also gave the right to operate the refinery and therefore there was no liability in nuisance for the inevitable consequences of working the refinery.[17] On the other hand, if a body is merely carrying out an activity it is empowered to do by statute, and provision has been made for a claim in nuisance, there will be no need to prove negligence and liability may arise.

It is no defence that a person has "come to" the nuisance even if the person arrived long after the nuisance commenced and that person's predecessor had not complained about it. Thus, it is not a valid defence if, for example, a person knowingly purchases a house which is close to a noisy factory.

Public nuisance

6–007 Public nuisance is an unlawful act or omission which materially affects the comfort and convenience of a class of people who come within the sphere of its operation. A civil claim can only be instigated by a private individual who has suffered "particular" damage, in excess of that suffered by others. It is then up to the Attorney-General or local authority to bring a criminal prosecution. This includes personal injury as well as property damage.[18]

When an automobile was damaged by the emission of acid from a factory, it was held that particular damage was suffered above and beyond that suffered by others in the area.[19]

Reasonable conduct cannot be a nuisance. A court will always have regard for the "give and take" principle expected between neighbours. An action for nuisance against a neighbouring property owner for noise during temporary building and redecoration would be unsuccessful, provided the noise was restricted to reasonable hours and not carried on late at night. Lord Wright has stated:

> ". . .a balance has to be maintained between the rights of the occupier to do what he likes with this own, and the right of his neighbour not to be interfered with. . ."[20]

While public nuisance has a potentially wide application in cases of pollution where there has been actual damage—such as in an accident—*an action can only be instigated by a private individual who has suffered special damage.*[21]

[17] *Allen v. Gulf Oil Refining Ltd.* [1980] 2 W.L.R. 188.
[18] *Halsey v. Esso Petroleum Company* [1961] 1 W.L.R. 683.
[19] The rest of the area had been affected by noise and smuts deposited in the smoke from the factory. *Halsey v. Esso Petroleum Co. Ltd.* [1961] 1 W.L.R. 683.
[20] *Sedleigh-Denfield v. O'Callaghan* [1940] A.C. 880, 903.
[21] *Solihull Metropolitan Borough Council v. Maxfern Ltd. and Another.* [1977] W.L.R. 127.

The Rule in *Rylands v. Fletcher*

The rule laid down in *Rylands v. Fletcher*[22] imposes strict liability so that there need not have been any fault on the part of the person found liable. As originally stated, it was said that: 6–008

> ". . .the person who for his own purposes brings on his lands and collects and keeps there anything likely to do mischief, if it escapes, must keep it at his peril and, if he does not do so, is prima facie answerable for all the damage which is the natural consequence of its escape."[23]

The rule has been further refined to require the land to have been put to "non-natural" use. In recent years this provision has restricted the scope of application of the rule.[24] The production of electrical goods on an industrial estate was held to be a natural use of land. In the *Cambridge Water Company*[25] case on the other hand, it was decided (*obiter*) that the storage of solvents in a factory did come within the definition of "non-natural" use.[26]

The Court of Appeal did not consider the rule in *Rylands v. Fletcher* in coming to its decision in the *Cambridge Water* case. However the House of Lords decision (as discussed previously) appears to have considerable potential particularly if the foreseeability of the impact of industrial and other types of pollution improves as long as any pollutant can be said to be under the "control" of the alleged polluter.

Under the rule in *Rylands v. Fletcher* there can never be a claim for pure financial loss which is not a direct result of physical damage.[27]

Defences

The defences to liability under the rule in *Rylands v. Fletcher* are somewhat limited. An absolute defence is an act of God or the operation of natural forces "which no human foresight can provide against, and of which human prudence is not bound to recognise the possibility." This is usually very restrictively interpreted.[28] In a relevant case where artificial pools constructed by damming a natural stream collapsed, an act of God was the defendants' winning defence. The dams were well constructed. However, as a result of a particularly violent storm, which witnesses described as the worst 6–009

[22](1865) 3 H. & C. 774.

[23]Blackburn J. in *Rylands v. Fletcher* (1865) 3 H. & C. 774.

[24]*British Celanese Ltd v. A. H. Hunt (Capacitors) Ltd.* [1969] 1 W.L.R. 959

[25]As discussed previously in Chapters 2 and 3.

[26]*Cambridge Water Co. v. Eastern Countries Leather & Hutchings and Hardings Ltd.* [1994] 2 W.L.R. 53, H.L.

[27]*Cattle v. Stockton Waterworks Co.* (1874-75) 10 Q.B. 453.

[28]*Tennant v. Earl of Glasgow* (1864) 2 Macph. 22 (Ct. of Sess.), H.L.

in living memory the dams collapsed and several bridges were washed away. An action for damages in respect of the last bridge was brought. Notwithstanding *Rylands v. Fletcher* the defendant was found not liable.

The occupier will also not be liable if the escape is due to the unforeseeable act of a third party, or if there is express or implied consent to the act by the adjoining landowner.

In the case of a body having statutory authority, similar defences will apply as those relating to private nuisance.

As with public nuisance, *Rylands v. Fletcher* potentially has a wide application to environmental pollution as pollution incidents frequently involve an escape of material. Increasing restrictive interpretations of this rule have however led to fewer actions being brought under it. Recent developments just described may suggest a reversal of theis trend.

Tort of negligence

6–010 To establish liability under the tort of negligence, it is necessary to demonstrate that a duty of care was owned, that the duty was breached, and that as a consequence damage has been suffered. In addition, the damage caused must be of a reasonably foreseeable kind and occur in a reasonably foreseeable manner.

In the past, negligence has been less popular than nuisance in the environmental field, partly because of the necessity to prove fault on the part of the defendant. A further problem likely to be encountered is the foreseeability of the damage. In the case of existing contamination upon land, the act which caused the pollution in the past may not have been prima facie unlawful at the time.

It is not necessary for the plaintiff actually to prove negligence; the plaintiff may be able to rely on the doctrine of *res ipsa loquitur*. Under this doctrine, if there is no explanation as to how an event occurred, the cause was under the control of the defendant at the time of the incident, and the accident was one that would not ordinarily occur without negligence, the onus will be on the defendant to prove that no negligence occurred. In one case, a regional water authority was held to be negligent for failing to warn the plaintiff of the potential danger in taking water for agricultural use from a polluted stream.

The basis for the decision was that the polluted water in the stream was under the control of the Water Authority. Since pollution would not normally occur without negligence, and the Water Authority were unable to provide an explanation for the pollution, it was inferred under the doctrine of *res ipsa loquitur* that the Water Authority was responsible.[29] The doctrine does not eliminate argu-

[29] *Scott-Whitehead v. National Coal Board* [1987] 53 P. & C.R. 263.

ment over whether damage suffered by the plaintiff is recoverable; that remains a live issue.

Tort of Trespass

An action lies under the tort of trespass when there is unlawful interference with land. The interference must be intentional or negligent and also sufficiently direct.[30] **6–011**

In the *Jones v. Llanwrst* case, sewage had collected on land down river from an outflow.[31] Trespass was determined as it was a natural and foreseeable consequence of the escape for the sewage to flow and collect downstream. In the more recent case of *Esso v. Southport Corporation*[32], where cargo jettisoned from an oil tanker into a river which carried it onto the shore, it was decided that trespass did not occur because the tide and winds could have carried it anywhere. Through the verdicts of these cases, it can be interpreted that an action in trespass is unlikely to be successful where pollution is airborne as the wind could carry the pollution anywhere.

Unlike nuisance and negligence, trespass does not require claimants to prove they have suffered damage and is actionable *per se*. This can make it very attractive as a course of action if an injunction is required where there has been direct interference with land.

Trespass has rarely been used in pollution cases because of the requirement for direct interference. A potential action in trespass is often capable of being actioned in nuisance or under the rule in *Rylands v. Fletcher* which may have a wider application. This is due to the fact that pollution will often occur as a consequence of an act and will not be sufficiently direct to guarantee success if an action under trespass is brought. Only a person with an interest in land is able to bring an action in trespass.

The Future

While there are many grounds in tort that are relevant to the environment, actions are increasingly likely to be based on breach of statutory duty. This is because there are existing provisions for civil liability in some statutes and there are incoming proposals from the European Commission which will almost certainly include provisions relating to strict civil liability.[33] Furthermore, it is widely accepted that actions brought at common law are procedurally expensive, complex and time consuming. **6–012**

[30] *Esso v. Southport Corporation* [1956] A.C. 218.
[31] *Jones v. Llanwrst Urban District Council* [1911] 1 Ch. 393
[32] [1956] A.C. 218.
[33] Discussed in Chapter 2.

CONTROL OF POLLUTION ACT 1974

6–013 The Control of Pollution Act 1974 (COPA 1974) has to a large extent been replaced by the Environmental Protection Act 1990 and the Clean Air Act 1993. Some provisions remain in force relating to noise pollution. They were mostly enacted to deal with a particular problem in a particular way. These provisions also suffer from the limitations of all reactive legislation, due to their narrow band of application.

Noise

6–014 The local authority has the power to serve a notice imposing requirements over how works are carried out on construction sites—specifying the type of machinery that may be used, the hours during which it may be used, and the level of noise which may be emitted from the premises.[34] It is a criminal offence to breach the limits. Application for a consent from the local authority may be made in advance of commencing construction works. The consent can have conditions stipulating noise levels attached.[35] British Standards Institute standards and Codes of Practice are in force in this area.

Noise abatement zones

6–015 Local authorities are empowered to designate certain areas as noise abatement zones and measure the level of noise emanating from premises within the zones. They are required to carry out reviews from time to time to decide how to exercise those powers. Maximum noise levels for the zones are placed in a public register and these levels should not be exceeded except with the consent of the local authority. It is a criminal offence to breach levels in the noise level register.[36]

There is also provision for a "noise reduction notice" to be served upon premises stating that the noise emanating from the premises should be reduced to a specific level. It then becomes a criminal offence to exceed that level. It is a requirement in respect of noise caused in the course of a trade or a business that the best practicable means have been used for preventing or counteracting the effect of the noise.[37]

Regulations may be made to limit the level of noise caused by

[34] COPA 1974, ss.60-61.
[35] COPA 1974, s.61.
[36] COPA 1974, s.65(5).
[37] COPA 1974, s.66.

plant and machinery.[38] The Secretary of State may also issue codes of practice as a guidance for those affected by these provisions.[39] They have been used to control intruder alarms, model aircraft and ice cream van chimes.

CLEAN AIR ACT 1993

Pollution of the Atmosphere

Regulations can be imposed under the Clean Air Act 1974 as to the type and content of fuel used in motor vehicles, after consultation with those affected in the motor industry.[40] Regulations can also be made, after consultation, on the sulphur content of oil fuel used in furnaces or engines. It is a criminal offence to fail to comply with regulations made under this section. Regulations are in force relating to the lead content in petrol and the sulphur content of gas oil.[41] **6–016**

There are detailed powers for a local authority to engage in investigation and research into air pollution and publish the results. These include powers to take measurements and samples. Occupiers may be required to give information about pollutants emitted from their premises. A detailed notice procedure must be followed by the local authority.

ENVIRONMENTAL ASSESSMENT

The Town and Country Planning (Assessment of Environmental Effects) Regulations 1988 as amended[42] require certain development projects to undergo Environmental Assessment before planning permission is considered. An "Environmental Assessment" is the process through which information about the environmental effects of a project is collected and taken into account by the local planning authority. **6–017**

The Regulations were enacted pursuant to the European Community's Environmental Assessment Directive of July 1985.[43]

[38] COPA 1974, s.68.
[39] COPA 1974, s.71.
[40] Clean Air Act, s.30.
[41] *Ibid.*, ss. 30–32.
[42] The Town and Country Planning (Assessment of Environmental Effects) (Amendment) Regulations 1990 (S.I. 1990 No. 367 *inter alia*).
[43] 85/337.

Projects Subject to Environmental Assessment

6–018 A project is subject to Environmental Assessment if it fits within categories laid out in Schedule 1 and Schedule 2 of the Regulations.[44]

Schedule 1 identifies various classes of project that are *always* subject to the assessment procedure. Schedule 1 projects include those dealing with crude oil, thermal power, nuclear power, radioactive waste, melting of metal, and asbestos.

Schedule 2 identifies types of project grouped within 12 industries that are subject to Environmental Assessment when, in the view of the Department of the Environment (DoE), the projects are:

- of more than local importance;
- on a smaller scale and placed in sensitive or vulnerable locations such that they will have significant effect on the environment;
- unusually complex and potentially the cause of adverse environmental effects.

Schedule 2 covers energy projects such as thermal power stations and electricity production. Covering the chemical industry, Schedule 2 addresses the treatment of intermediate products and production of chemicals. Covering infrastructure projects, Schedule 2 also addresses urban, road, harbour, airport, and industrial estate development. It includes waste disposal projects, holiday villages and hotel complexes.[45] Schedule 2 is also applied to mixed use developments, including one or more of the following:

- business parks
- conference centres
- hospitals
- offices
- hotels
- residential developments
- schools
- warehouses
- retail uses
- leisure facilities[46]

[44]Scheds. 1 and 2 have been subject to frequent revision.

[45]HMSO, *Environmental Assessment: Monitoring Environmental Assessment and Planning 1991*, Department of the Environment Planning Research Programme, p. 9, para. 2.10, 2.12.

[46]HMSO, *Environmental Assessment: Monitoring Environmental Assessment and Planning 1991*, Department of the Environment Planning Research Program, p. 20, table 13

Consultation with the Local Planning Authority

If it is difficult to place a particular project within the categories defined in the Schedules, a developer can seek guidance by: 6–019

- Discussing the Project confidentially with the local planning authority. The results will be only an indication of how the local planning authority will react.
- Formally requesting a pre-application opinion. The local planning authority has three weeks to respond. The documents concerning the project which have been submitted by the developer are available for public inspection.

Components of Environmental Assessment

If an Environmental Assessment is necessary, the planning authority will require an environmental statement. An environmental statement is the document containing information listed in Schedule 3 to the regulations, which the DoE has indicated should include: 6–020

- a description of the proposed development;
- an assessment of the existing environmental qualities and characteristics of the development site and related areas;
- an assessment of both the direct and indirect effects which the development will have on the environment;
- an explanation of any mitigating measures included in the development plan in order to ameliorate adverse environmental effects;
- a non-technical summary of the project.

Critical Issues

When creating an individual environmental statement, the developer will first need to identify the issues involved. In order to select the critical issues, the developer needs to assess all aspects of the project. The following are examples of the type of aspects that should be included: 6–021

- wildlife/ecology
- landscapes
- water quality
- water table/river levels
- traffic
- archaeology
- flooding and land drainage
- noise.

Planning Project Team

6–022 Planning project teams for large developments with the above characteristics would typically consist of a town planner, a landscape architect, a consulting engineer and an archaeologist. In addition, a range of experts might be involved such as wildlife consultants, hydro-geologists, drainage engineer consultants, highway consultants, soil scientists, agricultural and economists, noise engineers, economic advisors.

HAZARDOUS SUBSTANCES

6–023 Certain substances are capable of causing harm to both humans and the environment if they are directly emitted into the environment. Emission limits set in authorisations[47] and environmental quality standards[48] are the primary methods of controlling potentially polluting substances. However other substances are released into the environment in a variety of ways. Every day products ranging from plastics and nylons to agricultural fertilisers contain substances which are potentially harmful. Release may come through incidents involving the manufacture, storage, transport or disposal of these products. To limit their effect on the environment the following control systems have been set up which fall outside the ambit of the EPA or water legislation.

The Control of Industrial Major Accident Hazards Regulations (CIMAH)

6–024 United Kingdom and European Community law has responded to the dangers exposed and highlighted by disasters at Flixborough in the United Kingdom, Seveso in Italy, and Basle in Switzerland. All three were the result of accidents occurring during the manufacture, processing or storage of potentially hazardous substances. Incidents of this nature have increased awareness both of the widespread use of hazardous substances in domestic products, and the residual risk of harmful releases from chemical plant and chemical manufacture processes.

In 1976, at the Seveso plant in Italy, a chemical reactor went out of control, releasing a cloud of poisonous gas that killed animal and plant life in the area and caused illness amongst the local population. Subsequently in 1982, the "Seveso" Directive, as it is com-

[47]Discussed below in Chapter 4.
[48]Discussed below in Chapter 5.

monly known,[49] created tight controls for prevention of major accidents.

In 1986, a warehouse storing one thousand tonnes of agrochemicals at a pesticides factory adjacent to the River Rhine in Basle, Switzerland caught fire. Approximately 30 tonnes of poisonous chemicals entered the River Rhine and caused extensive ecological damage. The incident prompted the European Community to extend the provisions of the "Seveso" Directive to cover storage of hazardous substances.

The "Seveso" Directive requires Member States to ensure manufacturers take necessary steps to prevent accidents and, if they nevertheless do occur, to limit the consequences. Manufacturers must in particular identify potential hazards, adopt appropriate safety measures, and provide their employees with adequate training and safety equipment. They must notify the appropriate authority if their activity involves one of the 178 chemicals listed at Annex III of the Directive. Notification is also required if prescribed substances are held in storage.

The Control of Industrial Major Accident Hazards Regulations 1984 (S.I. 1984 No. 1902) (CIMAH) issued under the Health and Safety at Work Act 1974, implement the Seveso Directive in the United Kingdom. The Regulations apply to industrial activities which involve dangerous substances, such as toxic explosive and flammable materials.[50] The onus is upon manufacturers who fall within the Regulations to show that they have identified any major industrial hazard, taken adequate steps to limit or prevent the consequences of such a hazard, and provided adequate training, information and equipment for on-site employees.[51] **6–025**

Provision is also made for the manufacturer to notify persons likely to be affected by a major accident.[52] As a result of these provisions the emergency services in the local vicinity will be fully aware of the risks and contingency plans should an accident occur.

If an incident does occur it must be reported to the Health and Safety Executive who in turn must report it to the European Commission.[53]

Another accident which triggered legislation was the explosion at the Flixborough works of Nypro (United Kingdom) Ltd. Nypro operated a petrochemical installation which produced chemicals for nylon manufacture. The explosion resulted in 28 deaths and several serious injuries on site. In the surrounding area, 53 people were recorded as casualties due to the release of the chemical cyclohexane.[54] As a direct result of the explosion, the Notification of Installa-

[49] 82/501.
[50] CIMAH, reg. 2.
[51] CIMAH, reg. 4.
[52] CIMAH, reg 11(2).
[53] CIMAH, reg. 5.
[54] The Flixborough Disaster, Report of the Court of Inquiry (HMSO 1975)

tions Handling Hazardous Substances Regulations 1982[55] were introduced in the United Kingdom. The Regulations prohibit activities using a notifiable quantity (as defined at Regulation 2 and appearing in Schedule 1) of a hazardous substance unless the Health and Safety Executive is given three months notice.[56] Notice must also be given if quantities of a hazardous substance are changed.[57] Change will include an increase or a decrease in the maximum quantity of any hazardous substance subject to notification. The information provided is used in defining priorities for inspection, and to enable the manufacturer controlling the industrial activity to prepare an emergency on-site plan and the local authority in whose area the activity is situated to prepare an emergency off-site plan for dealing with a major accident.

Control of Substances Hazardous to Health Regulations (COSHH)

6–026 A further piece of subordinate legislation designed to promote health and safety is the Control of Substances Hazardous to Health Regulations 1988[58] (COSHH Regulations) made under the Health and Safety at Work Act 1974.

The COSHH Regulations place the onus on employers to assess the health risk of hazardous substances to employees and other persons. The Regulations apply to all work activities which use or produce substances hazardous to health. In order to help the employer decide what steps need to be taken and how best to implement an overall scheme of safety management, six important activities are identified:

(a) assessment of risk;
(b) prevention or control of exposure;
(c) use of control measures;
(d) maintenance, examination and testing of control measures;
(e) health surveillance and;
(f) information, instruction and training.

The Director General of the Health and Safety Executive instructed inspectors that Control of Substances Hazardous to Health Regulations were to be given a high profile when they came into force on October 1st, 1989. Since then, it has been noticeable that the Regulations have indeed been widely pursued in that the majority of employers are familiar with their requirements.

[55] S.I. 1982 No. 1357.
[56] Notification of the Installations Handling Hazardous Substances Regulations 1982, Sched. 2, part 1
[57] *ibid.*, 1982, reg. 4
[58] S.I. 1988 No. 1657.

The Planning (Hazardous Substances) Act 1990

The Planning (Hazardous Substances) Act 1990 is a direct derivative of parts of the Housing & Planning Act 1986. The 1990 Act, however, contains provisions concerning hazardous substances which are completely separate from the planning legislation. The object of the 1990 Act is to circumvent a control system which was only activated by the introduction of a hazardous use arising from development of land. This left no control over a new hazardous use which was introduced or intensified without development occurring. The 1990 Act came into force in June 1992. **6–027**

Outline of Provisions

The Act regulates the presence of hazardous substances on, over or under land in excess of a controlled quantity. The Planning (Hazardous Substances) Regulations 1992 (S.I. 1192 No. 656) enacted under Section 5 of the Act, specify the substances that are hazardous and the quantity which is to be the controlled quantity of any such substance. Consent, if hazardous substances are present in excess of the controlled quantity, must be granted by one of the hazardous substance authorities which are: **6–028**

(a) In Greater London and the metropolitan areas—the London Boroughs and the metropolitan district council;[59]
(b) In non-metropolitan areas—the district councils;
(c) In the National Parks—County Councils (except the Peak Park and Lakes District where control rests with the planning board).

Where urban development corporations and housing action trusts act as local planning authorities they will function as hazardous substance authorities. A hazardous substances authority is required to consult with the Health and Safety Executive in prescribed cases.[60]

Consents may be granted unconditionally, subject to any condition that the authority thinks fit, or refused if this is deemed appropriate. Regard must be given to "material considerations." Section 9(2) outlines these as including:

- current or contemplated use of the land to which the application relates;
- the way in which land in the vicinity is being used or is likely to be used;
- any planning permission that has been granted for development of land in the vicinity;

[59]Planning (Hazardous Substances) Act 1990, s.1.
[60]*ibid.*, s.7.

- the provisions of the development plan[61]
- advice given by the Health and Safety Executive or Health and Safety Commission following consultations—advice given by the HSC is only a material consideration if there have been consultations with the Commission under section 7(2).

A right of appeal to the Secretary of State exists where a hazardous substance consent has been refused or where conditions have been imposed on a grant of consent. In order to determine an appeal, the Secretary of State may hold a public inquiry if requested to do so either by the hazardous substances authority or the applicant. If dispute on a point of law exists, there is a right of appeal to the High Court from the Secretary of State's decision.[62]

If a breach of the legislation occurs, a hazardous substances contravention notice will be issued. This will detail what steps are to be taken to remedy the breach.

The Environmental Protection Act 1990 has introduced various amendments to the Planning (Hazardous Substances) Act 1990.

Environmental Protection Act 1990

6–029 The Environmental Protection Act 1990 gives the Government the widest general powers in relation to hazardous substances. Prior enactment, The White Paper on the Environment, "This Common Inheritance"[63] stated that:

> "The Environmental Protection Act 1990 will give the Government powers to obtain information on chemicals so that it can assess the harm they could do to man and the environment. The Bill also strengthens the Government's powers to control the use, supply, storage or import of chemicals. A new statutory committee, provided for in the Bill, will advise the Government on the selection of chemicals for assessment and control."

The Environmental Protection Act 1990 allows the Secretary of State to prohibit the importation, use or supply of injurious substances or articles to prevent damage to persons, animals or plants, or pollution of the air, water or land.[64] Injurious substances refer to both hazardous waste and toxic substances. The Department of the Environment have advised that these powers will be used primarily

[61]For a full definition of development plan, see Part II of the Town and Country Planning Act 1990. In brief the development plan is worked up by central government/county councils and local authorities with a view to creating guidelines as to future development in any given area.

[62]Planning (Hazardous Substances) Act 1990, s.21.

[63](Cm. 1200, 1990) page 178, para. 13.17.

[64]EPA 1990, s.140.

to implement European Community legislation within the United Kingdom, hence their wide wording. At the present time the Environmental Protection (Control of Injurious Substances) Regulations 1992 (Annex B) implements regulations concerning the use and supply of certain substances, including lead carbonates, sulphate and mercury compounds.

There are further provisions on hazardous waste in the European Community Regulation on Transfrontier Shipment of Hazardous Waste.[65]

Transportation of Hazardous/Dangerous Substances

The Road Traffic (Carriage of Dangerous Substances in Road Tankers and Tank Containers) Regulations 1992 and The Road Traffic (Carriage of Dangerous Substances in Packages, etc.) Regulations 1992, govern the carriage of dangerous substances by road tankers, tank containers, freight containers and other road vehicles. **6–030**

Both sets of Regulations impose duties on the operations of such vehicles used for the carriage of dangerous substances. They concern design, material construction and suitability of vehicles undertaking the conveyance by road of dangerous substances and take into account the quantity and characteristics of the dangerous substance being carried.

In addition, the former Regulation imposes duties on the operator regarding training of drivers who transport dangerous substances. The latter, in conjunction with duties placed on the operator, also imposes duties on the driver, over the conduct involved in operating the vehicle, which must display the required hazard warning labels

A duty is imposed on the consignor to provide correct and detailed information about the hazards relating to the substances, enabling the operator to comply with the Regulations.

The transport of hazardous substances by sea and air is regulated by the Merchant Shipping (Chemical Tankers) Regulations 1986[66] and the Air Navigation (Dangerous Goods) Regulations 1985.[67] The transport of such substances by rail is regulated by British Rail under the List of Dangerous Goods and Conditions of Acceptance by Freight Train and by Passenger Train or Similar Service.[68]

Radioactive Substances Act 1993

An obvious area of concern is that of radioactive material. Radioactive substances are used widely, including in the construction of **6–031**

[65]E.C. Regulation 259/93.
[66]S.I. 1986 No. 1068.
[67]S.I. 1985 No. 1939.
[68]Current editions are available from the British Railways Board, 222 Marylebone Road, London NW1.

nuclear weapons and in the development and use of nuclear power stations for the production of electricity. The main controlling provision is the Radioactive Substances Act 1993, which controls the keeping and use of radioactive materials on premises and provides for the disposal and accumulation of radioactive waste.

Radioactive material is defined in the Act which contains a general prohibition on its storage or use by any person or company for the purpose of a trade, profession or business unless they are registered under the Act by the Chief Inspector of HMIP. When registering, the Chief Inspector of HMIP will consider "the amount and character of the radioactive waste likely to arise from the keeping or use of the radioactive material on the premises in question."[69] A Certificate of Registration setting out the details of the registration will be given to the applicant. In addition a copy will be sent to the local authority where the premises are situated. The Chief Inspector retains the power to cancel or vary a registration at any time.

There is also provision requiring authorisation to be sought before disposal of substances which are known or reasonably believed to be radioactive.[70] A similar provision under section 7 applies to the accumulation of radioactive substances on premises, other than those operated by the Atomic Energy Authority for which a current nuclear site licence is in existence.

When granting authorisations for disposal or accumulation, local authorities within the affected vicinity will be sent details on request. Authorisations are granted on the recommendations of the International Commission on Radioactive Protection as expanded by the National Radiological Protection Board, a body of scientists who will advise on the safety standards applicable in each individual case. Their advice is governed by the allowable limits of radiation exposure permitted.

When local authorities receive notification of an authorisation, they are under a duty to notify interested public bodies.

The Chief Inspector of HMIP has the power to vary or revoke an authorisation at any time. In 1990, the Chief Inspector's powers were enhanced by the ability to issue enforcement and prohibition notices to persons not complying with the requirements of their registration.[71]

Nuclear Installations Act 1965.

6–032 Whereas the Radioactive Substances Act 1993 controls the keeping and use of radioactive materials, the Nuclear Installations Act 1965 ensures safety in the licensing and inspection of nuclear installations. There is also provision for compensation for injury resulting

[69] Radioactive Substances Act 1993, s.7.
[70] Radioactive Substances Act 1993, s.13.
[71] Radioactive Substances Act 1993, ss.21 and 22.

from the emission of radiation from nuclear sites. In addition, a site licence issued by the Health and Safety Executive is required before the site may be used for the installation or use of a nuclear reactor. Site licences are generally issued for nuclear power stations but have also been issued to research reactors and private commercial processing plants. Site licences will be required in addition to a certificate of registration under the Radioactive Substances Act 1993 which relates to radioactive substances as opposed to the installation itself. Site licences are not required by governmental departments, such as the Ministry of Defence.

Prior to granting site licences, section 3 of the Nuclear Installations Act 1965 provides for consultation with interested local bodies. Electricity boards are exempt from this requirement as electricity legislation provides separate similar provisions.

European Community Legislation

A paper produced by the Health and Safety Executive in April 1991 **6–033** on E.C. Directives and their impact on United Kingdom Toxic Substances legislation states:

> "United Kingdom legislation relating to the control of risks to health from toxic substances is sufficiently comprehensive and is generally robust and flexible enough to deal with these future proposals without major amendments"[72]

Like the United Kingdom, the European Community has responded to the increasing concern over the threat posed by dangerous substances during the past 20 years.

Overview

Specific Directives introduced in the late 1970s were aimed at generally controlling the discharges of dangerous substances into the **6–034** water environment and groundwater.[73] In addition, in the late 1970s and early 1980s, the Community addressed the problem of discharges and waste created by certain dangerous substances. These included titanium oxide waste, mercury discharges and the control of cadmium.

Classification, packaging and labelling of dangerous substances

Amendments to the 1976 E.C. Directive on the Classification, Pack- **6–035** aging and Labelling of Dangerous Substances were outlined by the Commission in January 1990. The classification, Packaging and Labelling of Dangerous Substances Regulation 1984 (S.I. 1984 No. 1244) implemented the provisions of the European Community.

[72] HSE, European Community Directives, Impact on UK Toxic Substances Legislation, April 1991.

[73] 76/464 and 80/68.

The new amendments will impose an obligation on suppliers of dangerous substances to notify the appropriate authority in the Member State before making them available in the marketplace. There will also be further obligations concerning the classification, packaging and labelling of dangerous substances. The main objective is to harmonise requirements in all Member States.

Notification and information for imports and exports

6–036 In 1988, the Council of the European Communities passed a Regulation establishing a common system of notification and information for imports and exports to and from non-Member States of certain chemicals.[74] It was directed at chemicals which are prohibited within the Community or severely restricted on account of their effect on health and the environment. These chemicals are largely produced for export to developing countries. Examples include certain varieties of pesticide.

The substances concerned are listed in Annex 1 to the Regulation. Each Member State must establish an authority responsible for notifying non-Member States of listed substances exported from that Member State. The appropriate state authority must also receive notification of imports to a Member State. The object is to create regularised control. Notification of imports or exports of prescribed substances must be passed to the European Community.

So far as disposal is concerned, the E.C. Directive on hazardous waste aims to approximate the laws of all Member States on the controlled management of hazardous waste. "Hazardous waste" is defined by references to Annexes I, II and III of the Directive which categorise the substances to be controlled. The Directive itself outlines objectives which can be generally applied to the Regulations, both European and national:

- the existence of special substances which necessitate more stringent control;
- the recognition that management of hazardous waste must be improved;
- the creation of a uniform definition of hazardous waste and the ability to monitor disposal and recovery in the most comprehensive manner possible;
- the foresight that technology will change and legislation must move with these advances.

The simple but vital questions that industrialists, manufacturers and transporters must ask themselves is: whether, where, and how they produce, supply, store or transport hazardous chemicals.

[74] 1734/88.

[75] Until Directive 91/689 is properly in force, the original Directive – 78/319 – remains current.

Answers to these questions will enable identification of the controls to be complied with both on a national and a European level.

HEALTH AND SAFETY AT WORK

Health and Safety law is a large and complex area of law defining duties relating to health and safety in the work place. Duties are imposed on employers, employees and the self-employed. **6–037**

The Health and Safety at Work, etc., Act 1974, was superimposed onto previous legislation, including the Factories Act 1961, Mines and Quarries Act 1954 and the Offices, Shops and Railway Premises Act 1963. Its purpose is to replace the requirements of earlier legislation with regulations and approved codes of practice under the Act.

There are also various regulations issued under the HSWA including the Control of Substances Hazardous to Health Regulations 1988[76] and the Control of Industrial Major Accidents Health Regulations 1984.[77]

Duties

The principles of safety responsibility and safe working are embodied in the 'general duties' section of the Health & Safety at Work, etc., Act 1974, sections 2 to 9. They are comprehensive in nature and designed to encourage employers and employees to take an active and responsible role. **6–038**

Objectives

By imposing these duties the Act aims to achieve three main objectives: **6–039**

(a) Serving the health, safety and welfare of people at work;
(b) Protecting people other than those at work against risks to their health and safety arising out of work activities;
(c) Consulting on the keeping and use of explosive or highly flammable or otherwise dangerous substances, and generally preventing unlawful possession and use of such substances.[78]

[76] Discussed above.
[77] Discussed above.
[78] This activity will be exercised by the Health and Safety Executive.

Enforcement

6–040 These objectives are to be enforced by the two bodies which were created by the Health and Safety at Work, etc., Act 1974. They are the Health and Safety Commission and the Health and Safety Executive.

The Secretary of State controls the Health and Safety Commission. The Commission controls the Health and Safety Executive. The Health and Safety Executive under the Health and Safety at Work etc. Act 1974 has the responsibility for licensing high hazard premises for fire purposes.

To enforce the legislation, the Executive is divided into inspectorates: the Nuclear Installations Inspectorate and the Explosives Inspectorate.

The Nuclear Installations Inspectorate is responsible for policy over hazardous nuclear installation and the assessment of major hazards. It is charged with constant surveillance of nuclear installation.

The Explosives Inspectorate is responsible for licensing and inspecting explosives factories and investigating accidents involving explosives.

Improvement and prohibition notices

6–041 Inspectors are given the power to issue improvement and prohibition notices when they have evidence to believe that health and safety legislation is being contravened. These can be issued whether there are breaches of the Act or a relevant statutory provision.

Public Access to Information

6–042 Freedom of information has not traditionally been a noted feature of United Kingdom law. Access to information held by the Government and its agencies has been hampered by the Official Secrets Act 1911. There have been limited powers for the procurement of information from the private sector. This trend has to an extent been reversed in recent years through the development of a system of public disclosure through the provision of registers. The indications are that there will be an increasing emphasis on "open" government which will include access to environmental data.

Survey of Pollution Control Legislation

6–043 The following sections give a summary of the more important public register provisions, including air pollution, water pollution, waste management, planning and environmental assessment control, the Environment and Safety Information Act 1988, the Food and Environmental Protection Act 1985 and genetically modified organisms.

Air pollution

The Control of Air Pollution (Registration of Works) Regulations 1989 implemented E.C. Directive 84/360 on air pollution from industrial plants subject to the registration requirements of the Alkali Works Regulation Act 1906, the "predecessor" to IPC control under Part I of the Environmental Protection Act 1990. They require the Secretary of State to maintain and publicly disclose the applications for the registration of works. Details must include maps of the works site; the nature of the work or proposed work on the site; the source, nature and amount of any noxious or offensive substance emitted into the atmosphere; and details of how the site will comply to other relevant legislation. Information relating to trade secrets or national defence is exempt from disclosure. **6–044**

Water pollution

The implementation of the Water Act 1989, replaced the water pollution control regime under Control of Pollution Act 1974 and the subsequent restructuring of the water industry transferred responsibility for registers to the National Rivers Authority through the Control of Pollution (Registers) Regulations 1989. The Regulations require the registers to meet certain standards such as indexing, chronological dating and rapid inclusion (within 28 days) of new data. **6–045**

The Water Resources Act 1991, together with the Water Industry Act 1991, replaces the pollution control provisions of the Water Act 1989 and contains several information provisions, including the dissemination of an annual report by the regional branches of the NRA. It also restates the pollution control register requirements, although these currently remain under the Control of Pollution (Registers) Regulations 1989. Other information must also be available to the public, such as physical criteria (water flow, locations of waterworks etc.). There is a provision for restriction of information disclosure in order to protect the confidentiality of the operations of a company or individual.

The Water Industry Act 1991 regulates the water service companies and stipulates that they, like the regional NRAs, must produce an annual report on their activities. Similar confidentiality exemptions apply to information disclosure. Additionally, the Secretary of State can freeze the publication of certain information if it is felt that disclosure is not in the public interest.

Integrated pollution control

6–046 The Environmental Protection Act 1990, which restructured pollution control and enforcement in the United Kingdom, also implemented several new public information provisions. HMIP is required to maintain registers for integrated pollution control. These registers must be made freely available to the public and list all applications for authorisations for emissions or discharge together with the grant and revocation of authorisations. Local authorities must do likewise for authorisations under the provisions for air pollution control under Environmental Protection Act 1990. Matters affecting national security or commercial confidentiality are excluded from the registers, although the Secretary of State can override such confidentiality if it is felt to be in the public interest to do so.

The Environmental Protection (Applications, Appeals, and Registers) Regulations 1991 detail the provisions for registers under Integrated Pollution Control. The registers must contain similar information to the Control of Air Pollution (Registration of Works) Regulations 1989, and apply to all companies which have received an authorisation since the introduction of the Integrated Pollution Control system.

Waste management

6–047 The Environmental Protection Act 1990 sets out similar register provisions for waste management authorities in relation to waste. Details of waste management licences must be shown on the Register with the same exclusions as are found in relation to Integrated Pollution Control. Waste regulation authorities must also draw up annual reports on their operations. Radioactive substances are covered within this part of the Act.

Planning and environmental asessment

6–048 The Town and Country Planning Act 1990 and a whole body of Statutory Instruments[79] implement E.C. Directive 85/337 on environmental impact assessment. The planning process in the United Kingdom has always had some degree of public participation through the publication of local planning applications and public consultation on draft structure and local plans. The legislation brought in to implement the Environmental Impact Directive also has some provision for public consultation, chiefly that the impact statement must be lodged for public review. Government guidance also recommends public consultation at the earlier stages of the process, but this is not mandatory.

[79]Extending and modifying categories of development requiring environmental assessment. Environmental Assessment (Salmon Farming in Marine Waters) Regulations 1988.

The Environment and Safety Information Act 1988

The Environment and Safety Information Act 1988, was introduced to reinforce provisions made in the Health and Safety at Work Act 1974 and the Food and Environmental Protection Act 1985. The Act requires the Health and Safety Executive to keep registers of improvement and compliance notices made under relevant legislation. The registers are open to public inspection and must be adequately indexed and updated, although there is provision for the protection of trade secrets (including manufacturing processes). **6–049**

Food and Environmental Protection Act 1985

The Food and Environmental Protection Act 1985, a hybrid Act covering both food safety and environmental protection, lays down information disclosure requirements for the pesticide industry. The licensing authority (the relevant Government Minister) must maintain, and make available to the public, registers giving details of licences issued under the Act. **6–050**

Genetically modified organisms

The Environmental Protection Act 1990 also directs the Secretary of State to maintain a register of consents for the release of genetically modified organisms into the environment. The usual provisions for public access and confidentiality apply. **6–051**

Major industrial accident hazards disclosure

The Health and Safety at Work Act 1974, comprises three sets of regulations: the partially implemented E.C. Directive 82/501 (the "Seveso Directive"), and two subsequent amendments to the Directive. The Act initiated inspection of factories by authorised inspectors whose reports are retained by the Health and Safety Executive and are currently confidential, although there are indications that this is being reviewed under the current policy of open government.[80] **6–052**

The Act requires manufacturers to prepare on-site emergency plans and local authorities to establish off-site emergency plans for a major accident. These plans must be supplied to the community potentially affected by a major accident without specific request. This information typically consists of the actions to take in the event of an accident, such as the closing of windows, extinguishing of naked flames and listening to the radio for further instructions. The general public can also obtain this information on request.

Amending regulations introduced in 1990 stipulate that the level of information provided to the public must at the least comply with the specifications listed in Annex V11 of the Seveso Directive. This

[80]Discussed above in Chapter 2.

includes additional details, such as a simple explanation of the operations on the manufacturing site, information on the nature of potential major hazards, and the way in which further information can be obtained. These amendments bring the United Kingdom into line with E.C. Directive 88/610, which itself was an amendment of the Seveso Directive and both extended the scope of operations to which the Directive was applicable and stipulated greater provision of information to the public.

To date, the progress of emergency plan provision has not been smooth in the United Kingdom to date. Environmental Data Services (ENDS) reported in March 1992 that over two-thirds of the on-site emergency plans submitted to the Health and Safety Executive had yet to be approved. Of the 331 reports submitted, only 86 satisfied the full information requirements.

Environmental data

6–053 The 1990 government White Paper, "This Common Inheritance", made several pledges to improve public access to environmental information. The long-standing Digest of Environmental Protection and Water Statistics is scheduled to be developed into a more coherent report on the United Kingdom environment, covering global and European issues as well as United Kingdom data. Other pledges (now fulfilled) include the implementation of the European Community Directive of freedom of access to information on the environment and implementation of an eco-labelling scheme.

European Community

6–054 Directive 90/313 on the Freedom of Access to Information on the Environment establishes new measures for public access to information. It guarantees freedom of access to environmental information relating to any public authority, company or individual without having to prove an interest. It covers information for all environmental media—air, water and land—but does not describe the systems necessary to allow public access to information. The permitted response time is up to a maximum of two months with restrictions in place for national security, trade secrets, draft documents and internal communications. Member States were required to implement this Directive by the end of 1992.

The United Kingdom government issued a consultation paper on the Directive in January 1992. This stated the Government's intention to implement the Directive through regulations (the Environmental Information Regulations 1992) issued under the 1972 European Communities Act and listed the bodies to which the regulations would apply, including several government departments and over 150 public bodies. However, the paper stressed the need to protect information which:

- Is given voluntarily by companies. The paper states that to do otherwise would jeopardise discussion of sensitive environmental matters;
- Is classified as sensitive. This includes national security concerns and commercial interests.

These restrictions have caused considerable debate. The House of Lords Select Committee on the European Communities report on Implementation and Enforcement of Environmental Legislation (March 1992) recommended that any refusal to disclose information under European Community Directive 90/313 should be subject to judicial review.

Other European Community Directives have had considerable effect. Directive 76/160 concerning the quality of bathing water requested that Member States must designate bathing beaches and monitor water quality during the bathing season (April–September). These annual monitoring results must then be submitted to the European Community. Many countries were slow to implement the Directive (including the United Kingdom) and the loose wording within the Directive allowed for differing interpretations of both "bathing beach" and "monitoring procedure." However, through sustained non-governmental organisation pressure, the monitoring results (compiled by the NRA) are now freely available to the public in the United Kingdom.

Other relevant Directives include:

- 76/161 which established a common procedure for the setting up and constant updating of an inventory of sources of information on the environment in the Community and defined procedures to create and update documentation centres, specialist centres and research projects;
- 90/1210 on the establishment of the European Environmental Agency and the European Environment Information and Observation Network: now located in Copenhagen the European Environmental Agency will be a major information resource. Its initial remit includes the production of a report every three years on the state of the environment, and also widespread information exchange and dissemination. It will also act as the central administration point for the proposed European Community Eco-labelling scheme;
- The European Fifth Action Programme which stresses the need for public participation and consultation in environmental regulation matters. Directive 90/313 is highlighted together with the development of information dissemination initiatives through the European Environmental Agency.

Voluntary Schemes

6–055 The European Community launched its proposed eco-labelling scheme in December 1992, although product criteria are still being developed. The appearance of the eco-label on a product will indicate that it has satisfied certain criteria, although space limitations will dictate that the criteria themselves will not appear on the packaging.

Successive drafts of the European Community's proposed Eco-Audit Regulation have resulted in a shift from mandatory to voluntary status for company compliance, but it retains extensive provisions for public information disclosure. Companies can enrol on a company-wide or site-by-site basis, and an environmental statement (built upon the results of the environmental review or audit) must be made freely available to the public. Furthermore, the statement must be written "specifically for the public in a concise, non-technical form."

The provisions of the British Standard for Environmental Management Systems (BS 7750) are more vague in relation to public information provisions. Although detailed procedures for record keeping, auditing and review are given, there is no specific commitment to public availability of anything beyond the environmental policy. Instead clause 4.9 states "policies shall be established concerning the availability of records."

Three other voluntary environmental management systems operating within the United Kingdom which have information disclosure policies are the International Chamber of Commerce Business Charter on Sustainable Development; the Chemical Industries Association Responsible Care Code and the Confederation of British Industry Environment Business Forum. As voluntary codes, however, these provisions are not binding.

Whether signatories to the above agreements or not, some companies have initiated a process of voluntary disclosure to the public by means of environmental information in annual reports or separate environmental reviews. Monsanto, Norsk Hydro, ICI, British Gas and British Airways are among the companies to produce such reviews to date.

Chapter Seven

E.C. LAW

It is only recently that the E.C. has played such a dominant role in the initiation of action on pollution control in Member States. Yet despite the pollution potential of the coal and steel industries, in the 1951 Treaty of Paris which established the European Coal and Steel Community, no reference was made to environmental protection. The same is true of the two Treaties of Rome, which established the European Economic Community and Euratom in 1957. To that extent they are the products of the thinking of their time, which appeared to place the goal of economic growth above all else. **7–001**

The very notion of "environmental law", in the sense of a cohesive body of legal measures designed to protect and improve the world about us, was unheard of in the Europe of March 1957. Not until the 1970s, when the level of public awareness of environmental matters became raised, does one begin to perceive the genesis of an E.C. environmental policy.

SOME GENERAL PRINCIPLES OF COMMUNITY LAW

Community law is derived from four basic sources: **7–002**

(a) The E.C. Treaty and Protocols, as amended by subsequent Treaties, the most recent of which is the Single European Act of 1986;
(b) Secondary legislation of the E.C. Institutions, *i.e.* Regulations, Directives and Decisions;
(c) The Jurisprudence of the European Court of Justice (ECJ) (and of the Courts of Justice of the European Coal and Steel Community and Euratom before the merger of the Communities in 1965);
(d) Treaties entered into by E.C. institutions on behalf of the Community.

TREATY LAW

7–003 The primary source of E.C. law is to be found in the Treaty of Rome as amended. It is a characteristic of that Treaty that its objectives are expressed in broad terms. Its Articles are the foundations upon which the edifice of Community law has been built. The formulation of detailed rules of law has been the task of the legislative and judicial institutions of the Community. Thus, over the years, a vast body of secondary legislation and case law has evolved.

E.C. SECONDARY LEGISLATION

7–004 Article 189 of the Treaty of Rome provides that:

> "In order to carry out their task, the Council and the Commission shall, in accordance with the provisions of this Treaty, make Regulations, issue Directives, take decisions, make recommendations or deliver opinions."

A Regulation has general application and is binding in its entirety and directly applicable in all Member States.

A Directive is binding as to the result to be achieved on each Member State to which it is addressed, but leaves the choice of the form and methods to each state's national authorities. Recommendations and opinions have no binding force.

The structure of Community secondary legislation is essentially hierarchical. A Regulation comprises rules of general application, binding in all Member States without the need for the national authorities to do anything further by way of implementing legislation. Directives, on the other hand, although binding in regard to the objective achieved, vest Member States with complete discretion as to the juridical vehicle employed at national level. Decisions are, by their very nature, of limited import. They may be addressed to individuals or Member States. As such, they are frequently used by the Commission as a means of enforcing the competition policy of the Community.

Of these three types of secondary legislation, the Directive is the most commonly used vehicle, in the environmental sphere, for implementing Community policy. This is largely due to the fact that the original juridical basis for Community action on the environment was Article 100 of the Treaty. This necessitated the use of Directives. Although later when reliance came to be placed additionally upon Article 235 this gave greater freedom of choice as to the method of implementation to be employed, the Directive retained its pre-eminence. Thus, because of the use of Directives, E.C. environmental policy is largely dependent upon implementing measures being taken in Member States for its practical effect.

DIRECT EFFECT

Community law, in all its forms, does not merely create rights and obligations enforceable as between Member States. It is also capable of creating rights (and obligations) which individuals may invoke before national courts, in the context of their legal relations either with Member States or other individuals. **7–005**

The tendency of a provision of Community law to confer rights and duties upon individuals (as opposed to Member States), which those individuals can enforce before national courts, is known as "direct effect". The tendency of a provision to create rights enforceable by an individual against a Member State is known as "vertical direct effect". Whether a provision has this effect is a question of interpretation.

The ground rules for establishing whether a provision is directly effective were established by the European Court of Justice as far back as 1963, in the landmark case of *Van Gend en Loos* v. *Nederlandse Administrasie der Belastingen*[1]. That case concerned Article 12 of the Treaty of Rome, which prohibits Member States from introducing between themselves any new customs duties on imports or charges having equivalent effect or from raising any existing duties. This provision went to the very root of the establishment of the Common Market for goods envisaged by the Treaty. The case was referred to the European Court of Justice by the Dutch Tariefcommissie for a ruling under Article 177 of the Treaty, on the question of whether Article 12 gave rise to rights which nationals of Member States were entitled to enforce before national courts.

The European Court of Justice answered this question in the affirmative. The wording of Article 12 contained a clear and unconditional prohibition amounting to a negative obligation. That obligation was not qualified by any reservation on the part of States which would make its implementation conditional upon any positive legislative measure enacted under national law. "The very nature of the prohibition makes it ideally adapted to produce direct effects in the legal relationship between Member States and their subjects".[2]

The principles enunciated in this case have been refined and developed by the court in its subsequent jurisprudence. In order to **7–006**

[1]Case 26/62, [1963] E.C.R. 1.
[2]*ibid.*, at p. 13.

satisfy the requirements for direct effectiveness, the provision in question must:

(a) Be sufficiently clear and precise;
(b) Establish an unconditional obligation;
(c) Be completely and legally perfect, requiring no subsequent measures to be taken by Community institutions or Member States with discretionary power in the matter.

A Regulation is, by its very nature, liable to be productive of a direct effect. However, the mere fact that an instrument is published as a Regulation in the Official Journal of the European Communities, does not automatically imbue it with the attribute of being directly effective. Whether it is possessed of the three characteristics essential and raises a direct effect is a question of interpretation. The substance, rather than the form of the instrument will be the determining factor. It may be that within an instrument published as a Regulation, there are provisions which lack sufficient clarity, fail to impose unconditional obligations or leave essential matters to the discretion of Member States. Such provisions, whatever the title of the legal instrument in which they are embodied, will not be held to have direct effect.

7–007 In contrast to Regulations, Directives are not expressed by Article 189 to be "directly applicable". Indeed, the fact that the means of implementation are left to the discretion of Member States tends to suggest that Directives are not designed to produce directly effective rules. In reality, the European Court of Justice has held that, provided a Directive possesses the necessary three characteristics, there is no reason why its provisions cannot have direct effect. In view of the Community's preference for the Directive as the primary vehicle for the implementation of its environment policy, it is important to examine the circumstances in which they may be held to have direct effect in a little detail.

In *Franz Grad* v. *Finanzamt Traunstein*[3] the court stated that the mere fact that under Article 189 only regulations were expressed to be directly applicable did not preclude other legal measures referred to therein from producing similar effects. To hold otherwise might undermine the useful effect (*effet utile*) of such measures, and render them impotent.

The principles set out in *Grad* were followed and refined by the Court in *Van Duyn* v. *Home Office*[4]. Miss Van Duyn was a Dutch National who wished to enter the United Kingdom in order to take up employment as a Secretary with the Church of Scientology at East Grinstead. The Home Office refused her leave to enter the country on public policy grounds, based on the fact that it considered the activities of the church to be socially harmful. She brought

[3]Case 9/70, [1970] E.C.R. 825.
[4]Case 41, [1974] E.C.R. 1337, [1975] 1 C.M.L.R. 1, [1975] 2 W.L.R. 760.

an action against the Home Office in the High Court in England. The High Court referred certain questions to the European Court of Justice under Article 177. One of the questions required the court to consider whether a Directive concerning the free movement of persons within the Community was a measure upon which individuals could rely. Advocate General Mayras, in his opinion, reiterated the criteria for direct effect originally proposed by Advocate General Gand in the *Lutticke* case,[5] which had been adopted by the European Court of Justice in subsequent cases, as follows:

> "the provision must impose a clear and precise obligation on Member States; it must be unconditional, in other words subject to no limitation; if, however, a provision is subject to certain limitations, their nature and extent must be exactly defined; finally, the implementation of a Community rule must not be subject to the adoption of any subsequent rules or Regulations on the part either of Community institutions or of the Member States, so that, in particular, Member States must not be left any real discretion with regard to the application of the rule in question".

M Mayras went on to say that:

> "When faced with a Directive, it is therefore necessary to examine, in each case, whether the wording, nature and general scheme of the provisions in question are capable of producing direct effects between the Member States to whom the Directive is addressed and their subjects."

The mere fact that Member States were given the choice of form and method of implementation which accord with their national law did not imply that a Directive could not be directly effective. The court adopted the same approach. It stated that:

> "In particular, where the Community authorities have, by Directive, imposed on Member States the obligation to pursue a particular course of conduct, the useful effect of such an act would be weakened if individuals were prevented from relying on it before their national courts and if the latter were prevented from taking it into consideration as an element of Community law."

There can be no doubt that many environmental Directives would be capable of giving rise to vertical direct effect. However, this presupposes that an individual with sufficient *locus standi* in the sense of having some cause of action before a court in a Member State was able to place reliance on a Directive. Such cases may in fact be rare in the environmental sphere.

[5]Case 48/65, [1966] E.C.R. 19, [1966] 3 C.M.L.R. 8.

THE SUPREMACY OF E.C. LAW

7–008 Directly effective provisions of Community Law, if invoked by individuals before the courts of Member States, may provoke a conflict between the domestic legal order and that of the Community. In such a case which law takes precedence? No guidance is provided by the Treaty.

The European Court of Justice has, however, made it clear that Community Law takes precedence over all national laws, whatever their nature, no matter how deeply rooted they may be in the constitution of a Member State.[6]

In *Administazione delle Finanze dello Stato SPA* v. *Simmenthal SPA*[7] the European Court of Justice held that to give legal effect to a national legislative measure which was incompatible with Community law would be to deny the effectiveness of the obligations freely entered into by Member States, and would strike at the very foundations of the Community. The court went on to say:

> "Every national court must, in a case within its jurisdiction apply Community Law in its entirety and protect rights which the latter confers on individuals and must accordingly set aside any provision of national law which may conflict with it, whether prior or subsequent to the Community rule."

COMMUNITY ACTION ON THE ENVIRONMENT—A BRIEF HISTORY

7–009 The Community was conceived as an economic community, founded on the so-called "four freedoms" free movement of goods, services, people and capital. The establishment of a regime to protect the environment might be seen as incompatible with the Community's goals of economic expansion and greatly enhanced living standards for its citizens. Checks and balances, however, were built into the Community's constitution.

Article 2 of the Treaty of Rome thus states:

> "The Community shall have as its task, by establishing a common market and progressively approximating the economic policies of Member States, to promote throughout the Community a harmonious development of economic activities, a continuous and balanced expansion, an increase in

[6] Case 11/70, *Internationale Handelsgesellschaft m.b.H. v. Einfuhr-und Vorratsstelle für Getreide und Futtermittel:* [1970] E.C.R. 1125, [1972] C.M.L.R. 255.

[7] Case 106/77, [1978] E.C.R. 629 [1978] 3C.M.L.R. 263.

stability, an accelerated raising of the standard of living, and closer relations between the states belonging to it."

The development of a Community policy on the environment has its genesis in measures taken in 1972–73. At the Paris Summit in 1972, Heads of State and Government of Member States emphasised the link between economic expansion and enhanced quality of life, and the importance of taking measures to protect the environment as a means of promoting the latter. These sentiments were echoed by the European Commission in its Proposal for a Community environmental policy in 1973.[8] There then followed the Commission's first action programme on the Environment.

THE PROGRAMMES OF ACTION ON THE ENVIRONMENT

To date five action programmes on the environment have been adopted: **7–010**

1 November 22, 1973 (O.J. C112);
2 May 17, 1977 (O.J. C139);
3 February 17, 1983 (O.J. C46);
4 October 19, 1987 (O.J. C328);
5 March 18, 1992 (O.J. C485);

These action programmes are both declarations of intent and discussion documents. They make proposals for action within a certain timetable. They have no legal effect. Not every proposal which they make has been adopted and translated into Community legislation.

The First Action Programme formulated the basic principles on which a Community environmental policy would be founded. It listed eleven principles which may be summarised thus:

(a) Prevention of pollution is better than cure; the ultimate aim of any environmental policy must be the elimination of pollution at source;
(b) Sound economic planning requires that environmental factors should be considered at the earliest possible stages of any decision-making processes;
(c) The person who causes pollution must bear the cost of preventing, eliminating or reducing it;
(d) Natural resources must be exploited in such a way as to avoid damage to the ecosystem;
(e) The ability of pollution to upset the delicate balance of that ecosystem must be recognised and guarded against;

[8] Bull E.C. Supplement 5/73.

(f) The "good neighbour" principle that activities carried on in one Member State should not be to the detriment of the environment of another Member State;
(g) The Community and its members have an important role to play on the international stage by co-operating with states and organisations outside the Community in the formulation of a global environmental policy;
(h) National environmental policies should be co-ordinated and harmonised within the Community. This should not, however, be achieved at the expense of progress at the national level;
(i) Different types of pollution require different levels of action (i.e. local, regional, national, Community, international). For each pollution type, it is necessary to establish the appropriate level of action;
(j) The First Action Programme envisaged three areas of action aimed at preventing and reducing pollution and nuisances, improving the quality of the environment and promoting co-operation with international organisations;
(k) Many of its proposals are aimed at achieving common standards and methodology for measuring pollution, and evaluating and dealing with its effects.

7–011 The Programme calls for harmonisation of the specifications of pollutants. In addition, it aims to promote co-operation in research and the dissemination of information, the latter with a view to raising the level of public awareness of environmental matters within the Community. Likewise included in the targets for action are natural resource management and conservation, the improvement of the quality of the working environment and planning. The emphasis is essentially on remedial measures.

The Second Action Programme focuses on moving towards greater emphasis on prevention. With the advent of the Third Action Programme, the prevention of environmental damage is the dominant theme. The Fifth Action Programme sets out an ambitious strategy for environmental management at Community level with quantified targets and the means of achieving them.

Five target sectors have been selected for special attention under the Fifth Action Programme: industry, energy, transport, agriculture and tourism for action between 1993–2000. The purpose, according to "Eurobrief",[9] is to:

(a) Improve environmental policy formulation;
(b) Make for better impact assessment;
(c) Step up research and development;
(d) Develop information, education and training;

[9] *Eurobrief: European Environmental Law Review*, June 1992.

(e) Promote sectoral and spatial planning in ensuring a more balanced geographical distribution of economic activities;
(f) Encourage the use of economic and fiscal instruments so as to reflect environmental costs in the price of goods.

The Fifth Action programme seeks to develop policies through information gained at forums with a multitude of qualified representatives. Each forum will have a different objective: to consult, implement, enforce, or eventually monitor the managerial policies that will be created.

THE LEGAL EXPRESSION OF COMMUNITY POLICY ON THE ENVIRONMENT

The action programmes are the expression of a strategic plan of action to protect the environment both within the Community and outside. They did not, in themselves, provide the legal vehicle whereby that plan could be implemented. It was necessary to revert to the Treaty of Rome to find a juridical basis for the implementation of an environmental policy for the Community. Historically, reliance has been placed on Articles 100 and 235 as the basis for measures taken. **7–012**

Article 100 enables Directives to be issued for the approximation of such provisions laid down by law, Regulation or administrative action in Member States as directly affecting the establishment or functioning of the Common Market. Article 235 permits appropriate measures to be taken where the Treaty has not provided appropriate powers to enable one of the objectives of the Common Market to be attained in the course of this operation.

Although reservations have been expressed about the use of Articles 100 and 235 as a legal justification for Community environmental measures, there is no instance where such a measure has been struck down by the Court of Justice for want of constitutional validity. Indeed, the environmental programmes of the Community may be said to have stood the test of time.

THE SINGLE EUROPEAN ACT

On July 1, 1987, the Treaty of Rome was amended by the Single European Act which had been signed in Luxembourg on February 17, 1986. In this instrument there is, for the first time, a title headed "Environment" under which one sees a clear and unambiguous jur- **7–013** idical foundation for Community legislation on the environment. Many of the principles enunciated in the Action Programmes are given constitutional status and provision is made for the full integration of the Community's environmental policy with its other policies. Article 130R thus provided as follows:

(1) Action by the Community relating to the environment shall have the following objectives:
- to preserve, protect and improve the quality of the environment;
- to contribute towards protecting human health;
- to ensure a prudent and rational utilisation of natural resources.

(2) Action by the Community relating to the environment shall be based on the principles that preventive action should be taken, that environmental damage should as a priority be rectified at source, and that the polluter should pay. Environmental protection requirements shall be a component of the Community's other policies.

3) In preparing its action relating to the environment, the Community shall take account of:
- available scientific and technical data;
- environmental conditions in the various regions of the Community;
- the potential benefits and costs of action or lack of action;
- the economic and social development of the Community as a whole and the balanced development of its regions.

(4) The Community shall take action relating to the environment to the extent which the objectives referred to in paragraph one can be attained better at Community level than at the level of the individual Member States. Without prejudice to certain measures of a Community nature, the Member States shall finance and implement the other measures.

(5) Within their respective spheres of competence, the Community and Member States shall co-operate with third countries and with the relevant international organisations. The arrangements for community co-operation may be the subject of agreements between the Community and the third parties concerned, which shall be negotiated and concluded in accordance with Article 228.[10]

Article 130S provides for new voting procedures in the Council of Ministers by extending the areas in which a qualified majority vote, as opposed to a unanimous one, will suffice.

Article 130T permits Member States to introduce stricter or more

[10]This is without prejudice to Member States' competence to negotiate in international bodies and to conclude international agreements.

extensive protective measures than those prescribed by the Community, provided that they are compatible with the Treaty. This provision is important, since different standards employed in laws designed to protect the environment as between different Member States may have the effect of distorting competition within the Community.

THE AMBIT OF COMMUNITY ACTION ON THE ENVIRONMENT

Well over 100 separate pieces of Community legislation concerning environmental matters have been passed in the last 20 years. In the field of pollution control, they may be classified under the following headings: water, air, chemicals, waste. Overwhelmingly, the Directive has been the preferred legislative instrument. In many cases, these have merely been framework Directives, regulatory skeletons which can only be properly effective once they have been "fleshed out" by detail provided in further, related "daughter" Directives. **7–014**

Water

The question of how best to tackle water pollution was a priority consideration in the early days of the development of environmental policy, and continues to maintain a high profile today. Directives have been passed designed to improve quality standards for surface water abstracted for use as drinking water and for drinking water itself.[11] Directives with similar aims relate to bathing water,[12] groundwater,[13] shellfish waters,[14] and fresh waters which support fish life[15]. Another significant Directive – 91/271 – deals with Urban Waste Water Treatment. This Directive imposes on any member state a mandatory obligation to facilitate the provision of waste water treatment by reference to the incidence of population. The extent of treatment depends, in turn, on whether treated discharges are to waters designated as being "sensitive" or "less sensitive". **7–015**

Dangerous substances entering the aquatic environment generally were tackled in an early framework Directive, followed by a number of daughter Directives concerned with establishing standards for specific pollutants. Two lists are created by the parent Directive, which basically classify substances according to their toxicity. Thus list one substances include DDT, mercury and

[11] 75/440 and 80/778.
[12] 76/160.
[13] 80/68.
[14] 79/923.
[15] 78/659.

cadmium, whereas list two substances include zinc, lead and ammonia. The goals are stated to be the elimination of pollution by the former substances and a reduction in pollution by the latter. Controls on the discharge, dumping, storage and injection of titanium dioxide were introduced in Directive 78/176.

Chemicals

7–016 Community action in this area has focused on measures to facilitate the safe handling of dangerous substances and preparations. These are substances which either individually or when mixed or combined are either explosive, oxidising, flammable, toxic, harmful, corrosive or irritant. Early efforts were geared towards achieving a uniform system for the classification, packaging and labelling of such substances.[16] This original Directive has been amended on a number of occasions so that the scheme of regulation now includes provisions governing the testing and notification of new substances.

Other Directives have made provision for prohibiting or restricting the marketing and use of certain dangerous substances, such as PCBs, PCTs, benzene and asbestos.[17] The use of certain mercury and persistent organochlorine compounds in pesticides has been outlawed.

The mid 1970s saw two major pollution incidents in Europe caused by the escape of toxic substances following accidents at chemical plants. These disasters, the 1973 chemical explosion in Flixborough, United Kingdom and the 1976 poisonous cloud burst in Seveso, Italy, heightened public awareness of the lethal potential of chemical installations. Mindful of the need to prevent future accidents of this magnitude, and after considerable consultation with the chemical industry, the Council of Ministers passed Directive 82/501 on the Major Accident Hazards of Certain Industrial Activities. The first section of the Directive imposes a general duty on manufacturers of substances which are toxic, explosive or flammable, to take all necessary measures to prevent major accidents or to limit their effects. The second section provides for the notification to the competent authorities of the carrying on of industrial activity involving certain substances.

Waste

7–017 Community action on waste effectively began in 1975 with the passing of a framework Directive,[18] which obliges Member States to take necessary measures to ensure that waste is disposed of without damage to human health or to the environment. To this end, the

[16]Directive 67/548.
[17]Directives 76/769, 82/806, 85/610.
[18]75/442.

Directive requires the establishment of responsible authorities in Member States charged with the duty of establishing regimes for the disposal of waste and the licensing of installations or undertakings handling it. Responsibility for the cost of waste disposal lies with the person creating or requiring it to be handled on the basis of the polluter pays principle. Other provisions of the Directive aim to encourage recycling or other similar beneficial exploitation of waste.

In 1978, Directive 78/319 on Toxic and Dangerous waste was passed, requiring that the storage and treatment of toxic waste be undertaken only by authorised persons. A scheme for licensing such persons was imposed by the responsible authorities who used established requirements to record, inspect and supervise those persons. Specific Directives have been passed regulating the disposal of PCBs and PCTs, waste oils and sewage sludge. The transfrontier shipment of toxic and dangerous wastes formerly merited a special regime provided for in Directive 84/631 (now repealed), central to which is the requirement to give advance notification of the movements of such wastes to the responsible authorities of Member States' across whose frontiers the consignments may pass. The Directive provided for the creation of a uniform notification document entitled a "consignment note", that contains, for example, information relating to the source and nature of the waste, the routes to be taken, safety measures, or third party insurance. Member States are required to nominate frontier crossing points for consignments of hazardous waste. Reference was made in the previous Chapter to the new Community Regulation – 259/93 – on the Transfrontier Shipment of Hazardous Waste.

Air

Historically, air pollution has been afforded a lower priority than **7–018** that given to water pollution in the development of the Community's environmental policy. In the mid 1980's concern on the part of Member States over the effects of acid rain, the depletion of the ozone layer and airborne fallout from nuclear disasters such as that which occurred at Chernobyl, served to bring the issue of atmospheric pollution into much greater prominence. The first Directive setting quality standards for air, adopted in 1980, relates to sulphur dioxide and smoke.[19] Limit values are established for both pollutants. Subsequent Directives have set air quality standards for nitrogen dioxide[20] and lead[21]. Motor vehicles and fuel have been specifically targeted and a number of Directives have been adopted in an effort to approximate the laws of Member States concerning lead in

[19] 80/779.
[20] 85/203.
[21] 82/884.

petrol and emissions from vehicles.[22] The Directive on the combatting of air pollution from industrial plants[23] and the Regulation on the protection of the Community's forests against atmospheric pollution[24] represent the first stage in the Community's onslaught on the problem of acid rain. The latter is designed to facilitate the monitoring of damage to forests in order to view and evaluate it and improve our understanding of its origin. Contemporary concerns relate to the need to legislate on matters including ozone, volatile organic compounds and solvents.

THE FUTURE OF EUROPEAN ACTION ON POLLUTION CONTROL-QUO VADIS?

7–019 The Community's environmental policy may be said to have come of age with the signing of the Single European Act. The diversity of approaches to pollution control in Member States combined with the wide discretion afforded to those states—inherent in the use of Directives—has rendered full implementation of the Community's environmental policy an elusive goal. Yet in the final analysis, a policy on the environment can only be truly effective if it can be translated into laws which are uniformly enforced in all Member States. As yet the Community lacks an environmental enforcement agency. Regulation 1210/90 has, however, provided for the establishment of a European Environment Agency to be located in Copenhagen. At present, its projected role is essentially limited to the gathering and distribution of environmental information important, though that is in relation to effect, to uniform enforcement. That role is, however, to be re-examined two years after the Regulation comes into force. There is nothing in principle to prevent the Agency from being vested with powers to enable it to function as watchdog and enforcer of the Community's environmental policy. It may only be a question of finding the necessary political will.

[22] *e.g.*, 82/2100, 70/220 as amended.
[23] 84/360.
[24] 3528/86.

Chapter Eight

ENVIRONMENTAL MANAGEMENT SYSTEMS

PIONEERING ENVIRONMENTAL MANAGEMENT PROGRAMMES

Some companies have been implementing environmental management programmes for a considerable time. Pioneering programmes in this area were typically driven by a sense of corporate responsibility, but the recent surge of E.C. environmental legislation and the overhaul of United Kingdom environmental law has prompted many companies to undertake some kind of environmental review. The concept of environmental management systems (E.M.S.) stems from this process: they attempt to define and structure the steps necessary to improve environmental performance, thereby reducing liability or litigation risk and enhancing public image. The International Standards Organisation (ISO) defines environmental management systems as: **8–001**

> "*Generic Management Control Systems* They will allow business and industry to set environmental policy and provide methods (through audits and environmental performance standards amongst others) to monitor and ensure that the environmental goals are met."

The European Commission is developing an eco-audit scheme with the objective of promoting Community-wide voluntary improvements in industry's environmental performance. This is to be achieved through the establishment of environmental management systems, periodic evaluations of the effectiveness of those systems and provision of information to the public on firms' environmental performance.

The drawing up of a formal standard for environmental management systems by the British Standards Institute BS 7750 is the first initiative of its kind in the world. It was prepared under the supervision of the Environment and Pollution Standards Policy Committee and came into effect on March 16, 1992.

BS 7750 specifies the elements of an environmental management system and is intended to apply to all types and sizes of organisations, including manufacturing facilities, offices and warehouses. The objective is to provide a structured management system, integrated within overall management activity to ensure compliance with stated environmental policies and objectives. It shares common management system principles with BS 5750 (EN 29000, ISO 9000) and organisations may elect to use an existing management system developed in conformity with BS 5750 as a basis for environmental management. However, BS 5750 certification is not required for BS 7750.

Many other Codes of Practice—such as the International Chamber of Commerce (ICC) Charter for Sustainable Development—also exist and stress the need for environmental management systems. One common feature all these schemes share is that they are voluntary, and require the support of organisations to be effective. The next few years should indicate whether such an approach will be functional.

ENVIRONMENTAL AUDIT

8–002 Environmental health and safety auditing developed in the early 1970s, largely among companies operating in environmentally sensitive sectors such as oil and chemicals. Since then, environmental auditing has spread rapidly, with corresponding development in the approaches to and the techniques of auditing. The public, with its increased awareness of environmental and safety issues, has become more vocal, forcing companies to respond to public concern with assurances that they are managing environ-mental risks effectively.

Major industrial incidents, such as the Bhopal, Chernobyl, Basle and *Exxon-Valdez* disasters, have repeatedly reminded companies that it is not sufficient to set corporate policies and standards on environmental, health and safety matters without ensuring that they are being implemented. Audits can help minimize the risk of unpleasant surprises in the future.

Increasing regulatory requirements, in some cases as a result of specific major incidents, have made it steadily more difficult for a company to ascertain whether a specific plant in a particular country is complying with all of the relevant legislation. The problem is compounded by the differences in environmental legislation between countries. The growth in environmental policies has led to a corresponding explosion of litigation and liability claims, particularly in the United States. In Europe there is growing emphasis on the responsibilities of individual directors and on making information available to the public.

Every corporation must be able to evaluate the performance of its environment, health and safety programmes. It must also be able to identify deficiencies, then implement improvements. Environmental auditing has become an essential management tool for making such evaluations.

Questions of Definition

At the outset, it is important to draw a distinction between auditing, and techniques such as environmental impact assessment (EIA). 8–003
The latter assesses the potential environmental effects of a proposed facility or process. The essential purpose of an environmental audit, on the other hand, is the systematic scrutiny of environmental performance throughout a company's existing operations. At best, an audit is a comprehensive examination of management systems and facilities, at worst, it is a superficial review.

The term "environmental audit" means different things to different people, while a variety of terms all in common use, have been used to describe the same type of activity assessment, survey and review. Furthermore, some organisations consider that an environmental audit addresses only environmental matters, whereas others use the term to encompass health, safety and environmental matters.

Although there is no universal definition, auditing as practised by many leading companies follows the same basic philosophy and approach, as defined by the International Chamber of Commerce (ICC) in its recent publication, *Environmental Auditing*. The ICC defines environmental auditing as:

> "a management tool comprising a systematic, documented, periodic and objective evaluation of how well environmental organization, management and equipment are performing, with the aim of helping safeguard the environment by (i) facilitation management control of environmental control of environmental practices; and (ii) assessing compliance with company policies, which would include meeting regulatory requirements."

Objective of Environmental Auditing

The overall objective of environmental auditing is to help safeguard the environment and minimize risks to human health. Clearly, 8–004
auditing alone will not achieve this goal, it is a management tool. The key objectives of an environmental audit are to:

- determine how well the environmental management systems and equipment are performing;
- verify compliance with the relevant national, local or other laws and regulations;
- verify compliance with corporate policies and standards;
- identify deficiencies with respect to the above; and
- minimize human exposure to risks from environmental, health and safety problems.

The Scope of the Audit

8–005 Audits can address one topic, or a whole range of issues. The greater the scope of the audit, the greater the size of the audit team, the time spent on-site and depth of investigation. Where international audits need to be carried out by a central team, there can be good reason for covering more than one area while on-site to minimise costs.

In addition, the scope of an audit can vary from simple compliance testing to a more rigorous examination, depending on the perceived needs of the management. The technique is applied not only to operational environmental, health and safety management, but it is increasingly applied to product safety/quality management and to areas such as loss prevention. If the intention of the audit is to help ensure that these broad areas are managed properly, then all of these individual topics must be reviewed.

Although some companies have a regular (often annual) audit cycle, audits are primarily determined by need and priority. Thus not all facilities or aspects of a company will be assessed at the same frequency or extent.

The Typical Audit Process

8–006 An audit is usually conducted by a team that will assemble factual information prior to and during a site visit, analyse the facts, and compare them with the criteria for the audit, draw conclusions, and report their findings. These steps are usually conducted within some kind of formal structure (an audit protocol), so that the process can be repeated reliably at other facilities and quality can be maintained. To ensure that an audit is effective, there are standard pre-audit, on-site, and post-audit steps that must be included.

Pre-Audit Steps

8–007 Pre-audit steps include the administrative issues associated with planning the audit, selecting the personnel for the audit team (often from different parts of the company or from a specialised unit), preparing the audit protocol used by the organization, and obtaining background information about the facility.

If auditing is new, the need for education of those involved in the audit process (the auditors or those being audited) should not be underestimated. This also applies to a multinational company extending an audit program from its home country to subsidiaries abroad. The time spent on explanation and education will pay dividends by ensuring that the audits are approached in a spirit of co-operation rather than perceived as a threat by the local management.

When the American conglomerate Allied-Signal proposed extending its auditing programme to its operations in Europe, it was particularly concerned with ensuring that the plants were properly briefed, that audits protocols were appropriate for European operations, and that audit teams understood the relevant Regulations. Pilot audits were conducted at selected plants. In addition, the audit process was introduced to stress the benefits of a co-operative rather than a "policing" approach.

Obtaining background information about a site and its processes can help focus its activities, and it saves resources by minimising the time spent on site by the audit team. The composition of the audit team will depend on the approach adopted by a particular organisation. Where there is a lack of internal expertise or resources cannot be devoted to the audit activity, companies frequently use independent consultants to conduct the audits for them. Other companies employ a mix of in-house staff and external consultants on each team to obtain an "independent" view. Some large companies use in-house staff only for audits, and have environmental audit groups for this specific function. Companies such as Union Carbide and Allied-Signal have their own dedicated audit staff, but also include an independent consultant on the majority of the audits they carry out.

On-Site Steps

As a first on-site step, it is necessary to develop an understanding **8–008**
of the controls that are in place or thought to be in place. These will include:

- formal procedures and practices;
- record keeping and monitoring;
- inspection and maintenance programs; and
- physical controls to contain spills.

The audit team gathers information on the various controls by observation, interviewing staff and the use of detailed questionnaires.

Evaluating the strengths and weaknesses of internal controls will provide the rationale for conducting subsequent audit steps. Auditors will look for indicators such as:

- clearly defined responsibilities;
- competence of personnel;
- appropriate documentation and records; and
- systems of authorisation.

It is more important to determine whether the system is effective than whether it is sophisticated.

The audit team attempts to verify that the steps and controls work as intended by gathering audit evidence. Evidence may be collected through inquiry, such as asking plant operators what they would do if there was a major chemical spill; observation such as watching specific activities/operations in progress; and testing such as checking records to confirm compliance with regulations.

All of the information obtained is recorded (usually on the audit protocol document and as working papers), and a comprehensive record of the audit and the state of the facility at the time is subsequently produced. Where a deficiency is discovered, it is noted as an audit "finding."

The audit team then integrates and evaluates the findings of individual team members. For some observations, an informal discussions with the plant manager will be sufficient; for others, a formal report will be appropriate.

Reporting the audit findings is usually done in a meeting with the plant management at the end of the team's visit. Each finding and its significance should be discussed with the plant personnel. Prior to leaving the site, the audit team will often provide a written summary of findings for the plant management, to ensure that there are not surprises in the final audit report.

Post-Audit Steps

8–009 Following the on-site work, the next step is to prepare a draft report, which is reviewed by the plant management to confirm its accuracy. It is then distributed to senior management according to the requirements of the company.

The other key step is to develop an action plan to address the deficiencies. Some companies ask for recommendations for corrective action to be included in the formal audit report. The plant will then base its plan on implementing these recommendations. Other companies require the audit report to state only the facts and the deficiencies, with no reference to how they should be corrected. It is then the responsibility of the plant to devise the means of remedying the failings.

Once an audit program is in place, as part of its evidence, future audits will include past reports and progress in the implementation of any recommendations made therein.

For companies with a range of sites being audited, attention must also be focused on effective ways to using audit findings to prioritise sites. Several companies have developed simple scoring systems, paralleling those used in other audit functions, such as fire safety, so that corporate staff can focus on overall findings and measure performance over time.

Extending the Audit Process

Although audits largely focus on a company's processing operations, there are variations on the theme, and different types of audit are used for different situations, including pre-acquisition audits, pre-sale audits and issues audits. **8–010**

Pre-acquisition audits

Concern about potential liabilities has promoted the dramatic increase in environmental auditing prior to acquisition. Pre-acquisition audits are a means of identifying actual or potential problems and taking these into account in the final negotiations of the deal. Time scales are often very short. However, the information obtained on past operations (perhaps before the present owner), current activities, and past incidents, for example, can be invaluable. **8–011**

Pre-sale audits

Less common than pre-acquisition audits but becoming more popular, are audits conducted by the owner prior to selling a plant or a subsidiary company. A growing number of major organisations, such as Dutch chemical company DSM and Finnish conglomerate Neste, undertake pre-sale audits as part of corporate policy. The rationale is that the company will then know the status of environmental issues before the plant is sold, and can take action to remedy any problems it deems appropriate. Equally important, it can present the results of an independent audit to a potential purchaser as confirmation of the situation. Should any environmental problems arise after the sale, a base line has been established against which issues of liability can be decided. **8–012**

Issues audits

Some organisations apply the audit technique to a specific issue that may have implications for the whole company, such as waste. The United Kingdom-based oil multinational, BP, has carried out audits examining the impact of ozone depletion and the implications of public concern about tropical deforestation. **8–013**

Advantages of Auditing

8–014 Auditing brings benefits to business and the community at large. A rigorous process of environmental auditing will help to:

- safeguard the environment;
- verify compliance with local and national laws;
- indicate current or potential future problems that need to be addressed;
- reduce exposure to litigation, incidents and adverse publicity;
- increase employee awareness of environmental matters;
- assess training programmes and provide data to assist in training;
- enable companies to build on good environmental performance, give credit where appropriate and highlight deficiencies;
- identify potential cost savings, such as from waste minimization;
- assist the exchange and comparison of information between different plants or subsidiary companies;
- provide an environmental data base for planning, plant modification and emergency planning; and
- demonstrate company commitment to environmental protection for employees, the public and the authorities.

Future Trends

8–015 As more companies view the environment as a competitive issue, the number and type of audits will increase. The number of companies operating audit programmes will grow, particularly at the medium-size/small company level. More companies will extend auditing to facilities outside their domestic locations. Simultaneously, the scope of audits will be expanded. Many companies that already have environmental audit programmes will extend them to cover health, safety and product safety. New ways of assessing the environmental performance of products, both scientific and perceptual, will be developed to respond to the "green consumer" phenomenon. In many cases, audits will be increasingly required by business partners, not just in the sale of assets, but also in negotiating insurance cover.

Demands from other groups, such as environmentalists or the local community around a plant, for information about company activities will lead to pressure on companies to disclose the results of their audit findings. This increase in auditing activity is likely to lead to more standardization of auditing techniques, procedures and reporting.

At present, there are no standards for the conduct of an audit or the skills/experience required of auditors. The growth in demand for these services will lead to pressure to ensure quality control.

FORMALISED ENVIRONMENTAL MANAGEMENT SYSTEMS

Evidence of good management practices includes regular management review of the company's environmental policy, objectives and programmes and the fostering of a sense of responsibility for the environment among employees at all levels. **8–016**

Two formalised systems have now been developed to the stage of pilot testing:

- The proposal for a E.C. Regulation allowing voluntary participation by companies in the industrial sector in a E.C. Eco-audit scheme; and
- BS 7750 specification for environmental management systems.

The Eco-audit

Early drafts of the Eco-audit proposal indicated that the scheme would be mandatory for manufacturing companies operating within the E.C.. Later drafts were heavily revised and the scheme downgraded to voluntary status, therefore turning the proposed Directive into a Regulation. A final draft, the Proposal for a Council Regulation, allows voluntary participation by companies in the industrial section in a Community Eco-audit scheme. **8–017**

In contrast to the environmental management system BS 7750, which is applicable to all types of organisations, the Eco-audit scheme will only be open to industrial activities, together with operations involving the production of electricity, gas, steam or hot water, and the waste management industry.

Companies will be able to seek registration in the scheme on a site by site basis. Once a company or site has elected to participate in the scheme, it will have to observe all the rules and procedures laid down by the Regulation. Applications for Eco-audit will be handled by competent bodies within each Member State. The competent body need not be a government group—an independent technical group will also be acceptable.

Eco-audit includes commitments by site management to undertake the following tasks: **8–018**

- An initial environmental review comprising a comprehensive analysis of four key environmental performance areas:

issue-based (energy efficiency, waste management and product planning); impacts (to air, soil, water); performance in relation to E.C. and national standards and other evidence of "good management practices";

- An environmental protection system to be established from the results of the review. This includes a written environmental policy and details of environmental objectives, programmes, management system and audit programmes. The system must relate the activities of the specific site to the operations of the whole company and utilize good management practices. Energy, raw materials, production processes, accident prevention, staff and public information must be included within the environmental protection system;
- An environmental statement to be prepared for each site. It will have to be written "specifically for the public in a concise, non-technical form" and include a description of activities; an assessment of significant relevant impact; a summary of relevant data; details of policy, programme and objectives for the site; and evaluation of performance and a deadline for the production of the next statement;
- An environmental statement of validation by an accredited auditor working according to professional codes of practice to be developed by the Commission. Their validation will signify that the statement complies with the Eco-audit Regulation, indicate technical validity and the reliability of given data and information;
- Disclosure and submission. Once the environmental statement is validated, it will be submitted to the Member State's competent body, who will maintain a database of sites participating in the scheme. It will also be "kept at the disposal of the public";
- Periodic environmental audits to assess the effectiveness the environmental protection systems must be carried out at intervals between one and three years, depending on the environmental impact of the site. The audit will assess management systems, determine compliance with regulations, and ensure conformity with company policies.

This process is summarised in Figure 1.

There are a number of ill-defined points in this process:

- It is not clear what the environmental statement should cover: in particular, the extent to which this document should detail the external environmental impacts of the site needs to be verified.
- Independent auditing and verification will be performed by people independent of the activities they audit. The Government resisted a suggestion that the individuals undertaking an audit must be accredited to an external body. Feeling that

8–019

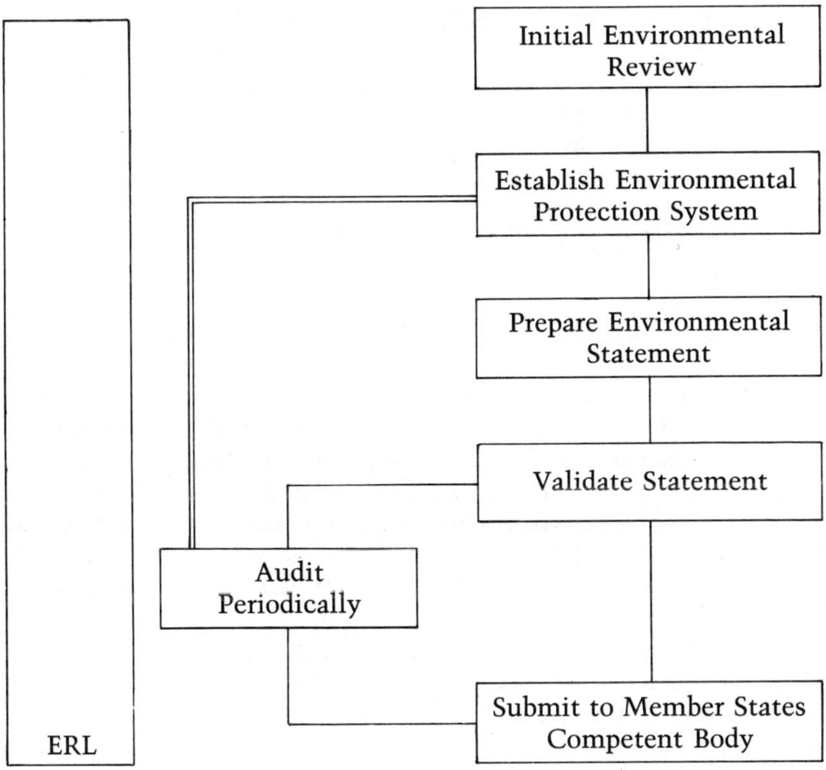

Figure 1: Summary of process to receive E.C. Eco-Audit accreditation

this would constitute excessive cost to small and medium size companies, the Government suggested to the E.C. that a company's own personnel could undertake the audit providing they have received sufficient training to be competent. Actual verification procedures for an audit have been long debated. However, it has been decided that the "independent verifier" for an audit must be an external, *i.e.*, not work for the company under review.

The Eco-audit logo

Companies registered under the Eco-audit scheme are entitled to advertise their participation in the scheme by using the scheme logo. It may be used on corporate brochures, headed paper and reports and in corporate but not product advertisements. The logo would always have to be accompanied by one of the following statements of which sites were participating in the scheme: 8–020

- "All our problem sites in the E.C. participate in the Eco-audit scheme";
- "All our production sites in (name of Member State) participate in the Eco-audit scheme";
- "The following production sites of our company participate in the Eco-audit scheme."

Use of the logo for sites in breach of E.C. or national environmental rules is forbidden.

British Standard 7750

8–021 British Standard 7750 has been issued subject to review by the technical committee responsible for drafting no later than September 1, 1993. The Standard is currently being piloted by some 250 organisations in over 30 industries. The results will not be made available for individual organisations unless they choose to release it, but will be incorporated in the revised Standard when it is published. Any changes to the draft E.C. Eco-audit Regulation will also be reflected.

British Standard 7750 was developed at the same time as the E.C. prepared work on the Eco-audit Regulation. A commitment has been made by the British Standards Institute and E.C. to take account of developments in the other system.

Scope of British Standard 7750

8–022 This is an innovative approach. The conclusion of a formal standard for environmental management systems, BS 7750 was the first initiative of its kind in the world. It was prepared by the British Standards Institute (BSI) under the supervision of the Environmental and Pollution Standards policy Committee and came into effect in March 1992.

British Standard 7750 specifies the elements of an environmental management system and is intended to apply to all types and sizes of organisation, such as manufacturing facilities, offices and warehouses. The objective is to provide a structured management system, integrated within overall management activity to ensure compliance with stated environmental policies and objectives. It shares common management system principles with BS (EN 29000, ISO 9000) and organisations may elect to use an existing management system developed in conformity with BS 5750 as a basis for environmental management. However, BS 5750 certification is not required for BS 7750.

Organisations which elect to implement a full environmental management system must commit to the prevention of adverse environmental effects, not to detection and amelioration after occurrence. The components of an environmental management system conforming to BS 7750 include an internal review, an environmental policy, organisation and personnel, monitoring environmental effects, objectives and targets, an environmental management programme, a management manual, an organisation's operational control, environmental management records, environmental management audits, and an environmental management review.

THE BS 7750 ENVIRONMENTAL MANAGEMENT SYSTEM

8–023

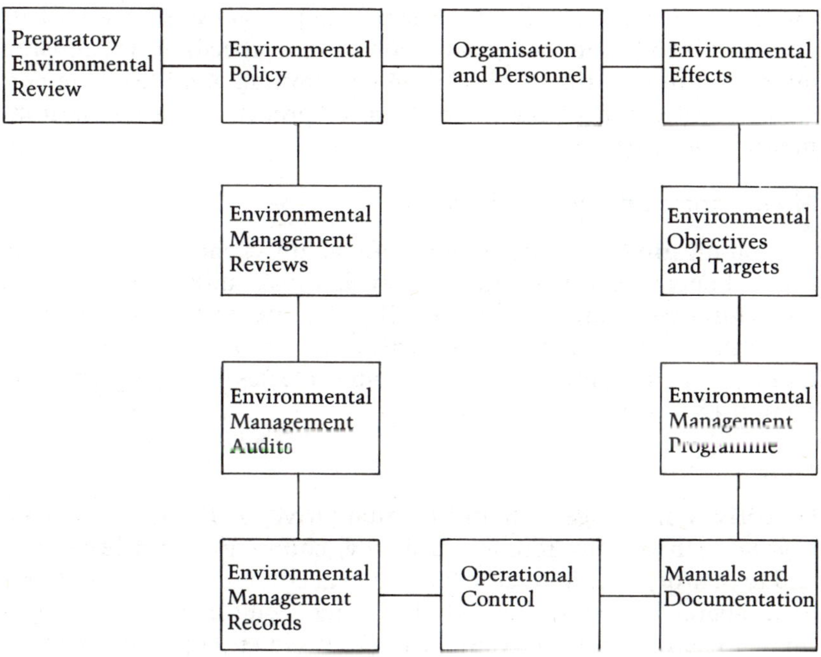

Figure 2: Summary of process to receive accreditation for the BS 7750 Environmental Management System

An internal environmental review

An internal review establishes the organisation's current position 8–024 on the environment. The environmental review should assess all legislative and regulatory requirements, and evaluate and register significant environment effects. It should also examine all existing environmental management practices and procedures, while assessing feedback from the investigation of previous incidents and non-compliance.

An environmental policy

8–025 An environmental policy must be initiated, developed and actively supported by management at the highest level. It should be prevention oriented, go beyond relevant regulatory requirements, and demonstrate commitment to continual improvement in environmental performance. It must be understood, implemented and maintained at all levels of the organisation, and publicly available.

Organisation and personnel

8–026 The organisation should define and document the responsible authority and key environmental personnel. It should identify in-house verification requirements and procedures, appoint a management representative who will ensure that requirements are implemented and maintained. This management representative will be responsible for establishing and maintaining procedures that ensure direct communication with and proper training of all levels of personnel, while motivating them toward a proper regard for environmental concerns.

Monitoring environmental effects

8–027 The monitoring of environmental effects must encompass the life-cycle of operations. The organisation should establish and maintain procedures to examine and assess all of the direct and indirect environmental effects identified as significant. They should also establish open communication to interested parties regarding environmental effects and management.

Objectives and targets

8–028 Objectives and targets should be quantative, achievable, and consistent with the environmental policy, complying with legislative and regulatory requirements. Personnel accountability and performance appraisal should be included when demonstrating commitment to continual improvement in environmental performance.

The environmental management programme

8–029 The environmental management programme should designate responsibility for targets at each function and level of the organisation and identify the means by which targets are to be achieved. Commitment should be highlighted for all personnel—especially management and senior levels. Developments of new products or services should address the environmental effects from all stages of their life-cycle, and new installations or modifications to processes and plants should cover all stages of development.

The management manual

A management manual and other documentation should provide an adequate description of the environment management system, collate environmental policy, objectives, targets and programmes, document key roles and responsibilities, describe interaction of system elements, cover abnormal operating conditions, incidents, accidents, and potential emergency situations. **8–030**

Operational control

An organisation's operational control should ensure the controlled execution of functions, activities and processes which affect, or have the potential to affect, the environment at any point in their life-cycle. The operation control should establish and maintain procedures for verification to check compliance with specified requirements and maintain records of the results. It should also define the responsibility and authority for initiating investigation and corrective action in the event of non-compliance. **8–031**

Environmental management records

Environmental management records should be kept to demonstrate compliance with the requirements of the environmental management system, and to track progress towards environmental objectives and targets. It should include pertinent contractor and procurement records, results of audits and reviews, and training verification. **8–032**

Environmental management audits

Environmental management audits determine the effectiveness of the environmental management system in fulfilling the organisation's environmental policy. They should determine whether or not environmental management activities conform to the environmental management programme, and are implemented effectively. **8–033**

The environmental management review

The environmental management review should encompass the entire organisation and all its activities, products and services, ensuring the continuing relevance of the environmental policy. It should guarantee the continuing suitability of environmental targets and objectives, update the evaluation of environmental effects, and check the efficacy of audits and follow up action. **8–034**

HOW ECO-AUDIT AND BS 7750 WILL MESH

8–035 It remains to be seen if companies will seek to gain both accreditations. Non-manufacturing operations will only be able to seek BS 7750 accreditation. Those already accredited with BS 5750, will add BS 7750 as a logical "upgrade" to their management system. The cost of implementing BS 7750—estimated at £70,000 for a company employing 75 people—may also be a deciding factor.

Appendices

APPENDIX 1: LIST OF STATUTORY INSTRUMENTS

No.	*Title*	*In force*
1147	The Water Supply (Water Quality) Regulations 1989	1/09/1989
1148	The Surface Waters (Classification) Regulations 1989	1/09/1989
1149	The Controlled Waters (Lakes and Ponds) Order 1989	1/09/1989
1150	The Control of Pollution (Revocations) Regulations 1989	1/09/1989
1151	The Control of Pollution (Consents for Discharges etc.) Secretary of State Functions) Regulations 1989	1/09/1989
1152	The Water and Sewerage (Conservation, Access and Recreation) (Code of Practice) Order 1989	1/09/1989
1154	The Director General of Water Services' Register (Inspection and Charges) Order 1989	1/09/1989
1155	The Water Reorganisation (Pensions etc.) (Designated Persons) Order 1989	1/09/1989
1156	The Trade Effluents (Prescribed Processes and Substances) Regulations 1989	1/09/1989
1157	The Control of Pollution (Discharges by the National Rivers Authority) Regulations 1989	1/09/1989
1158	The Control of Pollution (Radioactive Waste) Regulations 1989	1/09/1989
1159	The Water Supply and Sewerage Services (Customer Service Standards) Regulations 1989	1/09/1989

1160	The Control of Pollution (Registers) Regulations 1989	1/09/1989
1161	The Water Reorganisation (Pensions etc.) Regulations 1989	1/09/1989
1162	The Water Appointment (Monopolies and Mergers Commission) Regulations 1989	1/09/1989
1186	The Reservoirs (Panels of Civil Engineers) (Reappointment) Regulations 1989	15/07/1989
1263	The Sludge (Use in Agriculture) Regulations 1989	1/09/1989
1378	The Rivers (Prevention of Pollution) Act 1951 (Continuation of Byelaws) Orders 1989	1/09/1989
1379	The Water and Sewerage (Works) (Advance Payments) Regulations 1989	1/09/1989
1380	The Water (Local Statutory Provisions) (Consequential Amendments) Order 1989	1/09/1989
1381	The Water Reorganisation (Pensions etc.) (Amendment) Regulations 1989	1/09/1989
1382	The Water Reorganisation (Pension etc.) (Designated Persons) (Amendment) Order 1989	1/09/1989
1383	The Water Supply and Sewerage Service (Customer Service Standards) (Amendment) Regulations 1989	1/09/1989
1384	The Water Supply (Water Quality) (Amendment) Regulations 1989	1/09/1989
1461	The Companies Act 1985 (Modifications for Statutory Water Companies) Regulations 1989	1/09/1989
1462	The Local Government Superannuation (water) Regulations 1989	1/09/1989
1465	The Water Authorities (Successor Companies) Order 1989	9/08/1989
1530	(C.51) The Water Authorities (Transfer of Functions) (Appointed Day) Order 1989	1/09/1989

1531	The Water Reorganisation (Holding Companies of Successor Companies) Orders 1989	19/08/1989
1532	The Water reorganisation (Successor Companies) (Transfer of Loans) Order 1989	1/09/1989
1557	(c.52) The Water Act 1989 (Commencement No. 2 and Transitional Provisions) Order 1989	1/04/1990
1561	(c.53) (S.128) The Water Act 1989 (Commencement No. 3 (Scotland) Order 1989	28/08/1989
1588	The Local Government (Direct Labour Organisations) (Competition) Regulations 1989	1/10/1989
1590	The Town and Country Planning General Development (Amendment) (No. 2) Order 1989	29/09/1989
1939	The Water (Pensions and Compensation) (Transfer of Liabilities) Regulations 1989	17/11/1989
1968	The Water (Consequential Amendments) Regulations 1989	27/11/1989
2017	The Water Reorganisation (Capital Allowances) Order 1989	15/11/1989
2018	The Water Reorganisation (Nominated Holding Companies) (Extinguishment of loans) Order 1989	15/11/1989
2278	The Water Act (Commencement No. 4) Order 1989	1/04/1990
2286	The Surface Waters (Dangerous Substances) (Classification) Regulations 1989	1/01/1990
2314	The Reservoirs Act 1975 (Application Fees) (Amendment) Regulations 1989	1/01/1990
2479	The Water Undertakers (Rateable Values) Order 1989	23/12/1989
72	The Internal Drainage Boards (Finance) Regulations 1990	24/01/1990
118	The National Rivers Authority (Levies) Regulations 1990	31/01/1990

119	The Water Supply (Water Quality) (Scotland) Regulations 1990	1/07/1990
120 (s.12)	The Controlled Waters (Lochs and Ponds) (Scotland) Order 1990	1/05/1990
121 (s.13)	The Surface Waters (Classification) (Scotland) Regulations 1990	1/05/1990
126 (s.15)	The Surface Waters (Dangerous Substances) (Classification) (Scotland) 1990	27/02/1990
173	The Drainage Rates (Forms) Regulations 1990	1/03/1990
503	The Local Government Superannuation (Funds etc.) Regulations 1990	1/04/1990
564	The General Drainage Charges (Forms) Regulations 1990	1/04/1990
1013	The Nitrate Sensitive Areas (Designation) Order 1990	1/06/1990
1083	The Water (Target Investment Limited) Order 1990	11/06/1990
1187	The Nitrate Sensitive Areas (Designation) (Amendment) Order 1990	7/06/1990
1629	The Trade Effluents (Prescribed Processes and Substances) (Amendment) Regulations 1990	31/08/1990
111	Litter (Fixed Penalty Notices) Order 1991	
324	The Control of Pollution (Silage, Slurry and Agricultural Fuel Oil) Regulations 1991	1/09/1991
1409	The Water (Compulsory Works Powers) (Notice) Regulations 1991	17/07/1991
1597	The Bathing Waters (Classification) Regulations 1991	01/01/1992
1837	The Water Supply (Water Quality) (Amendment) Regulations 1991	01/01/1992
337	Highway Litter Clearance and Cleaning (Transfer of Duties) Order 1991	1/04/1991
472	Environmental Protection (Prescribed Processes and Substances) Regulations 1991	1/04/1991
476	Litter (Relevant Land of Principal Litter Authorities and Relevant Crown Land) Order 1991	1/04/1991

507	Environmental Protection (Applications, Appeals and Registers) Regulations 1991	1/04/1991
508	Disposal of Controlled Waste (Exceptions) Regulations 1991	1/04/1992
513	Environmental Protection (Authorisation of Processes) (Determination Periods) Order 1991	1/04/1991
561	Litter (Designated Educational Institutions) Order 1991	1/04/1991
719	Litter Etc. (Transitional Provisions) Regulations 1991	1/04/1991
961	Litter (Animal Droppings) Order 1991	1/05/1991
1043	Litter (Statutory Undertakers) (Designation and Relevant Land) Order 1991	13/05/1991
1324	Street Litter Control Notices Order 1991	1/07/1991
1325	Litter Control Areas Order 1991	1/07/1991
1991/1624	Controlled Waste (Registration of Carriers and Seizure of Vehicles) Regulations 1991	14/10/1991
1837	Water Supply (Water Quality) (Amendment) Regulations 1991	3/9/1991
2285	Water (Prevention of Pollution) (Code of Practice) Order 1991	22/9/1991
2790	Private Water Supplies Regulations 1991	1/01/1992
2839	Environmental Protection (Duty of Care) Regulations 1991	1/04/1992
31	Environmental Protection (Controls on Injurious Substances) Regulations 1992	28/02/92
337	Surface Waters (Dangerous Substances) Classification) Regulations 1992	20/03/92
339	Trade Effluents (Prescribed Processes and Substances) Regulations 1992	20/03/92
462	Environmental Protection (Waste Recycling Payments) Regulations 1992	1/04/1992

588	Controlled Waste Regulations 1992	1/04/1992
614	Environmental Protection (Processes and Substances) (Amendment) Regulations 1992	1/04/1992
693	Burning of Crop Residues (Repeal of Byelaws) Order 1992	12/03/1992
1583	Environmental Protection (Controls on Injurious Substances) (No.2) Regulations 1992	31/07/1992
2415	Export of Dangerous Chemicals Regulations 1992	20/11/1992
2997	Public Information for Radiation Emergencies Regulations 1992	1/01/1992
3240	Environmental Information Regulations 1992	31/12/1992
3280	Genetically Modified Organisms (Deliberate Release) Regulations 1992	1/02/1993
1	Environmental Protection (Controls on Injurious Substances) Regulations 1993	31/01/1993
1366	Crop Residues (Burning) Regulations 1993	29/01/1993
199	Environmental Protection (Non-Refillable Refrigerant Containers) Regulations 1994	2/03/1994
232	Batteries and Accumulators (Containing Dangerous Substances) Regulations 1994	1/03/1994 or 1/08/1994

APPENDIX 2: SELECTED E.C. DIRECTIVES

(i) Water for drinking

80/777/EEC on the approximation of the laws of the member states relating to the exploitation and marketing of natural mineral waters.

80/778/EEC relating to the quality of water intended for human consumption.

(ii) Wastewater

91/271/EEC concerning urban waste water treatment.

(iii) Quality for various uses

75/440/EEC concerning the quality required of surface water intended for the abstraction of drinking water in member states.

76/160/EEC concerning the quality of bathing water.

78/659/EEC on the quality of freshwaters needing protection or improvement in order to support fish life.

79/869/EEC concerning the methods of measurement and frequencies of samples and analysis of surface water intended for the abstraction for drinking in the member states (reference methods for 75/440/EEC).

79/923/EEC on the quality required of shellfish waters.

91/676/EEC concerning the protection of fresh, coastal and marine waters against pollution caused by nitrates from diffuse sources.

(iv) Discharge of dangerous substances

76/464/EEC on pollution caused by certain dangerous substances discharged into the aquatic environment of the Community.

This Directive has given rise to several "Daughter Directives".

82/176/EEC on limit values and quality objectives for mercury discharges by the chlor-alkali electrolysis industry.
83/513/EEC on limit values and quality objectives for cadmium discharges.
84/156/EEC on limit values and quality objectives for mercury discharges by sectors other than by chlor-alkali electrolysis industry.
84/491/EEC on limit values and quality objectives for discharges of hexachlorocyclohexane, in particular lindane.
86/280/EEC on limit values and quality objectives for discharges of certain dangerous substances included in List I in the Annexe to Directive 76/464/EEC (covers DDT, PCP and CTC).
88/347/EEC amending Annex II to Directive 86/280/EEC relating to aldrin, dieldrin, endrin, isodrin (the 'Drins'), hexachlorobenzene (HCB), hexachlorobutadiene (HCBD), and chloroform.
90/415/EEC amending Annex II to Directive 86/280/EEC on limit values and quality objectives for discharges of certain dangerous substances included in list I of the Annex to Directive 76/464/EEC.
80/68/EEC on protection of groundwater against pollution caused by certain dangerous substances.

(v) Controls over industry

78/176/EEC on waste from the titanium dioxide industry.
82/883/EEC on procedures for surveillance and monitoring of the environments affected by wastes from the titanium dioxide industry (reference methods for 78/176/EEC).
83/ 29/EEC amending Directive 78/176/EEC.
87/217/EEC on prevention and reduction of environmental pollution by asbestos.
89/428/EEC on procedures for harmonizing the programmes for the reduction and eventual elimination of pollution caused by waste from the titanium oxide industry.
92/112/EEC On procedures for harmonising the reduction and elimination of pollution caused by waste from the titanium dioxide industry.

(vi) Controls over products

73/404/EEC on the approximation of the laws of the member states relating to detergents.

73/405/EEC on the approximation of the laws of the member states relating to methods of testing the biogradability of anionic surfactants.
82/242/EEC amending Directive 73/404/EEC.
82/243/EEC amending Directive 73/405/EEC.
86/ 94/EEC amending Directive 73/404/EEC.

(vii) Sewage sludge disposal

86/278/EEC on the protection of the environment, and in particular of the soil, when sewage is used in agriculture.

(viii) Information exchange

77/795/EEC+ establishing a common procedure for the exchange of information on the quality of surface freshwater in the Community.
83/189/EEC+ on laying down a procedure for the provision of information in the field of technical standards and regulations.
86/ 85/EEC+ establishing a Community information system for the control and reduction of pollution caused by the spillage of hydrocarbons and other harmful substances at sea.
86/574/EEC+ amending 77/795/EEC.
88/346/EEC+ amending 86/85/EEC to include major inland waters.
90/2/EEC amending 77/795

(ix) Public procurement of works and supplies, and products and assessment

89/106/EEC on the approximation of laws, regulations and administrative provisions of the Member States relating to construction products.
90/531/EEC on the procurement procedures of entities operating in the water, energy, transport and telecommunications sectors.
90/683/EEC concerning the modules for the various phases of the conformity assessment procedures which are intended to be used in the technical harmonisation directives.

(x) Waste

75/442/EEC Framework Directive on Waste
91/156/EEC Amending 75/442
259/93/EEC Regulation on the Transfrontier Shipment of Wastes
76/403/EEC Disposal of PCBs
91/157/EEC Batteries and Accumulators

(xi) Other

82/501/EEC	on the major accident hazards of certain industrial activities.
87/217/EEC	amending Directive 82/501/EEC.
88/610/EEC	amending Directive 82/501/EEC.
85/337/EEC	on the assessment of effects of certain public and private projects on the environment.
85/374/EEC	on the approximation of the laws, regulations and administrative provisions of the member states concerning liability for defective products.

+A "Decision" rather than a "Directive".

APPENDIX 3: PROPOSED E.C. DIRECTIVES

COM(93)721	Bathing Waters
COM(88)559/ COM(91)373	Civil liability for damage caused by waste
COM(91)102	Landfilling of waste
COM(93)425	Hazardous waste
COM(92)9	Incinerators for hazardous waste
COM(93)202	Ozone
COM(92)277	VoCs
COM(92)572/ COM(93)626	Vehicle emissions
COM(94)4	Major accident hazards
COM(90)319/ COM(92)483	Environmental data

INDEX